GRUESOME DISCOVERY

Kathy Porter was giving her mother a metal desk, which she planned to deliver that hot July day. Kathy and her fifteen-year-old daughter, Kendra, arrived at her mother's home at approximately 1:30 PM. As they had done hundreds of times before, Kathy and her daughter got out of their truck and went up the steps into the house.

The first thing Kathy and Kendra noticed when they walked through the door was an overturned chair in the living room with its seat cushion turned out onto the floor.

"We thought, well, Carolyn's cleaning, so she's doing something to this chair," Kathy said. "Then Kendra went into the kitchen and found Mother lying on the floor."

Dora Ann lay partly under the kitchen table in a pool of blood. Kathy rushed into the room and began calling to her mother, and Kendra went to look for her aunt Carolyn.

"I found her in the bathroom floor against the wall with a spear in her chest," Kendra later told investigators.

When she heard Kendra begin to scream, Kathy ran to the bathroom and panicked when she saw her sister's body.

"We just ran and got out of there," Kathy said.

BLOOD BETRAYAL

SHEILA JOHNSON

PINNACLE BOOKS
Kensington Publishing Corp.
http://www.kensingtonbooks.com

Some names have been changed to protect the privacy of individuals connected to this story.

PINNACLE BOOKS are published by

Kensington Publishing Corp.
850 Third Avenue
New York, NY 10022

All Kensington Titles, Imprints, and Distributed Lines are available at special quantity discounts for bulk purchases for sales promotions, premiums, fund-raising, and educational or institutional use. Special book excerpts or customized printings can also be created to fit specific needs. For details, write or phone the office of the Kensington special sales manager: Kensington Publishing Corp., 850 Third Avenue, New York, NY 10022, attn: Special Sales Department, Phone: 1-800-221-2647.

Pinnacle and the P logo Reg. U.S. Pat. & TM Off.

First Pinnacle Printing: September 2006

10 9 8 7 6 5 4 3 2 1

Printed in the United States of America

*For Carolyn Jean Dalton and Dora Ann Dalton,
and for those who will always feel their loss*

ACKNOWLEDGMENTS

Without the aid and cooperation of Sheriff Cecil Reed and District Attorney Mike O'Dell, of DeKalb County, Alabama, this book would not have been possible. These two gentlemen, and all those who have served on their staffs over the past decade, never gave up believing that justice would be served in the Randy Headrick case. They have all been a tremendous help, and I will always be grateful.

Thanks also to Stephen V. Smith and LaRue Cornelison, two true friends of law enforcement, whose excellent reporting and photography helped bring forward tips and information from those who read their stories in the area newspapers.

Thanks to all the DeKalb County sheriff's investigators, who were determined to break the case and see the murderer of two innocent women sent to prison. Their dedication to finding the truth is a continuing inspiration.

A special thanks to lead investigator Rhonda Jackson, who kept such careful, detailed records of every aspect of the investigation for five long years. Her supervision of the case stands as a textbook example of outstanding police work. And special thanks also to Terry Durham, the young man whose courage and integrity provided Rhonda Jackson and her team with the information that finally broke the case.

Most of all, I thank my late mother, Olena M. Beasley, for a lifetime of love and support, without which I would most likely have ended up as the subject of someone else's true crime book, instead of the author of my own.

CHAPTER 1

State Highway 75 is dotted with a string of small communities as it runs north to south through DeKalb County, Alabama. The upper end of the county is bordered by both the Tennessee and Georgia state lines, and most of its nine municipalities are situated along the highway, each little town blending almost seamlessly into the next. New brick ranch-style homes share space along the highway with small, older wood frame houses and single- and double-wide trailer homes, and small businesses of all types are scattered among the houses up and down both sides of Highway 75. Side roads, paved and unpaved, branch off the highway with other homes and small farms, and reconnect to other roads that form a spiderweb of gravel and asphalt covering the mountain. With its distinction of having the most total miles of roadways in the state, DeKalb County's citizens are easily able to travel to and from other communities in the county by a number of different routes. The residents of these adjoining neighborhoods pay little attention to town limits, and their city services are all but interchangeable. Fire and rescue personnel, law enforcement officers and even members of the communities, pitch in and help each other whenever needed, giving all those who live and work in the homes and businesses along the highway the benefit of more than one source of aid in the event of emergencies.

Friday, July 7, 1995, was a typical midsummer day in rural northeast Alabama. Skies were clear and bright, the thermometer hovered in the mid-nineties, and most of the families in the rural neighborhoods tried to beat the heat and humidity by finishing their gardening and yard work early in the day. Produce had been gathered from neat rows of vegetables growing in backyards, and now, in the heat of midday, people rested indoors. An occasional breeze helped to cool a small white frame house with blue shutters, located on the aptly named Shady Lane in Henagar, Alabama, on a dirt road just off Highway 75. Inside, Carolyn Jean Headrick, forty-four, and her mother, Dora Ann Dalton, sixty-two, had been busy since midmorning preserving food from their home garden. Air-conditioning helped keep them comfortable as they worked indoors, lowering the heat and humidity in the kitchen, but the pleasant breeze and the shade trees around the house were especially welcome that day.

Several years earlier, Carolyn had worked for a time as a caregiver in Chattanooga, Tennessee, sitting with elderly people and tending to their needs. Now she and her husband, Randy, lived with her mother, who was a heart patient. Carolyn didn't work outside the home; she never had, except for her stint as a sitter and companion. Instead, she stayed home to be with Dora Ann in case she became ill. Carolyn had a seventh-grade education and enjoyed reading Harlequin romances, occasionally making up stories of her own and writing them down in notebooks that she kept. Other than a few people she had met through her husband, she had no circle of friends that she regularly socialized with, and she didn't go out. She and her mother went to church and occasionally had other church members over for dinner on Sundays. Until Carolyn met her husband a few years earlier, her personal life had been very reclusive and isolated, with members of her family as her only frequent contacts.

Carolyn's widowed mother, Dora Ann Dalton, had worked at a leather company in Chattanooga for twenty-six years before retiring in 1989 due to disability because of her heart condition. Dora Ann's husband died in 1990, and from that time until Randy Headrick appeared on the scene, the two women lived alone in the modest little house. Dora Ann enjoyed cooking and reading the Bible, and her other children visited and called her on the phone regularly, staying in touch with their mother and sister.

Around 1:00 P.M. on that hot July day, Dora Ann finished preserving sauerkraut and preparing a large pot of green beans to can after lunch. Before she sat down to eat some watermelon, which was cooling in the refrigerator, she took a minute to phone her daughter Kathy Porter. Kathy was giving her mother a metal desk, which she planned to deliver that day, and she told Dora Ann she'd bring it over as soon as her family finished their lunch. Dora Ann told Kathy that Carolyn was vacuuming and re-arranging furniture in the room where they planned to put the desk. The room was used by Randy, who kept his arrowhead collections and Indian craft supplies there. The desk would provide additional convenient storage for Randy's growing stockpile of beads, animal bones, and leather.

When he finished his lunch, Kathy's husband loaded the desk onto their gold Mazda B2000 pickup truck, and Kathy and her fifteen-year-old daughter, Kendra, headed for the Dalton home. Before she left her house, Kathy looked at the clock: it was 1:17 P.M. She arrived at her mother's home at approximately 1:30 P.M., backing the truck up into the yard to unload the desk. Other than Dora Ann's red Chevrolet S10 pickup sitting in the carport, there were no other vehicles parked at the house and no sign of anyone else around. Then, as they had done hundreds of times before, Kathy and her daughter got out of their truck and went up the steps into the house.

The first thing Kathy and Kendra noticed when they

walked through the door was an overturned chair in the living room, with its seat cushion turned out onto the floor.

"We thought, 'Well, Carolyn's cleaning, so she's doing something to this chair,'" Kathy said. "Then Kendra went into the kitchen and found Mother lying on the floor."

Dora Ann lay partly under the kitchen table in a pool of blood. Kathy rushed into the room and began calling to her mother, and Kendra went to look for her aunt Carolyn.

"I found her in the bathroom floor against the wall with a spear in her chest," Kendra later told investigators. When she heard Kendra begin to scream, Kathy ran to the bathroom and panicked when she saw her sister's body.

"We just ran and got out of there," Kathy said. "Kendra had seen our pastor's vehicle at the Cabbage Bowl restaurant on the way down to Mother's house, and we went up there and he got help."

The Reverend Joseph Carl Turman and his wife, Lee Ann, had stopped that afternoon for a late lunch at the Cabbage Bowl, a popular restaurant on Highway 75 between the towns of Ider and Henagar, on the north end of the county. The Cabbage Bowl served as a regular meeting place for many of the businesspeople and community leaders from both towns, and Turman stopped by frequently for meals or to have coffee and visit with the restaurant's other customers. As pastor of the Ider Church of God, he spent much of his time ministering to those who attended his church and socializing with his many friends of other denominations. Joey Turman was the kind of man that community residents knew they could always turn to for help, someone who truly believed that his duties as a pastor extended far beyond the doors of his own church.

Turman's lunch was interrupted when two of the members of his congregation, Kathy and Kendra Porter, burst into the restaurant and ran to him. In their panic, Turman was the first person the two women thought to turn to for help. They believed he would know what to do. Both women were crying hysterically, and Turman finally managed to calm Kathy enough so that she could catch her breath and tell him what was wrong. He was deeply shocked when she cried out that she and Kendra had just found Dora Ann and Carolyn lying dead in their home.

Turman fought down a rising feeling of panic and phoned a friend, Donald Smith, who was working at his Ace Hardware store in Henagar. He asked Smith to come to the Cabbage Bowl as quickly as possible; it was an emergency, he said. Without waiting for details, Smith immediately dropped everything and sped toward the restaurant while Turman placed his first call to 911. When the dispatcher answered, he tried his best to stay calm and give as much information as he could.

"Nine-one-one, what is your emergency?" the dispatcher asked.

"Yes, ma'am, I'm at the Cabbage Bowl in Ider. My name is Joey Turman. We've been reported, just here, that a woman and her daughter's possibly been murdered at their home and robbed."

"Where at, sir?"

"Right across from the old skating rink, there's a dirt road right across the road from the old skating rink. First house on the left. I'm going there now to keep everybody out and—"

"Okay, sir, just stay on the line with me for just a moment, hear? You say they're possibly murdered?"

"I don't know, you've got to ask the lady, she's here, a [church] member of mine, and she is badly upset, and I'm going to check everything out."

"Okay, sir, when you get to that residence, I want you to call back on nine-one-one."

"Yes, ma'am, I'll call you right back."

By that time, Smith had arrived at the restaurant and rushed inside in time to overhear the last part of Turman's conversation with the 911 dispatcher. He realized the situation was extremely serious, and as soon as Turman phoned Kathy's husband, Stanley Porter, telling him to come quickly to the Cabbage Bowl and take care of Kathy and Kendra, Turman and Smith sped south on Highway 75 toward the house on Shady Lane.

Smith skidded to a stop in front of the house, and Turman got out and hurried inside. When he got to the kitchen and saw Dora Ann Dalton's body, then found Carolyn Headrick lying in the bathroom, he quickly ran back outside and motioned for Smith, who came to the front porch and stood watching through the door as Turman once again called 911.

"Nine-one-one, what is your emergency?"

"I have an emergency! I just called the lady, from the Cabbage Bowl—"

"Yes, sir."

"I'm at the residence, the residence, and we need some help quick."

"Okay, sir, can you tell me what's going on?"

"Ma'am, I found two people dead, possibly dead, in the house."

"Okay, I'm going to transfer you to the Ider Rescue Squad and I'm going to get everybody en route. Have you checked to see if either one of them are breathing, or anything?"

"No, ma'am, I don't think I can. It's . . . it's bad."

The 911 operator then connected Turman with the Ider Police Department, whose dispatcher clearly wasn't expecting a call of such urgency on such a quiet summer afternoon.

"This is a transfer from DeKalb nine-one-one," the operator said. "We need your police officer en route to Shady Lane to secure the area; a possible murder has gone on at this residence."

"Ah . . . okay," said the Ider dispatcher. "Give me a name."

"Dora Ann Dalton is the one that lives here, it's her home," Turman broke in. "The rescue squad has come out here before for her."

"Okay. Ah . . . my officer is in Fort Payne. Let me see—"

"Just get somebody down quick, hurry, please!"

The 911 operator assured Turman help was on the way, and checked with the sheriff's dispatcher to see which of the county officers might be patrolling in the area. Then the Henagar Police Department was contacted.

"This is a transfer from nine-one-one. Can you get your police officer and first responders to the Dalton residence on Shady Lane?"

"All right, I'll get them en route."

The 911 operator told Turman to hang up and go wait out at the front of the house for help to arrive; then the operator called the county dispatcher.

"You need to contact Ider police station, ten-seventeen. Ider police station, ten-seventeen. We've got a murder. Shady Lane, shows up as being a Henagar address, but it's gonna be between there and Ider, on the left. The residence will be the first dirt road after Moore's Skating Rink, on the left. Two murders."

When Henagar fire chief Winston Busby and fireman Reed Smith answered the first responder call to the Shady Lane address at 1:46 P.M., they happened to be quite nearby, on County Road 134, directly behind the skating rink, just across Highway 75 from the dirt road turnoff. Busby told the Henagar dispatcher they would be on their way to the scene, and the two men arrived at the Dalton house just three minutes later. Both men had misunderstood the call and believed they were going to the aid of a heart attack patient; the rescue squad had responded to the address before, for Dora Ann had needed emergency treatment for her heart condition on more than one occasion.

When Winston Busby and Reed Smith pulled into the driveway, they found Donald Smith and Joey Turman standing out in the front yard, both men looking very upset and agitated.

"Where's the patient?" Busby asked Turman.

"One is in the kitchen," Turman told him, "and one is in the bathroom."

Busby later told investigators that he couldn't quite understand why there were two people at the same time and the same location, both having heart attack symptoms. He immediately went into the kitchen, where he found Dora Ann's body lying partially under the table with drying blood pooled around her head. Busby realized with a shock that he was definitely not dealing with a heart attack when he saw that Dora Ann appeared to have been shot in the forehead and stabbed with a long spear, which remained embedded in her body. Busby quickly went back outside to the city truck he was driving and was on his radio reporting to Henagar that the call was 10-17, all units, when Henagar assistant police chief Robert Hales pulled up in his patrol car. Hales was closely followed by county deputy Jim Mays, who quickly ushered everyone out of the house and asked if the scene had been secured. On hearing that it had not been checked out, Mays sent Reed Smith and Officer Hales back inside to search, room to room, in case the killer was still there. When the two men went down the hallway, they saw Carolyn's body in the bathroom. She appeared to have been shot with a gun more than once and stabbed in the neck with a large knife, then speared in the chest. Both the knife and spear were still in place.

The shower curtain was closed, so Smith picked up a long stick from the bedroom across the hall and slowly pulled back the shower curtain so Hales could see if anyone was behind it. To their relief, no one was hiding there. Then, after checking the rooms in the rest of the house and finding them clear, they went back outside and Hales went to his car to radio in to his dispatcher and make sure that the county investigators were on the way. He and Smith then continued their search of the property, walking around outside the house and searching several sheds, storage buildings, and a tent that had been set up on the grounds. They found no one, and by the time they finished, several investigators and even more law enforcement personnel were beginning to arrive at what DeKalb County sheriff Cecil Reed would later describe as one of the worst murder scenes in the county's history.

CHAPTER 2

DeKalb County deputy Lamar Hackworth was right in the middle of a busy but routine first shift. It was just past midday, but he had already made a round trip from the sheriff's office in Fort Payne, Alabama, to a Chattanooga, Tennessee, doctor's office with two inmates in need of medical care. He waited while they were treated; then he returned them to the county jail. As soon as he turned over his two charges to the jailers, he was asked to take another inmate for a doctor's appointment in Rainsville, Alabama, the town immediately south of Henagar on Highway 75.

"As I was getting back into the car from the doctor's office, I heard nine-one-one dispatch giving a nine-one-one call of a possible homicide on Shady Lane in Henagar," Hackworth said. "I was told to be en route to assist the units that were responding, so I dropped the prisoner off at the Henagar Police Department and went on to the call."

On his arrival at the murder scene, Hackworth saw several people he knew from other law enforcement agencies and city departments. Deputy Jim Mays and Henagar street department worker Eugene Camp were putting up crime scene tape, and Hackworth parked his car along the road while another arrival, Lieutenant David Smalley, from the Henagar Fire Department, moved his first responder vehicle from the driveway to make room for other emergency units that were on their way. Hackworth and Smalley helped to finish putting up the crime scene tape as several other vehicles pulled up, lining both sides of the already narrow road in front of the house. Hackworth then began a job that would take several hours and would later prove to be very important to the investigation of the murders. He started a list of the names of everyone who came into the house before it was taped off, then continued with another list of those people who crossed the crime scene tape during the following hours.

Investigator Rhonda Jackson, of the DeKalb County Sheriff's Department, and another officer, Investigator Clay Simpson, arrived at the Dalton home around 3:01 P.M., responding to emergency calls from the sheriff's dispatcher. Jackson would be tapped by the sheriff to serve as lead investigator in the case, her first time to head up the investigation of a homicide. With her keen eye for detail and her meticulous record keeping, she was an ideal choice for the job. Jackson, a striking young brunette who had worked her way up through the ranks the hard way, from rookie patrol deputy to experienced investigator, was just as determined as she was attractive. Knowing she would be judged by her colleagues on the skill with which she handled the investigation of this double homicide, she began to walk through the house with Simpson, taking careful note of everything she saw.

"We entered the residence through the front door into the living room," Jackson said. "There was a chair overturned in the corner, with what appeared to be a brown leather sheath lying near it. The chair's cushion was against the couch."

Jackson also noticed an afghan, a pillow and a binder notebook lying on the floor beside the overturned chair. The ceiling fan and a window air conditioner were both running.

As the investigators moved from the living room into the kitchen, where rumpled throw rugs lay on the floor, they found the ceiling fan turning overhead and a pedestal fan sitting with its cord stretched across the kitchen floor. It was plugged into the electric wall receptacle but was not turned on. Dora Ann Dalton's body was lying, fully clothed, on the floor, positioned partially on her side with her head under the kitchen table. She was wearing dark blue shorts, a light-colored top, white socks and tennis shoes.

"A large amount of blood was under the victim's upper body," Jackson said. "A spear around five or six feet in length had been stuck into her right side, and there was an additional stab wound visible to the back and one bullet wound to the middle of the forehead. Her glasses were lying on the floor beside the body."

As they looked around the kitchen, nothing seemed out of place and there were no evident signs of a struggle. Glass jars of freshly preserved sauerkraut, still warm to the touch, sat in neat rows on the countertop, and a pot of green beans was steaming on the stove. The house's back door was closed. Jackson noted that Dora Ann appeared to have been sitting at the table eating watermelon when her killer struck without warning; half of a small watermelon lay broken into pieces on the kitchen floor, and the other half sat on the kitchen counter covered with aluminum foil.

Jackson and Simpson then moved down the hallway to the bathroom, where Carolyn's body was slumped against the wall in a semiseated position, with her legs bent and her right shoulder against the commode. The left side of her head was wedged against a wooden towel rack. The investigators noted three gunshot wounds to her head, and she had been stabbed in the throat with a large bowie knife, which had been left in the wound. A seven-foot homemade Indian spear had been used to stab Carolyn in the chest; it, too, had been left in her body. A pattern of blood spatters extended from her wounds toward the doorway, and the blood was already coagulated.

Like her mother, Carolyn was fully clothed. She wore blue jeans, a light-colored top, white socks and tennis shoes. Her reddish brown hair was pulled back into a ponytail, and a small floral picture had fallen off the bathroom wall and lay in the floor by her right leg.

Jackson and Simpson moved on to the other rooms in the house, starting with Dora Ann's bedroom. There they found a middle dresser drawer open, with underwear lying on the floor and hanging out of the drawer. Dora Ann's oxygen machine was on the right wall, and a small fan sat on top of the machine. A dresser drawer containing Indian-style bric-a-brac sat in a chair, and three decorative Indian plates were lying on the bed along with their holders. The doors were standing open on the wardrobe, and clothes were lying scattered about on the floor.

In Carolyn and her husband Randy's bedroom, a purse was sitting on the bed with its contents partially dumped out. Several papers and other miscellaneous items were scattered over the bed. In another room, which was the room where Randy kept most of his Indian artifacts and craft supplies, a twin bed had been moved away from the wall and a vacuum cleaner was sitting behind it. There were spears mounted on the wall behind the bed, along with some empty holders. Decorated Indian staffs and walking sticks stood in the corner of the room, along with a .22 long rifle. A box of shells for the rifle was sitting on a nearby wall shelf, and a large dresser that appeared to have been moved from the room was sitting out in the hallway with Indian jewelry and several other items lying on top.

After this initial inspection of the house, Jackson and Simpson and another colleague, Investigator Jimmy Phillips, determined that there had been no forced entry, and nothing obvious appeared to be missing. There were no signs of a struggle or of any resistance by either of the two women. The investigators decided it was time to contact the Department of Forensic Sciences in Huntsville, Alabama, to request their assistance in working the crime scene. They also requested the help of one of the most experienced crime scene investigators in the state, Danny Smith. Smith worked for Richard Igou, district attorney (DA) of the Ninth Judicial Circuit of Alabama, as the circuit's investigator. The Ninth Judicial Circuit consisted of

DeKalb County and the adjoining Cherokee County, and Danny Smith regularly assisted sheriff's investigators in both counties when his experience and expertise were needed. While Phillips phoned the forensic department, Sheriff Cecil Reed contacted Danny Smith and asked him to come lend a hand with the investigation.

Around 5:00 P.M., Danny Smith arrived at the house on Shady Lane and began his own walk-through of the crime scene. After he conferred with the other detectives and learned there had been no forcible entry, no apparent robbery and no signs of a struggle, he entered through the front door and walked into the living room.

Much of what Danny Smith noticed coincided with the observations already made, except for one thing: the brown leather knife sheath he saw lying near the overturned chair looked like the right size to fit a twelve-inch bowie knife, and there was an empty display space on the wall behind the chair. It appeared that the knife had been hanging on the wall and had been taken down and possibly used as one of the murder weapons.

Danny Smith then walked through the double doorway at the northeast corner of the living room, which led into the kitchen. When he viewed Dora Ann's body, he noted that, judging by the position of her feet, she might have been standing at the kitchen counter and was attacked without warning from behind.

When he looked at Carolyn's body in the bathroom, Danny Smith saw that the gunshot wound to her right temple appeared to be a contact wound. There was gunpowder on the vanity at the front edge of the lavatory, and Smith felt she was most likely standing when at least one of the wounds occurred. The spray pattern he noticed on the towel near her head indicated that the contact gunshot wound happened after she came to rest in the sitting position, where she was found. The towel rack beside her body looked as though it had been pushed against the wall as she fell, gouging a small hole in the Sheetrock and knocking the picture off the wall, which the other investigators had seen lying on the bathroom floor. Other than that, there was no sign of a struggle in the room.

In the bedroom where Carolyn had been vacuuming and moving furniture, Smith saw that there were several Indian-type weapons hanging on the wall, with at least two places on the wall where something had obviously been displayed, but had been taken down. The empty spaces, he noticed, were the right size and shape to accommodate the two long spears that had been used to stab the two victims.

Strangely, no bullets or spent casings were found in the house; the only piece of evidence of that type was a small shaving of lead that was found underneath the kitchen table. Just as strange was the lack of an obvious motive for such brutal murders. A few things had been thrown about, as though the killer or killers wanted it to look as though there had been some type of a search for valuables, but nothing actually seemed to have been taken. Jewelry and other items were lying untouched in plain sight on the dresser top; if theft had been the motive, surely those items would have been quickly and easily snatched up.

What reason could there have been for the murders? The two women were very well-known and respected in the community, and they had no enemies. Their home was neat and comfortable, but modest; it was not the type of house to attract burglars in search of expensive, easily fenced items or a stash of currency. No motive for the double homicide had yet become apparent, but that was soon to change. During her further search of the house the following day, Rhonda Jackson would find and seize evidence that provided a great deal of motivation for murder: 325,000 dollars' worth, to be exact.

CHAPTER 3

Around an hour after the initial crime scene investigation began, a growing crowd of people were standing outside in the yard at the Dalton/Headrick home while the investigators worked inside. Murmurs began to spread through the group when they saw a red 1995 Ford F-150 pickup truck approaching on Highway 75. The truck drove past the Shady Lane turnoff, then turned around, came back and turned onto the road heading toward the residence. Behind the wheel was William Randall "Randy" Headrick, Carolyn's husband and Dora Ann's son-in-law.

"Headrick was met by our officers on the road and was told what was going on," Sheriff Reed later told Jimmy Phillips. "That's the main thing I remember, when he drove on past and then turned around and came back. I talked to him, but I didn't say anything to him about how the victims were killed."

No one else at the scene gave Headrick any details about the murders, or about the weapons that the killer or killers had used. He appeared to be in a state of shock as he sat on the tailgate of his truck, head down, staring at the ground, waiting to be questioned.

A young reporter for the Rainsville, Alabama, newspaper, the *Weekly Post,* had heard enough on his police scanner to know that something really big was happening up in Henagar, and he was the first member of the media to arrive at the crime scene. Stephen V. Smith was well-known and liked by all the area law enforcement personnel, and they knew he could be trusted not to interfere with their work. He always used good judgment and discretion when reporting or photographing at crime scenes, and on this day his reporter's instincts told him he'd better try to get a photo of Randy Headrick. Stephen Smith walked over in the direction of Headrick's truck and snapped a shot of him sitting there on the tailgate, apparently in a state of shock and disbelief. That photo, along with Smith's story about the murders, ran in the next issue of the *Weekly Post*. The picture of Randy Headrick was highly dramatic, it told a riveting story all on its own, and the following year it won Stephen V. Smith the first-place award in the Best News Photo category from the Alabama Press Association.

The time had come for someone to have a talk with the bereaved husband and son-in-law, and the investigators Jackson, Simpson and Phillips asked Danny Smith if he would interview Headrick. Smith began their conversation by getting some general information about the victims, and although he seemed shaken, Headrick had no problems answering Danny Smith's questions in considerable detail. He stated that he last saw his wife that morning when he left home on his way to work. She was still in bed when he left, he said, and he didn't see his mother-in-law, but he knew she was awake because he could hear her breathing machine running. As far as he knew, he said, the two women had planned to can beans that day. Carolyn didn't work outside the home, Headrick told Danny Smith; she stayed at home and took care of her mother, who was a heart patient.

Headrick, who had worked at Builders Supply in Fort Payne for several months, claimed that he had clocked in that morning around 6:30 A.M., took thirty minutes for lunch, then clocked out at 3:00 P.M. He bought hamburgers from a local drive-in at lunch, he said, but one of the other boys went to pick it up. He said he only left work one time during the day, and that was to make a delivery to a Fort Payne business. On his way home after work, he stopped at the bank in Rainsville, made a deposit, then stopped in Henagar, where he put gas in the truck, got some gas for the lawn mower and bought a pack of cigarettes. Then, he said, he drove straight home to find his house surrounded by law enforcement and emergency vehicles and barricaded by crime scene tape.

Headrick told Danny Smith that the police had told him that his wife and her mother had been shot, and he said that Kathy Porter, Carolyn's sister, told him they had been shot and stabbed. He said that he didn't know anything else, and he denied that anyone had told him what kind of weapons were used.

When Smith asked Headrick point-blank if he killed his wife and mother-in-law, Headrick did not hesitate or show any emotion when he simply answered, "No." But Smith noted that he avoided eye contact and looked away when he answered. Then Headrick gave the first of many statements that began to raise red flags for the investigators.

"Will your fingerprints be on the murder weapons?" Danny Smith asked.

"Yes, I guess they will," Headrick answered, "since I made them . . ."

Headrick stopped in midsentence, then became very quiet. He then said that he had fired the rifle found in the house, and that it would likely have his fingerprints on it. He had fired it last, around three weeks earlier, he said, when he shot a snake, down at the creek. Headrick stated that the rifle was a Ruger 10/22 clip-fed semiautomatic, and said he didn't know where the gun was in the house. The last time he saw it, he claimed, it was lying on a bed, but he said that his wife usually kept it standing in the corner of the bedroom.

"How did you know what weapons they were killed with?" Danny Smith asked.

"Someone in my family told me," Headrick replied.

When asked about a small amount of blood on his shirt, Headrick claimed that he had cut a metal band on a bundle of lumber at work that day, and the band had kicked back and cut the end of his middle finger on his left hand. He agreed to give a sample of blood to the forensic lab for comparison, and he also consented to the seizure of his clothing for testing.

The questioning went on to include details about the Headricks' marriage and Randy Headrick's strained relationship with his mother-in-law.

"I haven't talked to her in about a year," he admitted when asked if he got along with Dora Ann Dalton.

Headrick told Smith that he and Carolyn had been married for around five years—his second marriage and her first. They had no children, but there were two, a boy and a girl, from Headrick's previous marriage. Both of the children lived in Texas with their mother, he said. Headrick had been born in Etowah County in northeast Alabama, but later moved to Texas. When asked if he had a prior police record of any kind, he admitted to being arrested as a juvenile in Texas for larceny and for possession of an unregistered firearm.

While Headrick answered Danny Smith's questions outside in the yard, the other officers continued their work inside the home. Rhonda Jackson carefully videotaped the interior of the crime scene while Clay Simpson took photographs. The Department of Forensic Sciences in Huntsville had dispatched two of their investigators, Martha Odom and Richard Marx, to collect evidence and process the scene, and they arrived and started their painstaking work inside the house. Randy Headrick was asked if he would go voluntarily with Investigator Danny Smith to the Ider Police Department for further questioning. He wasn't under arrest, Smith told him, and he didn't have to answer any questions. But Headrick said that he understood and was anxious to cooperate, readily agreeing to continue the interview at the police station.

When they got settled in at the Ider Police Department, a small brick building on Highway 75, Danny Smith resumed his questioning by asking about the ownership of the home where Headrick, his wife and his mother-in-law lived. Headrick told Smith the home belonged to Dora Ann Dalton and had been deeded around a year earlier to Carolyn in the event of Dora Ann's death. Should Carolyn die before her mother, the house and all the property would go to Carolyn's sister Kathy Porter. He also said that Carolyn had $25,000 in one life insurance policy and $50,000 in another, and they had bought another $250,000 on her around a year earlier. He was listed as the beneficiary on all the policies, he said, and he thought there was $25,000 on Dora Ann, but he wasn't sure. According to Headrick, it had been his wife's idea to buy the $250,000 in additional insurance because she felt they needed more.

Headrick claimed he and his wife had discussed how the money was to be used. If something happened to her, he said, he was to hire a nurse to take care of her mother for the rest of her life, and set up trust funds for her nieces and nephews. He added that he and Carolyn had recently discussed dropping part of the insurance.

During the second interview, the subject of Headrick's prior convictions in Texas came up again, and this time around, the story began to change. Headrick admitted to Smith that he and a friend had been charged with possession of a pipe bomb, and that the incident involved his ex-wife. He had been in a vehicle with a friend, heading to the Huddle House to get a cup of coffee, he said, when the police stopped them and found a pipe bomb in the bed of the truck. Headrick said he was charged with aiding and abetting, and said that his friend had set off a bomb in the middle of the road in front of a woman's house, and the man later carried Headrick by the house to show him his handiwork. The friend, he claimed, told him he just did it to scare the woman, but Headrick finally admitted to Danny Smith that the bomb actually had been set off in front of his ex-wife's house and that the bomb had been made in his garage. He denied, however, that he had any prior knowledge of the existence of the pipe bomb until the night of his arrest for its possession.

Headrick told Smith that he had served four years in the federal penitentiary following the incident, and then two years on parole after he was released from prison and returned to live with his parents in their home across the road from the Daltons.

Headrick first met Carolyn, he said, when he went to the Dalton house to fix a leak in the bathroom. Later he called her and asked her if she'd like to join him wading barefoot in the creek. Since it was wintertime, he said, Carolyn thought that was funny. They began seeing each other regularly after that, despite the fact that she was older than Headrick. Around six months later, they were married.

Headrick again denied any out-of-the-ordinary problems in the marriage; they had argued, like most married couples, he said, but it never came to blows. They had argued three days before the murders because he had burned some romance novels before she could read them, and she became angry. He admitted that he had left home two or three times during the marriage, but he said that he never stayed away more than a couple of days. Headrick claimed he usually just went across the road to his parents' house, and said the last time he left was more than a year earlier. He denied that he'd ever been told by Carolyn or her mother to get his things and get out. Headrick said the last three weeks of his marriage had been the best, but Danny Smith told him that he'd heard that Mrs. Dalton had spoken to her minister and told him things were bad between her and her son-in-law. Headrick then said he didn't know what she might have told the minister, or why. Things at home were good, he claimed.

Following his marriage, Headrick spent three to four years working at Earthgrains bakery in Fort Payne, and told Smith he had been fired after being accused of "mooning" a man and woman while on the job. He denied that the incident ever happened, but said that he lost his job anyway because of their claims. Later he went to work at Builders Supply in Fort Payne, where he normally worked in the door shop. That shop, he said, had been closed for the past week and he had been working on the yard and out in the warehouse. He again outlined his whereabouts during the day in detail, adding that he only had left work one time that day, to make a delivery to Sola Electric around 6:30 A.M. He had not called home or returned home during the day, he said.

During this second interview, Headrick admitted to Smith that he'd had a girlfriend around a year earlier, and said that he had told Carolyn about the woman and that she had forgiven him. He claimed that nothing ever really happened between him and the woman, but like many of Headrick's statements, and countless others yet to come, that claim soon would be proven false. A complicated web of lies and betrayal was beginning to be woven, and many of Headrick's friends and family members, and even some complete strangers, would soon find themselves becoming entangled in its bloody strands.

CHAPTER 4

Randy Headrick's third interview with Danny Smith took place at 11:30 P.M., July 7, and several officers left the murder scene and came to the Ider Police Department to listen to the questioning. Headrick again was advised that he wasn't under arrest and didn't have to answer any questions, but he said he wanted to cooperate and wasn't uncomfortable with the other officers being present in the room during the interview. Smith then went over many of the same questions he had asked Headrick previously, and this time he was rewarded with some additional information.

Headrick began by telling the officers that neither his wife nor her mother had an enemy in the world, and that they had never hurt anyone. His mother-in-law, he said, was always helping others and had often loaned money to people in the neighborhood.

A great deal of new information came to light concerning the girlfriend Headrick claimed to have had a year earlier, with whom he had said "nothing happened." The woman was riding back and forth to work with him and they became attracted to each other, he said, but again he claimed nothing had ever happened between them. Headrick told Danny Smith he felt guilty and decided to tell his wife about the situation one afternoon; then he called the woman and talked to her and her husband on the phone, in Carolyn's presence. After discussing the matter for around six hours, he said, Carolyn forgave him.

Lately, Headrick told Smith, his life mostly consisted of going to work, then coming home, and he said that he never went anywhere anymore. His hobby of making Indian crafts and his interest in Indian history and relics began after he met Kenneth "Red Crow" Snapp, a self-styled Shawnee holy man who was well-known within the local Indian community for his outstanding craft work. Red Crow and his wife had taught Headrick how to make spears, arrows, knives, tomahawks and war clubs, and they had taught Carolyn how to do Indian-style beadwork. The Snapps were in the process of moving into another house, and Headrick said he had been helping them move for the past three weeks, going to lend them a hand after work and not getting home until late at night.

According to Headrick, his wife was still in bed that morning when he left for work. She kissed him good-bye and told him she loved him. He knew his mother-in-law was awake, he said, because he could hear her breathing machine running in her bedroom.

Headrick told Smith he clocked in at work between 6:15 and 6:30 A.M., delivered a truckload of building materials to Sola Electric in Fort Payne, then went straight back to work, never leaving again until he clocked out at 3:00 P.M. He took a thirty-minute lunch break, he said, and a coworker went to pick up hamburgers at a local drive-in, bringing them back to Builders Supply, where the two men ate their lunch on the loading dock between 11:30 A.M. and noon.

After lunch, Headrick claimed that he and another worker went to the warehouse and helped a truck driver unload a truck, then pulled and loaded a truck to be delivered on Monday. He only left the warehouse one time, he said, when he walked next door, got two sodas, and returned to the warehouse, where he and his helper took a ten-minute break. He locked the warehouse and went back to the office around 2:20 P.M. and talked to some of the other workers until he clocked out at 3:00 P.M. Then he drove to the bank in Rainsville, making a drive-through deposit, then headed home on Highway 75 to Henagar, where he stopped and got gas for the truck and the lawn mower, and cigarettes.

Headrick told Danny Smith he never called or returned home at any time during the day, and said that the last time he used his cell phone was when he tried to call home two days earlier, on Wednesday, but the line was busy. When Smith asked what he knew about what had happened to his wife and mother-in-law, Headrick insisted that all he knew was what he had been told by others when he arrived at his home. The police had told him his wife and her mother had been murdered; that they had been shot, he said. Later, he claimed, Carolyn's sister came up to him and told him that both of them had been shot and stabbed. No one else had talked to him about what kind of weapons had been used to kill the women, he claimed.

Smith then asked Headrick to name what kind of weapons were in the house and where they were kept. Headrick told him there was only one gun in the house, a 22-caliber Ruger rifle, and that it should have been standing in the corner of the bedroom, behind the door. The rifle was loaded, he said, but not chambered. Carolyn had a knife collection in the living room, Headrick said, with some of the knives displayed on the wall and others in cases. He went on to describe tomahawks, knives, arrows, war clubs and other items that were mounted on the wall in the bedroom across the hall from the bathroom, where Carolyn's body had been found. Then Danny Smith's repetitious questioning began to pay off. When naming the weapons in the house, Headrick failed at first to name the bowie knife, and spears used in the murders. But when Smith asked if there were any other weapons in the house, Headrick began to repeat his descriptions of the items, and this time he included the bowie knife, and the spears at the end of the list.

Headrick described the various weapons that he had made and how he had made them; then he denied that he had ever said his fingerprints would be on the murder weapons because he made them.

"If I did say that," he told Smith, "I don't know why."

Smith again asked Headrick point-blank if he killed his wife and mother-in-law, and he denied committing the murders or having any knowledge of them. But he admitted he hadn't spoken to his mother-in-law for the past year, and said they didn't talk. He said that he and Carolyn had some personal problems and claimed she didn't think they had sex enough.

Then the subject changed to Headrick's alleged girlfriend, with whom he had claimed "nothing happened." This time, Headrick's previous story began to break down rapidly. He admitted to Smith that he had spent two nights with the woman in two different motels in a nearby town, but again claimed "nothing happened," saying he couldn't get an erection. Strangely enough, Headrick then said that the woman became pregnant and accused him of being the father. He told Smith that he got a sworn statement from her later saying that he wasn't the father after all. Headrick then admitted that after he broke up with his girlfriend, her house had burned. He was accused of burning it, he said, but he told Smith he had taken a polygraph and passed it. He would take another polygraph in regard to the murders, he said.

Then, at 2:30 A.M., Headrick's questioning session ended and he left the Ider Police Department. His interrogation was to continue again the following day, when the officers continued to look for holes in his seemingly ironclad alibi.

CHAPTER 5

On the morning of July 8, work began early for everyone involved in the investigation of the murders of Carolyn Headrick and Dora Ann Dalton. Further searches of the crime scene were conducted, interviews were set up with a number of Randy Headrick's coworkers at Builders Supply, and a member of the Dalton family gave a long, detailed statement that provided a wealth of background information on Headrick's relationship with his wife and mother-in-law.

During a further search of the house on Shady Lane, Investigator Rhonda Jackson located the insurance policies on Carolyn and Randy Headrick that Headrick had described while being questioned the night before. She seized and retained them, along with deeds to the property, a "last will and testament" and other paperwork that might prove relevant to the case. Then, back in Fort Payne, a round of interviews began that were expected to either support or break down Headrick's alibi of being at work when the murders occurred.

Workers at Builders Supply were summoned, one at a time, to the DeKalb County Sheriff's Department, where they gave statements to the investigators Mike James, Rhonda Jackson, Jimmy Phillips and Clay Simpson. The men came in a steady stream, which started around 10:00

A.M. and continued until after 2:00 P.M., arriving fifteen to thirty minutes apart. One by one, they outlined their dealings with Headrick on the previous day.

First to arrive at the sheriff's department was a young man who had been temporarily employed for the summer as a loader. He told the investigators that he had worked that Friday, from 7:00 A.M. to 5:00 P.M., leaving for lunch from 12:15 to 12:55, P.M.and making a point of telling the officers that his time card would verify those exact times. He worked with Randy Headrick on two or three occasions the previous day, he said, and the last time he talked to him was around lunchtime.

"We talked about world economics and military history," the young man told Mike James and Rhonda Jackson.

"I don't remember seeing Randy after lunch."

Next to make a statement was another loader, working part-time at Builders Supply, who was at work from 11:55 A.M. to 4:00 P.M. on Friday.

"I know who Randall Headrick is, but I didn't see him yesterday," he said.

The next man interviewed talked to Investigator Jimmy Phillips, saying that by the time he got to work on Friday morning, Randy Headrick had already gone to deliver a load to Sola Electric. The man told Phillips that he saw Headrick, who was called "Bone Man" by some coworkers because of his work with animal bones in making his Indian crafts, when he returned from making the delivery. One of the employees in the maintenance department went to pick up lunch for himself and Headrick around 11:30 that morning. While Headrick was eating, the man being questioned said he spent around fifteen minutes talking with him.

"He didn't act any different yesterday than at any other time," he told Phillips.

He then said that around 12:30 or 1:00 P.M., Headrick went to the warehouse and another man, whom he knew as Joe, was sent over there to help him. The last time he saw Randy that day was around 2:30 P.M., when he, Randy and Joe were talking before they clocked out for the day.

Phillips then took a brief statement from another coworker, who said that he saw Headrick around 6:30 on Friday morning when they had coffee, and thought he might have seen him another time later that day in the company delivery truck.

The next man in line for an interview told Simpson that he remembered seeing Headrick on Friday, but he wasn't sure whether it was in the morning or the afternoon.

"He doesn't say much to anyone," the man said, "you have to start the conversation with him."

At the same time, in an adjoining office, Investigator Clay Simpson was interviewing a supervisor from Builders Supply, who told him that around 12:45 on Friday, Headrick told him he was going to the Builders Supply warehouse on the north side of Fort Payne to unload a truckload of materials that had come in from one of the company's suppliers. Headrick asked the supervisor if he would enlist another employee to help him with the unloading, and the supervisor sent Joe to the warehouse at around 12:50 P.M. The next time the supervisor saw Joe was around 2:30, and the next time he saw Headrick was at 2:45 P.M.

Another coworker told Phillips he saw Headrick twice that day, first around 9:00 A.M. and again about an hour later.

The last Builders Supply employee to be interviewed that day was Joe, the man who was said to have been working with Headrick unloading the truck at the warehouse from 12:45 to 2:30 P.M. Joe told Clay Simpson that he and Headrick were together at the warehouse unloading and loading trucks and that Headrick left only once, to go next door and buy soft drinks.

"He was gone for less than five minutes," Joe said. "Then we worked until about two forty-five or three."

So far, no gaping holes had turned up in Headrick's alibi, at least not in the statements taken from his coworkers up to that point. But while Phillips and Simpson had been finishing up those interviews, Rhonda Jackson and Mike James were on their way back up to Henagar to conduct yet another questioning session with Headrick. The interview took place at Headrick's father's home in Henagar, and started around 2:00 P.M. The two officers knew that repetition was a valuable interrogation technique, because subjects who were telling the truth usually answered questions in the same way they had previously answered. But those who had something to hide or were giving false or incomplete information, when asked the same question repeatedly on different occasions, would often ramble, change their answers or tend to give additional information that conflicted with what they had stated previously. By using repetition as they questioned Headrick, Jackson and James hoped to uncover more details that would fill out some of the gaps and inconsistencies in Headrick's personal information from the earlier interviews conducted the day before.

CHAPTER 6

Mike James began Headrick's interview by reassuring him that he and Rhonda Jackson weren't trying to embarrass him or give him a hard time.

"We just need to know what happened yesterday, so some of these questions you may have already been asked by the police, and if so, I apologize," James said. "We're not trying to be repetitive, it's just that I don't really know what you told the other investigators. And you understand you're not under arrest, or anything like that."

Headrick said he understood, and James then asked for a rundown of his activities on the day before, starting with the time he got out of bed. Headrick answered with an outline of his typical morning routine.

"I get up at five o'clock or five minutes till five, whenever the alarm went, go use the bathroom, and brush my hair," he said. "Then I put on a uniform, go into the living room, put on my boots, get my lunch bag, step on the porch, smoke a cigarette, get in my truck and go to Corner Market in Henagar. I buy usually a Mountain Dew or chocolate milk, and then I go to work."

James asked what kind of vehicle he drove, and Headrick confirmed that the red pickup he had arrived home in on the previous afternoon was his, and it was what he drove to work. He told James that he arrived at Builders

Supply about ten minutes until six o'clock on Friday morning, and started his workday by delivering a load of cardboard to Sola Electric, a Fort Payne manufacturing business. Headrick said he got back to work around 7:30 A.M. and spent the rest of the morning helping load trucks, taking a fifteen-minute break in the maintenance shop, then returning to help the loaders again until lunchtime. Then, he said, he called in an order to a local hamburger stand, which was picked up by another worker, and the two sat in the maintenance shop and ate their hamburgers. Headrick mentioned that another man came along during lunch and talked for a few minutes.

"Then about twelve oh-five, when I left the maintenance shop, I stopped by the woodshop on the way back up, grabbed my tickets and said, 'I'm gonna pull my load.' I went out and got in my truck, sat in it for a minute until the air pressure built up, and as I went out the gate, I saw a Milan Express truck pulling out, going to the warehouse. I pulled in behind him because I knew I was going to have to unload the truck.

"So I get over there, unlock the warehouse, let the guy inside and tell him that I'm gonna go get somebody to help unload. I met a supervisor and told him that I needed some help, and he asked how long it would take. I told him thirty-five, forty-five minutes to an hour. Then I went back over and about five minutes later one of our drivers showed up. He helped me unload the truck."

James asked for the name of the man who helped with the unloading, and Headrick said he couldn't remember, but described the man as a younger, stocky guy with a mustache.

"He helped me unload the truck and then I told him to stick around and I'd go get us a Coke. I went across the parking lot to the business next door and bought a drink out of their machine, two of them, two Pepsis," Headrick said. "Then I came back, gave him one, and we talked for about ten minutes. I started pulling my orders, so he stayed and helped me; then he left and I locked the warehouse up, plugged in the forklift, got in my truck and went back to Builders Supply."

"Okay, what then?" James asked.

"I stood around there by the loading office and talked to the loaders and everything else; then I went in and talked to the president of the company about a guy's job, how much he's paid and everything, and—"

"Who were you talking about?" Rhonda Jackson interrupted. "What did you mean about a guy's job?"

"There's a guy transferring from one department or taking another guy's job, and I wanted to find out how much his job paid," Headrick said.

"To see if you might want it?"

"Yeah."

James then asked Headrick if at any time during the day had he called home to talk to his wife or mother-in-law, and Headrick said that he had not.

"Do you normally do that?" James asked.

"Sometimes I do," Headrick answered. "I did on Wednesday or Thursday, I called from work and aggravated Carol. I called from the maintenance shop, bugged her a little bit, then ate my lunch. And sometimes I call her on my way home from work."

James asked Headrick how he first came to meet his wife, and Headrick launched into a long, detailed account of their courtship and their married life. At the time they first met, he said, he was living with his parents in their house across the road from the Dalton home, and he went over one day to fix a broken showerhead for Mrs. Dalton. He had been told she had a daughter living there with her, but after going over five or six more times to split and carry wood, Headrick had not yet seen her.

"I said, 'You know, I think you are putting me on, I don't think you've got a daughter,' and Mrs. Dalton called Carol and she came out and I got introduced to her. A couple of days later, I wasn't doing nothing, so I called over there and said, 'Mrs. Dalton, I'll tell you what, would you ask your daughter if she would like to come out and play in the creek barefooted with me?' It was winter, you know, and they thought it was funny and then she came out.

"We walked up to the barn and found a lot of the old things that are hanging on the outside of the shed; I took them over and hung them up for her, and she thought it looked pretty. I helped clean out that shed so they could have more storage, and I'd go over and split wood for them.

"We went out a few times for hamburgers and I'd go over there, I'd cook dinner here at my parents' house and invite them over, she'd come over when I was sick or wasn't doing good, and she'd stay with me. I'd come home in the morning and she'd come over here and make sure nobody bothered me, and when I'd come home [from working night shift] some mornings, she would bring breakfast or tell me to come over there and eat breakfast before I went to work."

James asked if Headrick and his wife ever had any kind of problems in their marriage.

"Oh, we had problems," Headrick answered. "We argued, we fought—you know, no blows—but we argued and fought."

"What would you argue about most of the time?" Jackson asked.

"You know, it was either something like, you know, maybe something her mother had done or something I had done, or, you know, things that other people had said or done, or just little things. We never got into no really heavy stuff because we always made up."

"Now you lived with both your wife and mother-in-law," James said. "Did that cause problems with your mother-in-law?"

"Just for a little while there," Headrick answered, "and I finally realized that if I didn't speak to her, but I treated her nice, then everything would be all right."

"You just didn't speak?"

"No, I didn't speak to her for a year, but you know . . . I won a safety award and I told Carol to tell her mother to get dressed and on Saturday I took them out to dinner and took them to Wal-Mart and let them shop, and, you know, I told Carol not to let her mama know it was my idea, and things like that, you know. On Father's Day, her mom bought me a new pair of sandals and a shirt and . . . ah . . . I remembered her at Christmas and her birthday and things like that, I'd get her cards."

"Now, is Carol your first wife?" James asked.

"No, Carol is my second," Headrick said.

James then seized the opportunity to steer the questioning into an area of great interest to the investigators.

"Okay, now of course, we've heard forty thousand things, folks have called us and we've heard, you know, rumors, and what I'm going to do next is to clear up some of these rumors so I can understand kind of where we stand at. Were you arrested at one time for something involving your first wife?"

"Yes, sir," Headrick answered.

"Okay, tell me about that, how you were arrested and how that came about—not necessarily the details of the arrest, but, you know, if you were charged and—"

Headrick interrupted, saying, "I was charged and I pled guilty to . . . ah . . . at the court-appointed lawyer's request, I pled guilty to aiding and abetting."

"Aiding and abetting what?" James asked.

"Ah . . . possession of an unregistered firearm."

"Okay, what kind of firearm was that?"

Headrick hesitated, then answered, "It was a pipe bomb."

"And was the allegation that you were going to have your ex-wife killed, or kill your ex-wife?"

"No," Headrick quickly said, "the man that went down with me, him and a couple of others, they decided, you know, maybe they could scare her a little bit and stuff, and maybe scare some sense into her and maybe make her come back home. The bad part about it was the guy had asked to use my garage to work on some stuff, and I never thought about it. The night I was arrested, it was the first night I knew about the bombing incident and he told me they had set one off in the middle of the street at a trailer park where my wife was staying with another woman."

James confirmed that the other man had been charged also and convicted, and asked Headrick how much time had he done in prison for the incident.

"I did four years in jail and two years on probation," Headrick said, then identified his federal probation officer, whose office was located in Gadsden, Alabama. He told James he had been off probation for four or five years, and said that he didn't communicate with his fellow pipe bomber.

"If he ever comes near me," Headrick claimed, "I don't know what I would do."

James then moved on to Headrick's military service.

"Let me ask you, somebody said that you were in the service; what branch of service were you in?"

Headrick said he had been in the U.S. Army, serving primarily as a diesel mechanic. During his time in the military, he said, he had been stationed in Alaska, Missouri, Louisiana and Georgia. When James asked if he ever had any problems while enlisted, Headrick said his wife left him once, taking their two children.

"Did you get an honorable discharge?" James asked.

"Other than honorable," Headrick said, "because I went AWOL on tour."

Headrick told James he had gone AWOL because his wife told him she would take him back if he would just come to her. She wanted him out of the military, he said, so she would have more of a chance at a career. She was going to college at the time, but was also in the army in a support company that rebuilt radios. She was currently living in Texas, Headrick said, with their two children.

James asked Headrick if the large amount of Indian artifacts found in the Dalton house were his, and if he was a collector.

"I collected the arrowheads," Headrick said, "and the rest I made."

Headrick again confirmed there was one gun in the house, a Ruger .22 stainless semiautomatic.

When the subject of Headrick's alleged girlfriend came up, he called her an "almost girlfriend" and told James, "See, everybody kept putting pressure . . . people kept putting ideas in Carol's head, just kept pressure on, and Carol was putting pressure on me, so was everybody else. Carol's sister was calling the girl and hanging up on her, and her husband was on her case, and all she did was ride to work with me at first. I tried talking to my brother-in-law and explaining that I didn't have no friends or nothing; she was the only friend I had then. After that, things developed and it just went on and went on and went on. She'd been having an affair with another guy, and when they broke up, I let her talk. I counseled with her and talked, and we became good friends."

When James began to move the questions toward the subject of the insurance policies and other paperwork Jackson had seized at the house earlier that morning, Headrick grew a bit more restless and began to give lengthier answers.

"Now you can go check," Headrick told the officers. "They found my will, and they should find where me and Carol sat down and figured what we would do if, you know, her mother didn't survive and something happened to us, her nieces and nephews would get everything. I made a verbal agreement with my wife that the money would be distributed amongst them for college money with two stipulations, that they go to church and that they never be arrested or have any problems with the police. I wasn't even supposed to administer the money or nothing, her brother-in-law was, and the house would [go to] her sister. It's in her mother's will. The deeds and titles are in Carol's name, and it's supposed to go to her sister, Kathy Porter, and I will see to it that she gets the deed, the same way with Dora Ann's little hidden income money that's in Carol's name in the bank."

Headrick told James that Dora Ann had a savings account in Carol's name, and said that Kathy was to get it all, including Dora Ann's truck. He then complained to the officers that he seemed to be under suspicion for the murders of his wife and mother-in-law.

"You know, everybody's looking at me like I'm gonna gain something here," he said. "What they were trying to imply last night, they kept bringing up the insurance and I tried to explain to them. I . . . the insurance, you know, I don't care about the insurance. I'd like to have my wife back. Ah . . . even though we had that large amount, I was not to gain by any of it. I'd promised her already what we would do with it and it would be done."

Jackson asked Headrick what he had promised his wife would be done with the money in the event of her death. He repeated his earlier account of the equal division between her nieces and nephews, with his brother-in-law supervising the trust accounts.

"He goes to the church and everything, and we figured he'd do a lot better job than anybody else, and he's honest. He would have got with it, you know, and done it because I would have contacted him and told him."

James told Headrick he was almost finished with the interview.

"I understand better now how things happened," he said. "Rhonda, you have any last questions?"

"I've heard also that you and Carolyn were planning on building a new house, is that right?" Jackson asked Headrick.

"We were looking at log cabins," he said. "We had contacted a contractor to build a house and it was too high, so we looked at one of the log cabins. You know, I had the deal all laid out; somewhere up there in the weeds, there's a basement layout. You know, the stakes are put up for a basement. I did all that, and everything, but we didn't have the money, we couldn't do it. So what we done was, we just put it off and thought, you know . . . we rode around and dreamed and the blueprints are over there at the house."

After asking the locations of savings and checking accounts that Dora Ann and Carolyn had, and whether or not Headrick had a safety-deposit box, the interview was concluded.

"Well, you know, we're sorry," James told Headrick, "and I'm sure there are still gonna be other questions we have, and we're gonna sit down and talk to you again. I'll tell you again, I'm sorry this happened, and we're going to do all we can to find out who did this."

Randy Headrick didn't realize that one of Carolyn and Dora Ann's close relatives would be questioned later that afternoon by Rhonda Jackson and Jimmy Phillips. That interview would cover many of the same subjects included in his interview, but from an extremely different angle. It would also bring another person of interest to the attention of the investigators: Shane, Headrick's younger brother.

The interview took place at Dora Ann's home, where Sheriff Cecil Reed was preparing to release the crime scene. Phillips began the session by asking if the relative would tell him about what had been going on between Carolyn and Randy during the past two or three weeks.

"Carolyn had gotten real depressed over a money deal between Randy and his sister," the family member said. "Carolyn had been making some little bead necklace sets and sending them over to a store in Fyffe for Randy's sister to sell for her. Time had rocked on and Carolyn hadn't gotten any money. Then one day the sister came over to see Carolyn about getting some cow skulls that she said Randy had sent her to pick up. Carolyn gave them to her, and when Randy came home, he got upset and said his sister had lied. Then a few days later, the sister came over again and talked to Carolyn. Carolyn was really upset with her because Carolyn didn't have any use for a liar.

"Randy's sister broke down and told Carolyn, 'I'm

gonna just tell you, me and Randy had this plan. The things that you've been making for me to sell, I've sold them because Randy owes me money.'"

According to the relative, Randy's sister then told Carolyn that she had already made over $200 on the bead necklaces and said that Randy told her it would be their secret and they wouldn't let Carolyn know anything about it.

"She thought a lot of Carolyn, and she told her that she had loaned him the money for a cellular phone, which he denied, but Carolyn began to doubt him and got real depressed."

The relative also told the investigators that Headrick's friend and mentor, Red Crow, who was in the process of moving, had been giving Headrick quite a few things, which had begun to pile up in Dora Ann's yard.

"Dora Ann had just spent money fixing up the house, and she asked Carolyn for them to move the stuff that was lying around in the yard. Carolyn moved all of it, except for three pieces that she couldn't lift, so she talked to Randy one morning while he was at work and told him that Dora Ann was upset and wanted the stuff moved. He said he would move them when he got there. He said, 'I've been nice to your mother, but no more,' and he was really upset with Dora Ann about it, but he did move it."

Phillips then asked the family member, "When Carolyn talked to you about all this happening, did she say anything about any insurance forms or life insurance?"

She had talked about the excessive amounts of insurance Randy had taken out on her life, the relative said, on Wednesday, just two days prior to the murders.

"Carolyn was real depressed and said that they had been really strained for money, and that she just didn't know anymore; she said they didn't have the money to pay the insurance premium that he had taken out on her. She told me it was a quarter of a million, a renewable term, and that she had asked Randy several times to drop it because they couldn't afford the premiums, but he wouldn't.

She said it was coming up, the term was ending, and she said that when it came up, she wasn't going to sign it again. She was not going to renew it. She also told me that day, 'I'm tired, I'm just so tired,' and was just real depressed."

Phillips asked the relative if Dora Ann had also discussed insurance or spoken about Headrick.

"Yes, Dora Ann called me one day, just tore up because of this particular insurance policy Randy had been pressing Carolyn to borrow against. I don't know if it was the property here or the policy, but it was through this insurance company, he was wanting her to borrow the money, and Dora Ann just stepped in and begged her not to. He had done this more than once. I called Carolyn and talked to her and she assured me she wasn't going to do anything like that, it wasn't her and Randy's home and she wouldn't do that."

The investigators were then told that Randy was constantly suspicious of several of the members of the Dalton family, complaining to Carolyn about them and claiming that when they came to visit, they were after something.

"He tried to tell Carolyn this, that they were after something, and he would tell Carolyn over and over, 'When you die, I won't get any of this place.' In other words, it wouldn't be his and the family wouldn't let him have anything. He said, 'They'll come and take everything that's here.'"

Jackson then asked if Carolyn had ever said anything about a mistake that she believed had been made on one of the insurance policies, the one for $250,000.

"She did tell me, yes, that Randy told her that he did not make her the beneficiary, that the insurance company had made a mistake. [She thought] the papers had been filled out to correct the mistake, but it never happened."

"It wasn't a mistake," Jackson said.

"It's what Randy told Carolyn," the relative said, "that the insurance company had made the mistake in the beneficiary."

"Did Carolyn believe that?" Jackson asked.

"Yes, she believed anything he told her. But then he said he told the insurance agent that Carolyn was the beneficiary and then Dora Ann was next; so that if something happened to him and Carolyn, then Dora Ann would be taken care of. If there was a mistake in the beneficiary, he would have never said that, but Carolyn just wasn't real sharp about things like that."

The investigators established that this had been Carolyn's first marriage, which took place when she was forty-one years old. The couple had been married four years at the time of the murders, and for most of those four years, there had been constant bickering and disagreements among Carolyn, Dora Ann and Headrick.

"When they first got married, things were real good," the family member said. "He treated Dora Ann and Carolyn real good; then an incident arose with a woman he was carrying back and forth to work. He just couldn't deal with the mistrust Carolyn had for him then, and it was like the entire marriage turned around. Dora Ann couldn't say anything or, you know, she was the troublemaker. If him and Carolyn got into it, he claimed Dora Ann was the reason."

When asked about Randy's affair with his former girlfriend, the relative said that Carolyn had talked about it a great deal.

"Carolyn didn't want to believe it was an affair, but she told me everything that she knew about the deal with the girl he was hauling back and forth to work. Carolyn believed that she was just after Randy, and that Randy liked her only as a friend and was giving her rides as a favor, but Randy would spend his off days at the girl's house. He would get up very early in the morning and leave and go to her house. And things that he had made for Carolyn began to start going missing, and when Carolyn would go to the girl's house, she would see the missing things and Randy would deny, 'These aren't the things I gave you, these are things just like them.'"

Then, one morning, it all blew up, the relative said, when Randy came home from work and told Carolyn that he had opened a closet at work and caught his erstwhile girlfriend and a black man together.

"Randy called her husband and told him about it, and the affair just kind of fell apart then. But Dora Ann and Carolyn were threatened by the girl at that time, she said the hurt and stuff and the damage that they had done in her marriage, she was going to do in Carolyn's."

"This may be a hard question for you to answer," Phillips then said, "but it's something I think we need to ask you. In your opinion, who do you think killed Carolyn and Dora Ann?"

The answer came promptly. "I believe Randy did."

"Even though he's got an alibi, you still feel that he's the one that actually killed them, or do you feel that he may have had somebody kill them?"

Again the family member answered quickly and with conviction: "If he didn't actually kill them, then he had to have gone over where everything was located in the house with whoever did kill them."

"Now, we went over with you and told you a little bit about the brutality of these murders," Phillips said, "and told you that it seemed to us to be a hate crime, a very brutal type of murder. If Randy didn't do it, is there anybody else that you might think would be capable of doing something like this?"

Again the answer came without hesitation.

"The only other person that even comes to my mind that I think might be capable of doing it would be Shane, and the only reason that I say that is because of drugs."

Jackson and Phillips immediately snapped to attention. This was the first time anyone they had interviewed had named a person other than Randy Headrick that they thought could possibly have been involved in the murders.

"Now, Shane is his brother, is that right?" asked Phillips, who had been acquainted with Shane Headrick for some time. "I know Shane, and he has definitely got drug problems."

Waylon Shane Headrick had just become a person of interest in the deaths of his sister-in-law and her mother, but whether he was actually involved—and, if so, to what degree—would not be determined any time soon.

CHAPTER 7

Another questioning session took place that same hot, muggy afternoon, across the road at the home of Randy Headrick's parents. Investigators Rhonda Jackson and Mike James conducted an interview that was informative at times, but took quite a bizarre turn at other times. Kenneth "Red Crow" Snapp, Randy Headrick's friend and advisor in all things Native American, sat down with the two officers and discussed his acquaintance with Headrick and his personal observations of Headrick's relationship with his wife.

Snapp, himself a member of the Piqua Sept of Ohio Shawnee Tribe, hoped to establish and gain state recognition of a similar Shawnee tribe in Alabama. He recruited a group of local would-be Indians to become a part of his tribe, and styled himself as their holy man and leader. His home served as a gathering place for his small circle of followers, and they met often to talk about Red Crow's versions of Indian culture and lifestyle, and to learn how to do various types of crafts.

Despite his many eccentricities, Red Crow was an excellent, meticulous crafter whose work in silversmithing, flute making and many other crafts was recognized as some of the finest in the Southeast. He was regularly invited to display and demonstrate his work at the prestigious Indian festival at the state park at Moundville, Alabama, where a group of Mississippian-era Indian mounds had been the source of archaeological study for decades. For some reason, Red Crow's crafting accomplishments served to lend him some degree of credibility as a spiritual advisor, and his loyal followers hung on his every word.

Mike James began the interview by asking Red Crow if he had been acquainted with the murder victims, Dora Ann Dalton and Carolyn Headrick. Red Crow said that he was not well-acquainted with Mrs. Dalton and told the officers that he had only met her a couple of times, but he said that he and his wife had both come to know Carolyn Headrick very well over the past two or three weeks. They had met, he said, through her husband, Randy.

"How did you come to meet Randy?" James asked.

"He'd been hearing about me, and his brother-in-law [who lived in Chattanooga] brought him in the store," Red Crow said. "We got to talking and found out we lived rather close. He wanted to learn more about Indian culture, and for his wife to learn more about Indian culture. It worked out, and I was teaching him stuff and giving him self-confidence and [helping him to be] more outgoing. Randy was very proud of that, he was very proud of that."

"Now, you met him, you said, through his brother-in-law?" James asked. "How did you come to know the brother-in-law?"

Red Crow replied that the man had come into the store a few times prior to his bringing Headrick there.

"We're talking about a store you own, a store in Chattanooga?"

"Well, four of us own it together. It's a Native American gallery, arts and crafts, supplies, an assortment of supplies," Red Crow said.

James asked if Red Crow had ever heard of Headrick or his wife having any trouble of any sort with other people, or if anyone had been causing them any kind of problems.

"None with his wife," Red Crow said, "but there's been several people that Randy's talked about, told me about, never mentioning names, which he was having problems with. Somebody was trying to harass him up and down the road about some things that he stood up for. . . ."

"Did he tell you what those things were?" James asked.

"Well, somebody was running around on their wife and he told them about it, told the man about it, his wife was running around on him, that's what it was," Red Crow said. "He told the man about it and he got angry about it and he got a little out of sorts about it. Randy's one that'll tell them the way it is, and a lot of people don't like that."

Red Crow then volunteered a statement that struck the investigators as absolutely preposterous, considering what they had already learned about Headrick.

"He stands for what's true and what's right," Red Crow pronounced. "He don't cut no ice with it, he's plainspoken."

Mike James chose not to comment any further on what he personally thought Headrick stood for, and decided to switch to another topic.

"You ever seen any kind of trouble between Randy and his wife or his mother-in-law?"

"No," Red Crow answered. "They had a relationship, from what I seen, was pretty much like me and my first mother-in-law, a pecking, ornery kind of thing, aggravating one another. But nothing, no; Randy was devoted over his wife, he was very proud of her and everything she did. Even on the sideline, he was trying to tell me that any way I could build her confidence up, so many people put her down."

James asked Red Crow if he thought Carolyn Headrick had perhaps had a learning disability and was a bit slow sometimes.

"Yeah, she was a little slow," Red Crow answered. "We work with people that are slow and with people with what we call environmental retardation. They're not re- tarded. It seems to bring them out, and basically, that's what we seen in her and Randy seen it too. He'd do any- thing to help her."

James asked Red Crow when had he last been in con- tact with Carolyn.

"About three days before, my wife had [spoken with her]. In fact, we was supposed to go tomorrow and spend the day with them. My wife had just come by and dropped off some stuff over there, and Carolyn brought out some tea."

"And you said your wife had talked to her the night before, that would have been Thursday night? She was killed on Friday."

"Yeah, it was Thursday night. My wife had told me about it. They were making plans for us to come over and spend the day with them and eat dinner with them."

James asked Red Crow how he found out about the murders.

"When I come in last night, a note was on the door and my wife heard some gossip about [the murders], and she was trying to find out about it and didn't know who it was. Finally she called last night to Randy's house and an in- vestigator answered, and she begged them to let her know who it was [who had been killed]. She told them we were friends, and that's how we found out who it was."

"What has Randy told you about it?" James asked.

"That he was at work and he can't remember any- thing, that his mind's spinning," Red Crow said. "I know that feeling because I've been there myself."

"Now, wait a minute, you've been there yourself, you know?" James asked.

"In other, different circumstances, but basically the same thing," Red Crow quickly clarified, "but not to do anything with the murder, but, you know, people helping, trying to get him in counseling or . . . all he's saying is 'They took my Carol, they took my Carol.'"

James asked if Headrick had indicated to Red Crow if he had any thoughts about who might be responsible for the murders, and Red Crow said he hadn't. James then asked if Red Crow had suspected that Headrick might have any kind of involvement.

"No," he replied, "I can certainly [say] he wouldn't. He'll find out [who was responsible]."

"That's what we're in the process of trying to find out now, is who they are," James said.

Red Crow then made another astonishing statement.

"I know enough about Randy's past to tell you one thing: if he did it, you'd never catch him until he was ready."

Rhonda Jackson quickly spoke up. "I don't understand—"

"He's government trained," Red Crow announced. "If he had done this, you would not have caught him until he was ready."

"'Until he was ready,'" Jackson repeated.

"He is government trained," Red Crow said again.

"What do you mean by 'government trained'?" Mike James asked.

"Vietnam," Red Crow said.

"Okay," James said, "he was in the infantry or SEALS or recon or what?"

"You have to talk to him," Red Crow said.

The last time the investigators had talked with Headrick about the time he had spent in the army, he had told them his military training had been in diesel mechanics, not covert operations. Headrick's supposed "government training" was evidently something that merited a closer look.

James then asked if there was anything that he and Jackson hadn't asked Red Crow that he thought they needed to know concerning the murders.

"Just that most people, you're gonna hear a lot of gossip, but I can tell you what I seen within the last three weeks or a month and understanding people, most people look at gossip. I look at people, look inside of them," Red Crow said. "What I seen with Randy and Carol, he's gonna have a hard time, but he'll come out of it. Each one of us have a different way of saying what relationships are. They had a relationship between them, they got along quite well and he liked being around me and my wife and him and her folks."

Rhonda Jackson found it odd that Red Crow had formed such deep opinions about Headrick's marriage and his psychological state in what seemed like a very short time, and asked, "How long did you say you had known them?"

"A little over a month," Red Crow answered.

"Little over a month. Okay," Jackson said. "Did Randy tell you how they were killed?"

"No. No, he didn't."

James asked if Randy was still there, at his father's home, where Red Crow's interview was taking place.

"Yeah," Red Crow said, "it took me all morning to get him to lay down and try to get some sleep."

Red Crow then volunteered that he wished he could help the investigators more.

"I've found out one thing in my, my dealings with people, that first impressions are ninety percent right. . . . I question that and start in gray areas."

"For the record," Jackson said, "and I'm not, you know, pointing a finger at you and your wife or anything like that, but where were you and your wife yesterday?"

"My wife [heard about it while she was] cleaning house in Sylvania, and I spent from ten A.M., Chattanooga time, till eleven-thirty at the store. I'm a silversmith there and have to run it sometimes when nobody else does."

"Who did you say owns the store with you?" Jackson asked.

"I didn't say," Red Crow answered smugly.

"Okay, all right, who owns the store with you?"

Red Crow named his three partners in the business, and stated that one was Jewish, one was white, and the other one was Native American.

"That's a fine combination," Mike James remarked.

"Do all of them go to the store on a daily basis?" Jackson asked. Red Crow told her that on Friday, one partner had been in and out all day, another was there for about half the day, and the third partner was celebrating a birthday and only came in once.

"When did you find out about [the murders]?" Jackson asked.

"It was last night, about eight P.M., Alabama time. I was listening to a tape on my tape player, and when I pulled in the driveway, I backed up and parked and sat and finished listening to it. Got out and looked on the door and there was a note on the door. When I started up the mountain here, my wife was just coming down the mountain, so I turned around and went back home and talked to her. Our phones were out, and all Dade County and the Sulphur Springs area too, for some reason. She'd been coming up the mountain to make phone calls back to the house."

Red Crow said the phones in his area were back in service around nine o'clock, and he and his wife went to spend the night with her mother.

"Then I went back in the house this morning to get ready to go and I had a phone call," he said, "and it was Randy asking me to come and help him, so I did."

That concluded Red Crow's statement, which had left the investigators with several very interesting avenues to pursue. Red Crow had made the statement that he knew enough about Headrick's past to assure them that if Randy did commit the murders, they'd never catch him until he was ready. But enough of Headrick's background was already known to law enforcement that they knew he was not government trained, as Red Crow had put it. Instead, an "absent without leave" charge had been at the apex of his military career.

When Red Crow told the investigators that Headrick "stands for what's true and what's right," the Shawnee medicine man's credibility took a serious hit. But later on in the investigation, during another questioning session, he made an even more telling statement when he announced to Rhonda Jackson that even if he had information incriminating Headrick in the case, he wouldn't reveal it to law enforcement. When it came to the value of his statements to the investigation, Red Crow had told the officers exactly what Randy Headrick wanted them to be told. And Headrick had proved that his friend Red Crow could be played like a fiddle.

CHAPTER 8

On Sunday, Randy Headrick was taken by his family to the emergency room at DeKalb Baptist Medical Center in Fort Payne. On arrival, he was helped to an examining room, where his mother told the emergency room staff that her son was refusing to eat or drink. He was shaking and incoherent, she said, and his "nerves were shot." While Headrick sat on the examining table, staring straight ahead, the family members explained to the ER staff that his wife and mother-in-law had been murdered on Friday. He had little to say except that he was not hungry and that he had to "go back to Carol." After being diagnosed as suffering from acute grief reaction, Headrick was prescribed medication for his troubled nerves and then returned to his parents' home.

Bright and early on Monday morning, tips, rumors and accusations related to the double homicide had begun to flood the county jail's switchboard. The DeKalb County authorities prepared to deal with a media frenzy that had begun to surround the case. As was his custom, Sheriff Cecil Reed already had spoken to some of his well-known "regulars," the local reporters who covered county law enforcement on a daily basis, some of whom had come to the crime scene over the weekend. They had been briefed, off the record, by Sheriff Reed. Because of the trust they had earned with Reed and his deputies, those local reporters had an advantage over their colleagues from larger media markets.

On Monday morning, the sheriff found his office crowded with television cameras and reporters from the big area TV stations and newspapers. From Chattanooga, Tennessee, to Huntsville and Birmingham, Alabama, the murders of Dora Ann Dalton and Carolyn Headrick were at the forefront of the news.

"This was one of the worst murder scenes I've ever been to," Reed told reporters. "I've been in law enforcement for thirty years and this is the worst I've ever seen."

After providing information on the discovery of the victims by members of their family, and how they appeared to have been killed, Reed addressed questions about all the fast-circulating rumors that Randy Headrick was a suspect in the murders. Reed confirmed that Headrick had taken out what he called a "large" insurance policy on his wife, naming himself as the beneficiary. However, he said, Headrick had a confirmed alibi and appeared to have been at his job in Fort Payne when the murders took place. Reed went on to describe the Native American artifacts that Headrick collected and made, saying that there were many such items around the house, and that the murder weapons were believed to have been taken from among them. Reed said Headrick was "a collector of unusual weapons," who also fashioned Indian paraphernalia using bone and metal, often selling the items at flea markets in the area.

The sheriff's department currently had neither a suspect nor a motive, Reed said, and drugs and sexual assault had been ruled out as motives. Early on in the investigation, it was believed that a pocketbook was missing from the residence, he told reporters, but it since had been found. Nothing else appeared to be missing from the house, but the gun used in the murders had not been recovered yet. Based on the preliminary autopsy reports, Reed said, it was believed that the weapon was a .22-caliber pistol and that the victims both had been shot at close range. A gun that was found at the house had been determined not to have been the weapon used to shoot the victims. At the present time, Reed said, investigators were actively searching for the missing murder weapon along the roadsides near the crime scene.

"I don't believe this was a random killing," Reed told the press. "I think this was someone who knew them and they probably knew their assailant. There was no sign of forcible entry, but it's not unusual on Sand Mountain for people to leave their doors unlocked. There has to be some motive here, and eventually the motive will be found."

Investigators from his department were working practically around the clock, Reed said.

"We have all our investigators assigned to this," he said, adding that anyone having any information about the murders should call his office.

"We'll take any lead we can get on this one," he said. "Everybody is a suspect. We have no prime suspect. We're asking for help. If anyone has any information, please contact us."

A reward from the governor's office had been requested that morning by DA Richard Igou, and Alabama governor Fob James responded quickly by issuing a proclamation later that same day offering a $10,000 reward for information leading to an arrest and conviction in the case.

"I hope an arrest will come soon," Reed said, "but you never know when you're dealing with this type of situation. This is not a smoking-gun case. We don't have any solid leads.

"This is a tough case," Reed told the people crowded into his office with cameras and microphones. "It's probably the most gruesome, grisly murder I've ever dealt with."

The residents of the rural mountain towns along

Highway 75 had no need to worry, the sheriff said, and repeated that he felt it was not a random killing.

"I feel like whoever committed these crimes had a reason they did it," he said.

While Sheriff Reed dealt with the press in his office off the lobby of the DeKalb County Jail, Investigator Rhonda Jackson sat in her tiny upstairs office reviewing the notes she had carefully taken over the long weekend she had spent, documenting evidence and conducting interviews. This was Rhonda's first time to be named lead investigator on a major crime, and all of her fellow investigators and a large number of uniformed officers had been assigned to the case full-time. She felt that her every action would be judged by her peers, and she was determined to supervise the investigation with the utmost professionalism. Rhonda had worked her way up through the ranks in county law enforcement, from desk job to patrol deputy to the county's first-ever female investigator, and her success or failure in the Headrick case would likely dictate the future of her career. She had been blessed with an extremely supportive husband and family, but there were times when she felt that her striking good looks were a curse. Despite their best intentions, her fellow investigators sometimes tended to treat her more like an attractive woman than a serious law enforcement officer. Because of this, Rhonda Jackson always went out of her way to conduct herself professionally in every aspect of her work. She intended to leave no stone unturned on the Dalton/Headrick murder case. That morning, during the media frenzy downstairs, Rhonda began the first page of what would become a huge file of notes documenting every phone call, every interview and every detail of the work done on the case. Her meticulous notes would prove invaluable to the outcome of the long, complicated investigation for which she was going to be responsible.

The first page she added to the file concerned a phone call Rhonda made that morning to the Alabama

Department of Forensic Sciences when she spoke with Brent Wheeler and Martha Odom, who had worked the crime scene on Friday evening. Their work was far from over, but Wheeler was able to report that the gun used in the murders could have been either a rifle or revolver. The bullet fragments were in bad shape, he said, and he probably would not be able to match them with the gun that killed Dora Ann Dalton and Carolyn Headrick, even if the gun were to be found. Wheeler said the spears and knife used as murder weapons would be checked for fingerprints, and he promised to notify Rhonda immediately if any prints were found.

Later that day, after the turmoil had subsided downstairs and Sheriff Reed had restored order to his department, he received a call from one of Randy Headrick's female relatives. She asked the sheriff if he would come to her place of business and talk to her, so Reed got in his car and headed there immediately.

The woman had received a collect phone call, she claimed, from a girl who said that she was at a hospital in an adjoining county and wanted the Headrick woman to come there to talk to her. The woman told Sheriff Reed that she went to the Jackson County Hospital in Scottsboro and met, as requested, with the girl, whom she identified by name. She claimed the girl had told her that on the day of the murders, she had been at a house in a remote community called Happy Hollow, an area on the far north end of DeKalb County that had long been notorious for its abundance of drug dealers and bootleggers. The Headrick woman told the sheriff that the girl had said that two men had come to the house with blood on their clothes, saying, "The job was done." And, the girl said, the men then burned their clothes outside in the yard.

The sheriff immediately passed this information along to the detectives. This was one of the first of countless numbers of calls and tips he would forward to them over the course of the investigation, and the first of many that would lead the authorities down far too many dead-end trails of lies and accusations. When she was located and questioned, the girl denied having been at the Jackson County Hospital, and said she did not place a collect phone call to the Headrick woman. In fact, she did not even know her. She had solid alibis for her whereabouts at the time of the alleged gathering in Happy Hollow, as well as for the supposed meeting at the hospital. Later on, when the Headrick relative's telephone records were subpoenaed, they showed there had been no collect calls from the Jackson County Hospital placed to the woman's phone, at home or at her business. Her tip turned out to be one of the many false leads, very likely an intentional one, that bogged down the investigation and wasted countless hours of valuable time in the search for a killer.

CHAPTER 9

Not all the tips the county officers received regarding the Headrick case on that Monday morning proved to be useless. Several witnesses came forward during the course of the day with some very valuable information about a red truck that had been seen leaving the murder scene at approximately 1:30 P.M. on Friday, July 7.

James Donald "Donnie" Watkins and his wife, Kim, were riding down Shady Lane on their way to a friend's house that afternoon. Kim commented to her husband about the large tent that had been set up in the side yard of the Dalton house, and when she looked back toward the road, she saw a red pickup truck cross a small wooden bridge on the dirt road ahead of their vehicle. Donnie, who was driving, thought that he saw the truck back out of the driveway of the Dalton house. He saw it spin out, fishtailing across the bridge and continuing on down the road at a high rate of speed. The truck appeared to be driven by a man with medium-length dark hair, which looked like it stuck out below his collar. Neither Donnie nor Kim could see anyone else in the truck. Donnie could tell that the truck bore an Alabama license tag, but neither he nor Kim could remember the tag number. Both agreed the truck looked like the one parked under the carport at the Dalton residence, a smaller model, like a Chevy S10.

Five houses south of the Dalton home on Shady Lane that Friday afternoon, two young women had been cleaning a house that had belonged to one of the women's deceased mother. As they worked to get the house ready for a tenant, they heard a vehicle on the road speeding past the house.

"Boy, that one was in a hurry," one of the women said as the other woman looked up in time to see the back end of what she described as a medium-sized dark red pickup going south on the dirt road at a high rate of speed.

The young women couldn't see who was driving the truck, or if there were any passengers, and couldn't remember if the truck passed by the house before or after they saw a police car go by.

Another statement concerning a red pickup came from the wife of an Ider business owner who was acquainted with Randy Headrick's friend Red Crow. The woman told Rhonda Jackson that she remembered a red truck coming to Red Crow's house on a recent occasion, but didn't know the name of the driver, who was a man with grayish hair. She said that Randy and Carolyn Headrick were there at the time, along with another couple, members of the local Indian community, whose Native ancestry was highly questionable. The man, whose nickname had been "Cowboy" up until he decided to reinvent himself and morph into an Indian, had begun calling himself "Crazy Bear," and his girlfriend, who claimed to be a medicine woman, was known as "Whitefeather." Both were very new on the Indian scene and had only recently begun to identify themselves as having Native ancestry. Although, according to others in their circle of acquaintances, the couple didn't have a drop of Indian blood in their veins. The investigators took note of their backgrounds and their presence at Red Crow's home, just in case they should become persons of interest in the case and might need to be brought in for questioning.

When the Dalton family member had been interviewed on Saturday and had stated that the only other person they believed could have been involved with the murders might have been Headrick's brother, Shane, Rhonda Jackson immediately set out to locate Shane Headrick. She soon learned he was living in Georgia with his girlfriend, Jill Shrader, who was working at a hospital in the Atlanta area. Shane and Jill were believed to be staying at a motel called the Lodge on Buford, in Chamblee, Georgia. Jackson contacted the Georgia Bureau of Investigation (GBI) to enlist their assistance in locating and questioning the couple. On Monday, two GBI agents went to the motel and found that Shane and Jill were registered in room 140. The agents questioned the motel employees about the couple and learned that Shane was driving a silver Ford Ranger pickup truck and Jill was driving a tan 1987 Nissan Sentra, but they were not in their room and the agents were unable to make contact with them at that time.

Another important development in the case came on Monday when Investigator Jimmy Phillips and Chief Deputy Eddie Wright interviewed the woman who had been identified as Randy Headrick's "girlfriend." She had plenty of information and she was ready to tell the two officers about her former suitor.

When she worked at the Earthgrains bakery in Fort Payne, she said, she had an eight- or nine-month affair with Headrick. He repeatedly told her that he and his wife were not getting along, and she said that he'd told her that if he could just get rid of his wife and mother-in-law, he'd have it made. The woman claimed that Headrick had been stalking her for the past year, since their breakup, and said that she had been getting a lot of hang-up calls at her home. She told the officers that she had a trap on her phone line at that time, but only one call had been traced so far.

The woman said that a fire had occurred at her home after the breakup with Headrick, and that it had been

ruled as arson, and she told them that Headrick was a suspect. In her mind, she said, she thought that Headrick had
gotten someone to kill his wife and mother-in-law, but she
had no idea who he could have gotten to do it.

After he got home on Monday evening, Investigator
Jimmy Phillips found that he had received two phone calls
at his home from an acquaintance of Headrick's. When
he contacted the man, Phillips was told that Headrick had
stopped by the man's home and told him that the police
were trying to give someone a break if they would tie him
in with the murders. Headrick claimed he had been advised by his lawyer that the police were going to make an
arrest in the case within the next week or so. The man told
Phillips that Headrick had said that he planned to sue the
sheriff's department on eleven counts of harassment
concerning the case, and said that Headrick claimed he
was being followed by the police, who were driving a
white car. The man also told Phillips that Headrick said
that he was going to get possession of Dora Ann's house
back from the Dalton family, and as soon as he got the
death certificates back, he planned to file on the insurance policies. Headrick, he said, had told him he had
"some of their stuff" in a storage building in the town of
Ider, and the man told Phillips that Headrick claimed he
was still taking medicine. He was still shaking, the man
said, but not as badly as he had seen him in the past.

Early on the morning of Tuesday, July 11, the two GBI
agents who had visited Shane Headrick and Jill Shrader's
motel phoned room 140 at the Lodge on Buford, and a
man they believed to be Shane answered the phone.
Around noon, the agents went to question Shane and Jill
at their motel room and found them packing their bags,
preparing to move to a less expensive motel in the Ma-
rietta, Georgia, area. They had been at the Lodge on
Buford for a week, they said, and prior to that, they had

lived in East Point, Georgia, at a motel that they thought was called the Good Nite Inn.

Shane Headrick, who had shoulder-length brown hair, told the agents he was currently unemployed, but usually he worked in sheet metal construction. Jill Shrader said that she worked as a registered nurse with a company that sent her to several different kidney dialysis units at hospitals and clinics in the Metro Atlanta area.

When asked if they had gone to the victims' funerals on Monday, the couple said they had gone to Alabama on Sunday, but they only stayed around for an hour and a half. They left because they felt "strange." Prior to that visit, they had been in Alabama two weeks earlier. They had not talked to either of the victims at that time, they claimed, but Jill said that she saw Carolyn and Dora Ann outside in their yard.

They were notified about the deaths, they said, on Sunday morning by Jill's mother and ex-husband; then Shane phoned his parents' home and they confirmed that the women had been murdered. When asked by the agents, Jill said that someone had told her the cause of death for both victims was their being shot with a shotgun, and then a spear was stuck in their hearts. Shane added, "My brother makes spears; they are all around the house." The agents asked how they learned the details of the deaths, and Jill replied that she had found out from her son, who was married to the daughter of Investigator Jimmy Phillips.

Shane and Jill were asked to contact the GBI agents as soon as they got settled into another motel, and they agreed to do so.

Investigator Mike James had scheduled an early-morning interview with a man who had contacted him after hearing of the murders, a former coworker of Randy Headrick's at Earthgrains bakery. He and Headrick had worked together for around two years, the man said, up until Headrick had been fired from his job.

"When you called me yesterday afternoon, you told me you'd had some problems with Headrick," James said.

The man told James that he and Headrick had been friends up until Headrick's behavior became erratic and began to pose problems at work. Eventually, the man said, he had no choice but to submit a complaint to Earthgrains regarding Headrick's sexual harassment of other workers, which eventually led to Headrick's termination.

"I was so afraid at that time because, knowing Randy, I mean, we'd had two years of association; I'm a Vietnam vet, so we used to get into talking about things, his military activity and his way of thinking. He scared me so much when [he was fired], I actually strapped a knife to my hand and slept on the couch for two or three nights. I strapped it to my hand so if I fell asleep, if he came in, then he wouldn't be able to knock it out and I would have something to fight with. That's how afraid of the man I was, and when I heard about [the murders of his wife and mother-in-law], it just sounds like that—that . . . you know."

The man told James that Headrick had claimed to have "a list of about three hundred people, nationwide, a military type of thing, that if he needed a favor done, he could have them come in and do it. He asked me would I like to get on this list. I didn't. I said, 'Randy, you don't need to talk like this to me, I don't want to hear any more about it or anything like that.' That's all I know, is that he said he had a list, and that if I had a favor that needed to be done, all he had to do was return the favor someday, if somebody called him to have it done."

James asked the man if he'd heard anything mentioned at Earthgrains about the affair that Randy had with his ex-girlfriend.

"Yeah, I heard something about it, rumors and hearsay," he answered, "that he even threatened to burn her house down, or something."

"You said that you and your wife had gone camping with

Randy and Carolyn. What was their relationship [like] when they were together?" James asked.

The man reported that the couple seemed cordial toward each other, but then added that Headrick had denied his marriage to another friend of his, and had been telling people he was divorced. He said that he had never heard Headrick threaten his wife, but went on to say, "It was his mother-in-law that he despised, talking about what a bitch she is and she's always down his throat. I don't know, I can't quote anything, but his attitude and all that toward her just sounded like, you know, 'If she was out of here, Carol and I would be fine.'"

When asked about Headrick's claims about his military service, the man, himself a veteran of two years in Vietnam, said that Headrick was vague about his alleged military experience. He would leave the impression that he had spent time there and knew all about Vietnam.

"I don't think he ever was, though," the man told James. "There was one time he had a dispute with a neighbor, and came to me and asked if I remembered any of my jungle tactics and stuff. He wanted to set up booby traps, like pungee sticks and log-swing types of devices. I can't remember if it was around his house or if it was his neighbor's property in the woods. He was always into that kind of thing."

James asked if Headrick was a collector of anything, and the man said, "Yeah, everything, from stamps to knives, Civil War stuff. . . ."

Headrick had told him that he had a stamp portfolio that was worth a lot of money, he said, but he had never seen it, adding, "Randy had a lot of stories, you know." He said Headrick did have a knife collection displayed in the house, which he had seen a couple of times.

"He had them all over his walls, and he took me back to his bedroom one time, and he had a whole box full of them. They were all thrown in together, a lot of cheap stuff. I didn't see anything that impressed me."

The man went on to say that he and Headrick shared

an interest in Civil War memorabilia, and Headrick claimed to have many different items, but he had never actually seen any of them.

James asked if Headrick had been interested in Indian artifacts at the time the two men were acquainted.

"Well, he talked about the Indian stuff and Civil War stuff, and . . . there's this friend of his that lives down on the river at Bridgeport during the summer, he's a fisherman, and the guy's got to have guns. I mean, you can't sit anywhere without sitting on a gun." The fisherman, he said, camped every summer at the same location, and fished for catfish, which he sold. He also had a great many guns, which Randy was always talking about.

"We're just looking at all aspects of this case," James said, "and we feel sure that Randy did not commit the murders himself because he has an alibi as to where he was. If he's involved in this, and that's a big *if,* who in your knowledge, as his friend, who would he have got to help him?"

"Somebody on this list that he told me that he had," the man said. "I never personally met anybody on it."

The man told James that the gun-happy fisherman was outgoing and friendly, but he had a son he described as "wild and crazy," off-the-wall and gun-toting, and said that the son disturbed him.

"That's a good possibility there," he said, "that he would be the one person I'd say that I had met personally."

James asked the man if there was anything else that he hadn't been asked about that he thought might be pertinent to the case.

The man laughed. "I wrote out a list last night," he said. "I got concerned for myself too, because, you know, me being the result of his termination at Earthgrains. I thought, well, if it happened and Randy was involved, I had a fear that the termination might have sparked this whole thing."

James asked if the man knew whether Randy had a drinking problem or did drugs.

"No. He said he used to, but he was in jail or prison or

something like that one time. He always told me, 'If I drink, I'd go crazy,' and that was what happened, how he ended up in the penitentiary. He said his face got all messed up in a fight and that he almost killed two guys in a fight, that he just went wild, and when he drinks, he was like an animal. I didn't question him about it; I didn't want to know. We never sat down and talked about it and got it all down, but he used to always mention about how this fight was, and how his face was half plastic, and hurts still."

James thanked the man and ended the interview, making careful note to take a trip over to the river to check out the fisherman and his son.

Earlier that morning, Chief Deputy Eddie Wright organized a search party made up of a number of his sheriff's deputies, rescue squad members and law enforcement personnel from several of the towns along Highway 75, and citizen volunteers from the communities in the area. The large group of people spent several hours conducting a careful, thorough search all along the sides of Shady Lane, the dirt road that passed by the Dalton residence, hoping to locate the murder weapon. Their efforts produced nothing—no gun, and no other useful clues of any sort. But Wright left the search with a strong feeling that the people of Henagar, Ider and the surrounding area were willing to do anything they possibly could if it would aid in the arrest and conviction of the person or persons responsible for the murders of Carolyn and Dora Ann.

Back at the sheriff's department, Rhonda Jackson spoke again with Donnie Watkins by phone, hoping he might have remembered some additional details about the red pickup he and his wife saw speeding away from the Dalton home around 1:30 to 1:45 P.M., the time the murders were believed to have been committed. Watkins said that he believed the pickup he saw was definitely not a full-sized truck; he thought it was a midsize to a smaller size, he said, about the size of a Toyota pickup, and was not a four-wheel drive. He told Jackson that the tailgate was solid red, and if it had any lettering on the tailgate, it was the same color as the truck. He remembered it had an Alabama tag, and thought its number might have begun with "28," which is the tag number prefix for vehicles registered in DeKalb County. The truck appeared to be a newer model, he said, possibly an '89 to '92 model truck, and looked to be in good shape. He and his wife were about thirty yards behind the truck, and he believed that it had just pulled out of the driveway of the Dalton house.

The search for red pickup trucks was on, and it would spread from DeKalb County to other surrounding counties and states, leading the investigators down an untold number of dead-end roads over the coming months.

CHAPTER 10

On Wednesday, Sheriff Cecil Reed announced to the press that the $10,000 reward requested of Alabama governor Fob James had been granted, and it would be given to the person who provided information leading to the arrest and conviction of the person or persons responsible for the murders of Carolyn and Dora Ann.

Reed once again told reporters that Randy Headrick "has an ironclad alibi," since his coworkers had said he was at work when the women died.

"The main question is," Reed said, "why would anyone use at least three weapons on a victim, when any one of them could prove fatal? Why did the killer overdo this?"

Reed said his officers were investigating "some bits and pieces of information we have received. Some tips need to be checked out, but we definitely need more to go on. Maybe the ten-thousand-dollar reward will help."

According to Reed, there was no indication that either of the two victims had an enemy anywhere in the world.

"We found no one who spoke a word of harm against these women," he said. "They all said they were quiet, stay-at-home types. They weren't employed; they were full-time homemakers."

Reed told the press about the life insurance policies on Carolyn Headrick, and said the companies would not pay the beneficiary until the case was settled. He said deputies were on their way from Huntsville to the state crime lab in Montgomery to deliver fingerprints from the crime scene, which would be matched with others on file at the Alabama Department of Public Safety.

"They have agreed in Montgomery to move our case ahead of everything else," he said. "We will know soon if there is a possible match."

Reed said again that robbery, sex and drugs had been ruled out as motives in the case, and the murder weapon had not been located. No blood had been tracked anywhere in the house, even though the shots were fired at close range, he said.

"I think the victims knew the killer, and the killer knew the victims," he told reporters.

While Reed conducted his press conference, Investigator Simpson and Investigator Phillips interviewed another woman who had worked with Randy Headrick at the Earthgrains bakery. She, too, admitted that she had had an affair with him, which lasted around one-and-a-half months. She worked at the bakery as a security guard at the time, and told the officers that she broke off the relationship when Headrick began talking to her about having her husband killed. He had a friend who lived on the river at Bridgeport, Alabama, he said, whom he could enlist to kill her husband. The woman said she then became afraid of Headrick and quit seeing him, but before their breakup, he told her that if he ever got in trouble with the law, he wouldn't be jailed. He would only go to the Veterans Administration Hospital for a short time because of his service record.

When Sheriff Reed returned to his office after meeting with the press, he received another one of those interesting tidbits that were coming in more and more frequently. A woman called him to say that she'd had an anonymous phone call saying that the wrong people had been killed; the victims were supposed to have been the wife and mother of another person in the same area with the last name of

Dalton. Reed doubted the accuracy of the information, but like all the other tips he received—no matter how far-fetched—the story of the anonymous call was treated seriously and was thoroughly checked out by the officers working on the case.

Investigators Rhonda Jackson and Mike James traveled to Kennesaw, Georgia, and met with GBI agents Larry Landers and Mike Lewis, who had spoken with Jill Shrader and Shane Headrick in Chamblee, Georgia. The officers went to the Smith Motel, where Shane and Jill had checked in when they left the Lodge on Buford. There, the officers conducted lengthy separate interviews with Shane and Jill.

Shane, who confirmed that he was Randy Headrick's brother, told James and Landers that on the day of the murders he took Jill to work around 4:30 A.M., then returned to the motel room. Jill called him around 10:00 or 10:30 A.M., he said, then between 12:30 and 1:00 P.M., calling him for the last time around 3:30 P.M. He stayed in the motel room and out by the pool all that day, he claimed.

Shane said he knew that Randy and Carolyn fought over Dora Ann, and told the officers that Randy had a .22 rifle. He said Randy had a $150,000 life insurance policy on himself and on Carolyn while he worked at Earthgrains bakery.

"I later heard he had got a second policy," he said, "but I don't know any details."

Shane then dropped a tidbit of information that immediately got the attention of the officers.

"Jill told me that Randy wanted Jill and her son to 'fuck up' Randy's ex-girlfriend," he said. "I do not know who killed Randy's wife and mother-in-law, but in my heart, I think that Randy is responsible for their deaths."

Shane also told the officers that he had heard Red Crow had a friend who had a red Chevy S10 pickup.

Jill Shrader's interview, conducted by Rhonda Jackson and Mike Lewis, was more lengthy and more productive than Shane's. Jill, forty-three, said that she and twenty-two-year-old Shane had been living together for just over a year and had known each other for three or four months before moving in together. The only relationship she had with Randy, she said, was as Shane's brother.

"I believe you had an occasion to talk to Randy one time about him trying to hire you and your son to do something for him," Rhonda said. "Can you tell us about that?"

"He was gonna go to Texas with me and my son and get some cranes that we were gonna bring back and sell and make some money off of them, whatever, and in order for him to do that, we had to do something for him. What he wanted us to do was for me to get in contact with his ex-girlfriend and get to where she would go somewhere with me, and my son was to do some dirty stuff to her and carve up her face and break a few bones, not kill her, but do some damage to her."

When asked who the ex-girlfriend was, Jill said she didn't know the woman's name.

"I just know it's a girlfriend of his. He told me she had a baby by him and that's caused him a lot of trouble and was still causing him trouble. He would park his truck across the road at his mom's because he was afraid they would do something to his truck. And he said she caused him to get fired from Earthgrains, the bakery in Fort Payne."

"Did he tell you what he wanted done to her?" Rhonda asked.

"He just told me a little bit. My son told me a little bit more, he said, 'Mom, he's sick,' he said he wanted no part of this stuff. We'd already decided that when we first started listening to him, but he kept on, you know, for several weeks wanting us to. He offered us all kinds of stuff. He told me I could have charge cards, go on a big shopping spree, he'd get me a card, he'd do this, he'd do that, you know. It was all kinds of stuff we were offered."

Rhonda asked Jill why she and her son didn't take Randy up on his generous offers.

"I'm not into anything like that, nothing," Jill said.

Jill said the attempt to hire her and her son took place in September of the previous year.

"There was several times he came by," Jill said. "He always waited till Shane wasn't there and he told me not to talk to Shane about it."

"Why did he not want you to talk to Shane about it?" Rhonda asked.

"I have no idea," Jill said, adding that she did tell Shane about it, but only just recently. She said Randy had never asked her to do anything to anyone else.

"Did he ever talk about Carolyn and Dora Ann in your presence?" Rhonda asked.

He had, Jill said, adding that she'd never heard him say anything good at all about either one of them.

"He called them evil bitches and that he'd like to drive something through their evil hearts and would like to figure some way of getting them out of his life. He said stuff like that, on and on, every time he talked about them at all, it was always something like that."

"Okay, all right. . . . Did he say what he would like to drive through their hearts?"

"No, I don't remember anything, but I tended to just steer away from Randy. I thought he was crazy; I thought that from the very start, when he started in with the stuff he wanted us to do to his girlfriend. I really thought he was just talking. And he'd go over stuff about how you could do things and you could not leave any clues and nobody would never know; just me and my son would do such and such, or whatever. He had ways of getting rid of everything."

"What was he talking about?" Rhonda asked.

"He had some kind of acid he could burn everything up with, that would just dissolve everything, where there would be nothing left. It would even dissolve bones, he said. He just, he said there was ways if you knew how to do them where nobody could ever trace anything back to you."

Outwardly Rhonda remained totally calm and professional, but her heart was pounding. This interview was becoming far more revealing than she had hoped.

"He was wanting you to do this to his girlfriend. Ah . . . is there some reason why he wanted somebody else to do it, he wouldn't do it himself?"

"I don't know, unless he thought they were watching him all the time because he was, like I said, he was real careful about everything. And his excuse to us was that he didn't trust her or her family," Jill said, "that there had been something about a safe and a bunch of drugs in a safe, like crack and marijuana and stuff like that, a whole lot. I mean pounds, not little amounts, that he got out of their house or something, and it was hid in the woods and nobody could find it, and he was the only one that knew where it was. But he'd already . . . some stuff had been done to them, as the house had burned and stuff had been stolen from them."

Rhonda asked Jill if Randy had ever said anything to her about the ex-girlfriend's house burning.

"You gotta realize Randy is just talk," Jill said. "You know, and I'm trying to remember exact stuff he's said, 'cause I try not to listen to him. I know that he said he'd got her some, but he wasn't through with her, that he wanted some more stuff done to her 'cause of what all she'd done to him."

Jill said that, to her knowledge, Randy had never solicited anyone else to do anything to the woman.

Rhonda asked if Randy had ever said anything else about Carolyn and Dora Ann, other than his statements about driving something through their hearts.

"Just that they bitched on him all the time—*bitch, bitch, bitch, bitch*—and stuff about their evil hearts and their tongues and crazy talk." Jill said Randy had never tried to enlist her and her son to do anything to Carolyn and Dora Ann.

"All right," Rhonda said, "did he ever tell you anything about the deal in Texas where he was charged with making a pipe bomb to blow up his ex-wife? Did he ever tell you about that?"

"Yeah," Jill answered, "he said that he was at work and had—I think the reason he told me this was to try to make me believe he was more fierce, because I would kind of laugh him off—he said that he was at work and he had a thing showing that he was at work, that there wasn't any way they could prove he was anywhere else, but he had his ways of doing stuff. He knows a lot of people, he said."

"Okay, let's go to Friday, July seventh," Rhonda said, "can you tell me your whereabouts on that day?"

Jill said she had gotten to work at a clinic in downtown Atlanta that day at around 5:45 A.M., and Shane had taken her to work and dropped her off. She said that she had gotten off work that evening at 4:15 P.M., when Shane picked her up.

"Do you know Shane's whereabouts during that time you were at work?" Rhonda asked.

"I know that I talked to him that morning after I talked to his dad, so it had to be somewhere between nine-thirty and ten A.M. And then I didn't talk to him again until later that afternoon, probably around two-thirty P.M., maybe between two-thirty and three."

Rhonda asked Jill if she had tried to call the motel room several times during the day.

"Well, I tried a couple of times and he said he was at the pool," Jill said.

"But you did talk to him on the phone both times?"

"Yes."

"All right. . . . Has Shane said anything to you about these murders? As far as . . . has Randy told Shane anything about these murders?"

"Shane certainly has not," Jill stated firmly.

"Okay," Rhonda said. "There was a small red pickup

seen in that area where these two ladies were murdered. Do you know anybody that may own a small red pickup?"

"I don't know the man personally," Jill said, "but Shane says the Indian friend that Randy has been running around with lately had a small red pickup."

Jill said that she was aware of Randy's interest in the Indian artifacts he collected and made, but she didn't know Randy's Indian friend or how they met.

"Okay, Jill, let me ask you," Rhonda said, "do you think Shane is involved in these murders?"

"I would think more toward that line if I knew he wasn't in Atlanta during the time of the murder," Jill admitted. "I don't even know what time the murders took place."

"Do you think Shane is capable of something like that?" Rhonda asked.

"I think he's definitely capable of murder," Jill answered surprisingly. "I don't like to think he would be capable of doing all the things that were done to them."

When Rhonda said that Randy appeared to have an airtight alibi, Jill replied, "I wouldn't doubt it."

"He was at work that day," Rhonda told her. "If Randy had planned this, to get somebody to do this job, would you have any idea who he would have gotten to do this?"

"No," Jill said, "I don't know of anybody other than what I've already talked about. That would be my first guess. I would think that would be the way it was, if it wasn't for the time difference, the time zone. And I'm still scared."

"That last statement you just made," Rhonda said, "are you saying that if it wasn't for the time difference—"

"That I would be inclined to think it was Shane," Jill said.

"Yes, right," Rhonda said. "I think you made the statement before the interview began, that Randy hated his wife and mother-in-law."

"I don't know of anybody I've ever seen that had that much hate toward somebody they were living with," Jill said. "It was just a strong hatred, but when he was with them, it was a different thing. Like when I saw him with Carol, it was honey and everything, and it was okay, and he had that look and action toward her. But when they weren't together, in front of just us and his family, it was a totally different thing. And if you didn't know any different, you would have thought that was the way he really felt about them when you saw them together."

On July 14, an article appeared in Fort Payne's daily newspaper, the *Times-Journal,* written by one of the area's top crime reporters, LaRue Cornelison. After working diligently to get information on the case, she finally had succeeded in getting Randy Headrick to come forward and make his first statements to the press since the murders. Six days after the murders, he talked to Cornelison at length and told her, "I'm ready to stand up and fight. I want the person who did it to get the electric chair. I'm going to keep looking and looking and try to find out for myself who did it. I told the police I'd help them any way I could."

Headrick said he and Carolyn shared Indian crafts as a hobby, and said the Native American keepsakes on the walls were some he and Carolyn made, plus some were gifts from friends.

"The police have been questioning Indians on the mountain," Headrick told Cornelison. "They think this killing was a ritual. But it's nothing. Me and my wife just enjoyed this as a hobby."

Headrick claimed he had a list of items taken off the walls, even though police had determined nothing had been removed except the spears and knife that were found in the victims' bodies.

"And there was a few dollars in my wife's purse that are missing," he said.

Headrick also spoke of the issues that he claimed had raised everyone's suspicions against him: the $250,000 life insurance policy on Carolyn, and his own criminal record.

The insurance policy, he said, was intended to be used to employ a full-time nurse for his mother-in-law in the event Carolyn died, because Mrs. Dalton was in poor health.

"I do have a past criminal record," he told Cornelison. "I came here to start my life over. In the past five years, all I've had is a couple of traffic tickets. I've lived a good Christian life and helped my neighbors. I did do time in prison—four years, and then two years on probation—for possession of an unregistered weapon, a pipe bomb." Headrick said he was in a truck with the man who made the bomb, and the bomb was in the back of the truck, when police arrested them.

"I want people to know I'm not trying to hide anything," he claimed.

In another, related article, which ran directly beneath the first on the *Times-Journal*'s front page, Cornelison interviewed Headrick's father, Waylon, owner of the Fyffe Antique Mall, who told her he had retained a lawyer to represent his son. Bob French, one of the best-known and most colorful defense lawyers in the Southeast, said that he would be representing Randy Headrick in all matters concerning the murder investigation. French, who had been known to introduce himself as "the notorious Bob French," was often deemed by his peers to be "the Gerry Spence of the South." He had defended Judith Ann Neelley some years earlier at her sensational DeKalb County trial for the brutal murder of Lisa Ann Millican, a young Georgia teenager who Neelley kidnapped and injected with drain cleaner, before shooting her in the back and throwing her body into Little River Canyon.

Neelley was found guilty and received the death sentence, but that outcome was not due to a lack of skilled defense. Bob French, an absolute master at his craft, used every trick in the book to try to exonerate his client despite the overwhelming evidence that convinced the jury of her guilt. French would do no less for Randy Headrick, but even though everything pointed to his new client being implicated in the murders of his wife and mother-in-law, there was still that ironclad alibi for French to work with, and he would use it well. In the meantime, he told the press that he would see to it that his client would be protected from unreasonable questioning by the authorities.

Waylon Headrick told Cornelison that his son had undergone a double trauma on Friday, first learning about the brutal murders and then immediately facing the police and being treated as a suspect. The questioning, he said, had left his son disoriented, and he was unable to work and was under a physician's care. He was sedated by doctors at the DeKalb Baptist Medical Center's emergency room on the night of his wife and mother-in-law's funeral services, and was currently being cared for at his parents' home.

"We were close to both of them," Waylon Headrick said of Carolyn and Dora Ann. "I have no idea at all who did this. I can't imagine them having an enemy who could do anything like that . . . or them even having an enemy."

Sheriff Cecil Reed told Cornelison that "everybody's a suspect at this point," and said that extensive questioning had taken place throughout the community, including family members and friends, particularly within the Native American community. The main one of those who had been questioned, Red Crow, also spoke to Cornelison at length. He told her that Randy and Carolyn Headrick were intensely interested in learning the authentic craft techniques, such as beadwork and making rattles, spears and other items. He explained that this was the reason that Headrick's home contained so many of the Native American pieces, and he said it was unfortunate the killer chose to use items taken from the wall, the spears and knife, to send what he called "a message for somebody. I believe somebody innocent got in the way. Shooting, stabbing and spearing has nothing to do with Native Americans," he said, "and for anybody to say Randy had anything to do with it is absurd. They were good people, had nothing to do with drugs or gambling. Most men would love to have a woman and most women would love to have a man to love them the way these two loved each other."

Red Crow said he and others in the local Native American community had been questioned by the sheriff's investigators, but he felt that none of those they had talked to had been able to be of much help.

"None of us know anything but what's been in the papers," he said. "I have nothing to hide. The Native American community is a network people don't understand. A true Native American can be recognized not by the regalia he wears. It is his way of life that sets the example."

Red Crow told Cornelison that he resented a television news report that said skulls were laid out in the Headricks' front yard to form symbols.

"Where did they get that?" he asked.

It was common practice among Indian craft workers, he said, to get skulls from slaughterhouses and clean them by leaving them outdoors in the weather and exposed to insects, and the bones from animal skeletons were left out to be cleaned in the same manner, then used for making jewelry and other items.

Red Crow said that Headrick did not claim to be Native American, and Carolyn did claim to be part Native American, but their interest in their artwork hobby was sincere.

"I could name four or five other families in the area who do the same thing," he said.

When Sheriff Reed was told about Red Crow's theory that the murders might have been some sort of family revenge gone wrong, a killing of innocents, Reed said, "We haven't decided if we are looking at that as a motive. We have not learned anything to substantiate that. . . . We are looking at anything that might pop up."

Reed told the reporter that no feedback had yet been received on the fingerprints lifted at the scene by the forensic team and sent to the state crime lab in Montgomery. Those, he said, could provide a suspect in the case if they happened to match prints that were already on record.

LaRue Cornelison would continue to use her considerable skill as an investigative crime reporter to provide readers of the *Times-Journal* with riveting coverage on the investigation into the murders, as well as the countless rumors and suspicions that made up the developing feud between the Headricks and the Daltons. She enjoyed an excellent relationship with area law enforcement, who had learned she could be trusted with sensitive information. As a result, LaRue was privy to much that was not disclosed to other members of the media. And her revealing interviews were a source of help to the investigators, who came to think of her more as a colleague than a reporter.

CHAPTER 11

Investigator Rhonda Jackson spent July 14 transporting Donnie and Kim Watkins to the Rainbow City, Alabama, Police Department, where they were to be hypnotized by Officer Dale Waldon in an effort to help them remember more details about the red pickup truck they had seen leaving the Dalton house on the day of the murders. Kim was hypnotized first, but wasn't able to give much more information about the red truck than she had given in her earlier statement. Donnie's hypnosis wasn't successful, and he came out of it during the relaxation state and said he couldn't hear Officer Waldon's instructions. Jackson rescheduled another hypnosis attempt for Donnie to be held at a later date, hopefully with more success.

The investigators made plans for several people to be interviewed on Monday, July 17, scheduling the meetings before noon and continuing on into the evening to accommodate those people who were unable to leave their jobs during the day. The first of the scheduled interviews was held at the sheriff's department. It began with a female relative of the Daltons' who had been visiting Dora Ann one day around two weeks before the murders, when Headrick and two other men drove up in a dark green pickup. Headrick came into the house and went to the back room. He came back out, carrying two spears, she said, and went back outside to show them to the two men. One of the men was about six feet tall, thin, with shoulder-length dark hair, and she estimated his weight to be around 140 pounds. The other man, she said, was short with a large gut and short brown hair. All the men were drinking iced tea while they were at the Dalton house, the woman added.

On Thursday, July 6, the day before Dora Ann and Carolyn were murdered, the two women had come to the relative's home and picked some green beans from her vegetable garden. The investigators noted that these were most likely the same green beans they had found steaming on the stove when they arrived at the crime scene the following day. The woman said that Headrick drove up to her house around ten minutes after Dora Ann and Carolyn arrived, at around 6:00 P.M.

On one occasion, she said, Headrick had told her that he and Carolyn were going to come into some money, and that they were going to build a house.

Another Dalton relative, a man, told the investigators that he was talking to Dora Ann and Carolyn around a week before the murders, and they told him at that time that they were both afraid of Headrick.

"They told me that they were afraid something was going to happen," the man said. "Prior to this, Randy told me in random conversation that he could kill anybody he wanted to and get by with it; that all he had to do was play insane."

The officers found this statement quite interesting, but things were about to get better. One of Headrick's coworkers was next in line for questioning, and he said Headrick had told him that he and his wife argued often. He also claimed that he and Carolyn had $90,000 in savings, and said that he was in the process of building a large house. The man also stated that for a period of about three weeks before the murders, Headrick had been quieter at work than usual. Then another significant piece of information was brought forward. On April 21, 1995, the man said, he had traded a .22-caliber revolver to a friend of one of Headrick's family members, swapping the pistol for a Yamaha guitar. The man provided the serial number of the revolver to the officers, then said that after the murders, he was told by the man he traded the pistol to that he had let his father have the pistol. The officers exchanged glances; that particular weapon would need to be located and checked out.

The next man in line for an interview met with the investigators that afternoon at his home, after he left work for the day. He was acquainted with all the people who were becoming key players in the investigation, and said he had known Headrick for around three months. He also knew Red Crow, and said he was at Red Crow's home on July 6, the day before the murders, and saw Headrick and Carolyn there. That night, around ten or ten-thirty, he said, Headrick called two other acquaintances of his, a man and woman, to ask them to move a Ford Escort station wagon for him the next day while he was at work, and the couple enlisted the help of the man being interviewed. After they moved the station wagon on the morning of July 7, the man said, he went back to his mobile home and was asleep when the woman came by that evening to wake him up and tell him about the murders.

The man then added another link to the slowly growing chain of evidence in the case. He had met Headrick, he said, through the same man who, the investigators had just learned, had swapped a Yamaha guitar for a .22-caliber pistol, and that man had been with him on the day of the murders until he left to go pick up his paycheck. He did not see him again until late that afternoon, he said, probably around six o'clock.

Later that evening, at the Ider Police Department, the investigators talked to a man who said that he had known Red Crow for around two and a half years, but as far as he could remember, he had only met Headrick once. He told the officers that he drove a 1982 Red Chevy S10 pickup, and had taken the tailgate off the pickup around a month earlier. On the day of the murders, he said, he was at his mother's house in the morning and most of the afternoon. He had recently been on a trip to Cherokee, North Carolina, he told the officers, leaving on Friday,

June 30, with the faux Indians Crazy Bear and White-feather, and returning home on Tuesday, July 4.

With new information having surfaced on both a small red pickup and a .22-caliber pistol, the investigators felt their long day of questioning had at least produced a few new leads to be pursued. But even though his so-called "airtight" alibi continued to hold up, almost every detail the officers uncovered pointed, in one way or another, directly toward Randy Headrick.

In Huntsville, Alabama, at the Alabama Department of Forensic Sciences, a memorandum was filed by forensic scientist II Richard B. Marx, who had collected evidence from the crime scene on the day of the murders. He described several items, including one spear, fifty-eight and three-quarter inches in length, another that measured seven feet three inches, and a Ruger Model 10/22 LR .22-caliber rifle with a black sling and loaded with eight live "CCI" .22-caliber rounds. He also listed eight fingerprint lifts from the scene, and noted that three days following the murders, a state contract driver had delivered a knife to the forensic lab that had been taken as evidence from the murder scene, which he described as a "Pakistan" hunting knife covered with blood.

Marx listed results of his examination of the items of evidence, and noted the seven-foot-three-inch spear had several red acrylic fibers on the shaft. Several partial latent fingerprints were found on the shaft, and one fingerprint was lifted for possible comparison purposes. No other suitable latent fingerprints were noted on any of the items. And if fingerprints on the murder weapons turned out to be those of Randy Headrick, it would not necessarily provide proof of guilt. After all, as Hendrick told Investigator Danny Smith at the murder scene, he made the spears himself. . . . Of course they would bear his fingerprints.

CHAPTER 12

On the afternoon of July 18, Jimmy Phillips drove to the Dade County Sheriff's Office in northwest Georgia to interview a woman who was acquainted with Randy and Carolyn Headrick. They had given her a ride to the Birmingham International Airport a couple of years earlier, she said. The approximately three-hour ride from north DeKalb County to Birmingham, from all indications, was a ride to remember, and the woman was eager to give Phillips the juicy details of the trip.

While Carolyn was apparently napping during the trip, Headrick spent the time entertaining his passenger. He told the woman—to her apparent surprise—that he had killed two men. He then told her how various women would tie him up and have sex with him. This information must have been intended to pique her interest in similar activities, for he went on to make a pass at her during the trip, she said.

She also stated that Headrick talked about violence "all the time," and told her that he could break her neck. This statement did not serve to make the woman any more receptive to Headrick's advances, if that had been his intention.

Phillips was also told during the interview that the woman had heard, prior to the murders, that Headrick and Carolyn were having some problems, and that she had also heard that Headrick was coming into a lot of money, supposedly from a car wreck he'd had.

On the drive back to Fort Payne from the Georgia interview, Phillips mulled over the wide variety of facts mounting up in the case. They all pointed to Randy Headrick, alibi or not, but nonetheless, Phillips and his fellow investigators kept doggedly following up on every tip they received. Sooner or later, they believed, they would receive that one critical bit of information or evidence that would break the case and put Headrick behind bars.

Rhonda Jackson spent a busy day on July 19, serving subpoenas and obtaining records from various locations around the county. Her first stop was at Farmers Telephone Cooperative in Rainsville, where she picked up phone records on Headrick's parents' home phone, their business phone, and on the phone at Dora Ann Dalton's home, with all the records covering the time period from May 1995 until July 1, 1995. The records after July 1 were not yet available, but the cooperative's telephone supervisors assured Rhonda that they would be turned over to law enforcement just as soon as possible.

Rhonda then served a subpoena to the First National Bank of Scottsboro's Henagar branch to obtain Headrick's banking records; then she went back to Fort Payne and visited the Woodmen of the World Life Insurance Society branch office with a subpoena for their insurance records on William Randall Headrick and Carolyn Jean Headrick. Rhonda was given the information and was told there was also an insurance policy on Dora Ann Dalton, but the records were not yet available. Like the telephone co-op, the insurance company promised her that they would contact her as soon as possible with the information on that policy.

After lunch and a stop by the sheriff's department to check her messages, Rhonda returned to the north end of the county and began a series of interviews with several of the people living in the Shady Lane area of

Henagar and Ider, hoping to locate someone who might have seen or heard something out of the ordinary on the day of the murders. The first person she spoke to, a neighbor who lived just across Highway 75 from the Shady Lane turnoff, near the old abandoned skating rink, said that he was at home waxing his truck on Friday, July 7. He was standing beside his carport when he heard a woman screaming through the woods from the direction of the Dalton house, crying, "Oh no, oh, my God!"

"I didn't see anything," he told Rhonda. "Then in a few minutes, I saw ambulances and police cars everywhere."

The man told Rhonda that the last time he had talked to Headrick was a couple of weeks before the murders.

"I was passing by their house and saw Randy and another man out in the yard working on cleaning some cow bones, and I stopped and talked to them," he said. Then he got to the good part of what he wanted to tell Rhonda, the part he felt might be of some use in the case.

"About a year ago, Randy approached me and wanted me to help him pull off a burglary," the man said. "He wanted me to drive him to a location and let him out, and pick him up at a different location. He was going to burglarize someplace. Randy told me he had a guy in LaFayette or Summerville, Georgia, that would buy anything he would bring to him. I told him I didn't want to be involved in this in any way, and I didn't want to know who it was, or anything. He never approached me anymore about this."

After this productive conversation, Rhonda stopped at several of the houses closest to the Dalton residence. She didn't learn anything useful: one man was home, but was asleep all day; another couple were home, but didn't see or hear anything; a man was at work in Chattanooga the day of the murders and didn't get home until 4:00 P.M.; and a woman was gone from her home that afternoon. But despite the fact that the day was late and all but one of the interviews had brought nothing new to light,

Rhonda still felt her time in the neighborhood had not been wasted.

The following day was an important one in the Henagar and Ider communities. A meeting was held at 10:00 A.M. at the Ider branch of the Citizens Bank of Valley Head, and the investigators Jimmy Phillips and Rhonda Jackson and Chief Deputy Eddie Wright were asked to attend. The purpose of the meeting was to set up a bank account for a reward fund that would be contributed by people in the towns, with the reward to be given to the person or persons who provided information that would lead to the arrest and conviction of the murderer of Carolyn Headrick and Dora Ann Dalton. The meeting proved to be an astounding testimony to the high regard within the community for the two victims. As of 10:30 A.M., only half an hour after the meeting began, Carolyn and Dora Ann's friends and neighbors had already raised over $9,800 in an effort to match the $10,000 reward offered on July 13 by the governor. Donations, according to church volunteers who helped with the reward fund, came in from businesses, as well as individuals. Donald Smith, the church member who had been asked to head the fund-raising efforts for the reward, said, "We didn't feel like we could do any less. The victims were well-loved by the community; it was a great loss. The two ladies were members at our church, and their other family are still members."

Chief Deputy Wright said later that he had never imagined such an outpouring of support, especially considering the small size and rural setting of the towns of Ider and Henagar.

"Those people really turned out that day, and I was amazed that they raised that much money so quickly. It said a lot about the people in the communities, as well as how they felt about those two ladies."

After the meeting, Rhonda Jackson met with Investigator Doyle York, of the neighboring Jackson County Sheriff's Department, and obtained from him the records on all Jackson County vehicle tag numbers that had been issued on red Ford Rangers and Chevy S10 pickups within the previous ten years. There were many, and each one would be thoroughly traced for any possible connection to the Headrick case.

When Rhonda returned to her office, a report had arrived from the Alabama Department of Public Safety concerning fingerprints from the crime scene that were forwarded to them from the Department of Forensic Sciences. Several of the prints were of insufficient quality to be identified, but a few were termed "fingerprints of value." One such print was found on a John Wayne collector plate, which was identified as the left index finger of Carolyn Headrick. Another print, also taken from a collector plate that was called "Spirit of the White Wolf," was identified as the right middle finger of Randy Headrick.

A report had also been returned that day from the Department of Forensic Sciences concerning results of some of the blood evidence tested by the department. As with the fingerprints, some of the samples submitted from the crime scene were too small or degraded to give readable results. But the bloodstain on Headrick's shirt did prove to be his own, as he had claimed.

As for the firearm evidence submitted for analysis, of the three bullets that struck Carolyn Headrick, one was too badly damaged to provide forensic evidence. The other two were determined to be .22 caliber, but were not fired from the Ruger .22 semiautomatic rifle that had been found at the scene. The bullet from the body of Dora Ann Dalton was also a .22, but no further information could be determined because of its badly damaged condition. A pink bath towel from the bathroom was found to have gunpowder particles on its surface, and gunpowder trace was also found to have been present in the bathroom sink.

Later that afternoon, Rhonda Jackson and Jimmy Phillips spoke again with Kathy Porter, who, along with her daughter, had first discovered the bodies of her mother and sister. After giving some thought to the time of the telephone call she received from her mother on the day of the murders, Porter told the investigators that the call could possibly have been made at around 12:35 P.M., instead of 1:00 P.M., as she previously had stated. This new information opened the killer's window of opportunity a bit wider than before, and Sheriff Cecil Reed, who was determined to find a crack in Headrick's alibi, set out to determine the time it would take to make the round-trip drive from Headrick's job site at Builders Supply in Fort Payne to the house on Shady Lane and back. During the coming months, Sheriff Reed would make the trip over and over again, traveling on all the possible routes that Headrick could have taken that day, and carefully timing and recording each drive.

"I made a whole lot of trips up there and back," he said. His instincts as an old pro in law enforcement kept telling him that the missing piece of the puzzle was right there in plain sight, and he was determined to do whatever he could to try and help his investigators uncover it.

On July 21, Rhonda Jackson scheduled an early interview with Red Crow's wife, Melva Snapp, a responsible, well-respected woman, who seemed to be very straightforward and sincere. She told Rhonda that she had known the Headricks for around six weeks prior to the murders. They first met, she said, when Carolyn's brother-in-law brought the couple into the Native American Connection in Chattanooga, the store that Red Crow owned along with three business partners.

"Randy found out we lived in Ider, and he started coming over to our house to see Crow," Melva said. "He started bringing his wife with him. Randy was interested in the Native American life, so him and Crow developed a friendship. When Carolyn started coming over, I taught her how to do beadwork."

Melva said that she and Red Crow had found another house at Sulphur Springs, a community to the north of Ider, and the Headricks had spent some time helping them move there.

"Randy and Carolyn were at our old house that we

were moving from, on Thursday evening around four-thirty or five, the evening before the murders. I left around five-thirty P.M. to go babysit for my son, and they were still there when I left. While they were there, Carolyn told me to come by the house the next day and get some vegetables out of their garden."

At the time of the murders, Melva was employed by DeKalb Baptist Medical Center and worked in the operating room. She was also picking up some extra work by cleaning houses on her days off.

"I had to clean a house Friday morning; then I went to another house around one-fifteen or one-thirty P.M., and I didn't find out that Carolyn and her mother had been murdered until around eight that night. I had heard the people talking at the second house I was cleaning, when the man told his wife that there had been a double homicide at Ider."

At the time she overheard the mention of the killings, Melva had no idea the two victims were Carolyn Headrick and her mother. She was totally shocked to learn later that evening that they had been murdered.

"The times Randy and Carolyn were around us, they seemed like they cared a lot about each other," Melva said. "They never quarreled or had harsh words toward one another in my presence. I didn't find out about Randy's past criminal record until I read it in the paper. I didn't know anything about Randy's family before this happened, and we didn't know about the insurance Randy had on Carolyn until I read it in the paper."

When Jackson returned to the sheriff's department after the interview, she stopped in at the office of the sheriff's chief clerk, Walker Driskill, to enlist his help in the search for the red pickup. Driskill called the DeKalb County Department of Revenue and requested the records on all red Ford Rangers and Chevy S10 pickups registered in DeKalb County from 1985 to 1995. The revenue department employees, eager to help with the case in any way they could, immediately went to work on the project. It would take some time and effort, but the revenue department workers were more than willing to devote whatever amount of time it might take, if it would help the investigators to catch a killer. Within two days, Walker Driskill handed Jackson a huge computer print-out with complete information on every red Chevy S10 and Ford Ranger registered in DeKalb County within the past ten years.

CHAPTER 13

When Headrick's former coworker at Earthgrains told the investigators about a friend of Headrick's who lived on the river and was a taxidermist who collected guns, the officers set out to identify the man and arrange an interview. On July 25, they arrived at Boggie's Taxidermy in Dutton, Alabama, just over the county line into Jackson County on the river near Scottsboro. John Boggie was willing to talk, but didn't have much useful information to share at that time. He told Rhonda Jackson and Jimmy Phillips that Headrick used to come by his taxidermy shop, usually about once a month or sometimes more often.

"I would give him hides, bones, teeth and stuff," Boggie said. "He was into the Indian artifacts, and I would give him the items to keep from having to bury them."

Boggie said that Headrick never made any statements to him about paying someone to kill his wife.

"The only thing he said was that him and his wife both made these Indian artifacts," Boggie said. "He mentioned two or three times several months ago that he had a girl-friend over in Section that supposedly had a kid by him."

On their way back to the sheriff's department from Boggie's interview, Jackson and Phillips stopped along the way to interview a couple of other people. Leonard Knight, who lived in Flat Rock on the Jackson/DeKalb county line, told the officers that he attended the Ider Church of God and had dated Dora Ann Dalton three or four times. Obviously saddened by the loss of his friend and her daughter, he told the investigators he didn't drive and had to have someone take him wherever he went.

"I went down to her house a couple of times on Sunday and ate dinner with her and Carolyn and Randy," Knight said. "I hadn't seen Dora Ann in a couple of weeks before they were killed.

"Dora Ann told me Randy was high-tempered," he said, "and from Carolyn's actions when I was around them, she seemed frightened of Randy."

After leaving Knight's home, the officers stopped by the home of Jim Travis on the outskirts of Henagar. They were astounded when they walked inside the small, tidy house and looked around. Inside the Travis home, they found themselves surrounded by a veritable museum of the very highest-quality Indian craft work, the walls and shelves filled to overflowing with all manner of objects that were all extremely detailed and authentic, and all done entirely by Travis himself. He was a highly respected, skilled artisan, very proud of his Iroquois heritage, and he was every bit as intelligent as he was talented. Travis, an older gentleman who lived alone, was open and cooperative, and didn't hesitate to tell the officers about his dealings with Headrick.

"I've known Randy Headrick for about two years," he said. "I met him at the flea market up on I-fifty-nine at Hammondville. I showed him how to make some Indian artifacts, and he would come over to my house and work in my shop."

Travis had no use whatsoever for liars, or for any type of deception or dishonesty, and was obviously displeased when he learned that Headrick had told him so many false tales about his past.

"Randy was a sarcastic, bully-type person," Travis said. "He never told me about being in prison. He told me he

served in Vietnam in the war, and said he was in the
Green Berets."

Travis said he never witnessed Headrick acting vio-
lently toward anyone, and said the last time he saw him
was at a powwow in Huntsville. Headrick was there with
his brother-in-law, Travis said.

The officers asked Travis if he owned any .22 pistols that
anyone had borrowed or stolen.

"I have two .22 pistols, both revolvers," he said. "No one
has borrowed them; I've had both of them for a long time."

The investigators left the home of Jim Travis knowing
that, after all their interviews of people who were supposedly of Native American descent, they had finally had the
privilege of meeting someone who was the genuine article, a man to be much admired for his talent, as well as
his ethics.

The following day began early for Rhonda Jackson. She
left her office with a handful of subpoenas for various
records from Earthgrains, Builders Supply and the Bakers
and Confectionery Union Local #611. When she contacted Farmers Telephone Cooperative, she was told that
the additional phone records from July 1 through July 14
on the Dalton residence and Headrick's parents' home
and business were ready to be picked up. She added a trip
by the telephone co-op to her list of stops to be made.

A new tip had come in from a bank security guard, who
said that a postal employee had mentioned to him some
comments Randy Headrick had made to her, so Jackson
stopped by the bank in Henagar to get further information from the man. She wanted to arrange an interview
with the postal worker as soon as possible.

After returning to Fort Payne, Jackson contacted
Shenandoah Life Insurance Company about a $12,000
policy on Dora Ann Dalton and was told that it was a
group policy that was only in effect from October 1985
to October 1989, and then had been terminated.

Jackson then phoned Etowah Steel Workers Credit
Union, but was told that Headrick was not a member of

that credit union, therefore he had no loans or bank accounts there.

Later that afternoon, a young man arrived at the sheriff's department for an interview. He had information that would serve to contradict the statement given the previous day by Boggie, the taxidermist. The man told Rhonda that he, a young woman, and Boggie had been at a house in Scottsboro around July 15, and said that Boggie had told him at that time that Headrick came by the taxidermy shop usually about twice a week. Boggie had told him, he said, that Headrick had made the comment that he was going to have someone do something to his wife.

"Boggie was not drinking at the time," the man said. "This was the first time I had ever seen Boggie."

The young woman who accompanied him to Scottsboro was standing nearby when Boggie made the comment, the man said, but she wasn't paying attention to the conversation.

Jackson made a note to reinterview Boggie; it seemed that some important details about his dealings with Randy Headrick might have slipped his mind at the time of their previous conversation.

Jimmy Phillips had been busy gathering some additional information on Headrick's past while Rhonda Jackson served subpoenas and made phone calls. He contacted a detective in Fort Worth, Texas, to see if he could locate the man who was arrested along with Headrick in the pipe bomb incident. He also asked the detective to obtain subscriber information on three phone numbers that showed up on Headrick's parents' home telephone bill: the calls were placed to Fort Worth and Arlington, Texas.

CHAPTER 14

Tips had been pouring into the sheriff's department on a continuous basis from the day of the murders; some seemed to be very valuable, but most were based on the rumors that continued to spread like wildfire among the communities up and down Highway 75. And several of the tips were downright ludicrous, but even those were thoroughly followed up.

As the weeks passed, it seemed as though every Saturday night in the Happy Hollow area generated Monday-morning reports that someone had "confessed" to his wife or girlfriend, implying that he was a dangerous, cold-blooded killer; and if she did not do as he demanded, she just might suffer the same fate as the two victims on Shady Lane. Apparently, many of the drunken bullies in north DeKalb County were using the murders to scare their women into line, and the more white moonshine whiskey they drank, the more elaborate and detailed their confessions became. Rhonda Jackson and her team were fairly adept at separating reports of these supposed drunken admissions of guilt from the other tips they received, but the officers couldn't afford to discount any unlikely tip they received, no matter how far-fetched the information might seem. All the anonymous phone calls, tips and rumors were carefully checked out regardless of their lack of credibility.

Several people had reported seeing what they believed to be a Builders Supply delivery truck—a flat-nosed, two-ton white model—in various locations along Highway 75 on the day of the murders. On July 31, Jimmy Phillips and Rhonda Jackson took a statement from Junior Frank Dalton, a Builders Supply employee who had driven a delivery truck that made some stops in the north DeKalb area on July 7. He told the officers he left Builders Supply in Fort Payne around 11:40 A.M. and stopped by Henagar Pawn Shop to make a payment on a guitar that he was buying there. He said he left there and went south on Highway 75 to make a delivery, then went to the Builders Supply store at Sylvania. When he left there, he went back to the Fort Payne store, arriving about 2:30 P.M. He didn't go any farther north that day than to Sylvania, he said. The investigators had been hopeful that, given the time frame of the deliveries, someone other than Junior Dalton might have been driving the white truck. Unfortunately, that didn't prove to be the case, and another promising lead turned out to be useless.

On August 1, Investigator Clay Simpson received a tip that a Valley Head man, John Mark Johnson, fit the description of the person several people had reported seeing leave the murder scene in a small red pickup. Interestingly enough, Johnson had shoulder-length dark hair, drove a 1984 red Chevy S10, and was heavily involved in the local Indian community. Simpson jumped to follow up on this information. Upon receiving a printout of Johnson's rather lengthy arrest records, he discovered that some years earlier, Johnson had spent time in prison on federal firearms charges. Simpson immediately set out to locate Johnson and make arrangements to interview him at the Valley Head Police Department. In a fairly short time, Johnson met Simpson and Valley Head officer Robert Hall there, and told them that he didn't know Randy Headrick. He could have met him, he said, at some of the many powwows that he had attended, but claimed that he didn't know him personally. Johnson admitted that he did know Red Crow very well, having met him at the Hammondville flea market. It seemed odd to the officers that Johnson was acquainted with Red Crow, Jim Travis, Crazy Bear and Whitefeather—and almost everyone else that Headrick knew in the Indian community—but still claimed not to know Headrick personally.

At the time, Johnson said, he and his wife, Laura, were separated and Johnson was living with his sister, whose home was in Ider. He was living there, he said, at the time the murders took place. Johnson told the officers he made Indian jewelry and other crafts, but claimed that he didn't make any type of weapons.

While Simpson and Hall talked to Johnson, Rhonda Jackson and Mike James went to the housing project in Valley Head where Johnson's wife, Laura, lived. Laura confirmed that she and Johnson were separated, and said she had seen Red Crow several times, but had never met Headrick.

"I've seen Red Crow at some of the powwows," she said, "but I've only talked to him one time at the flea market."

Laura said she and her estranged husband had a 1983 brown Chevy Malibu and a 1984 Chevy S10 red pickup. But she denied any further knowledge of the case.

"I don't know anything about the two women who were murdered in Henagar except what we've heard from other people," she said.

The interviews with John and Laura Johnson were a disappointment to the investigators, who couldn't make a connection to the Dalton/Headrick murders despite John Johnson's highly suspicious background and the many coincidental elements that could have linked him to the case. It had been a very promising lead, but like all the others thus far in the investigation, it just didn't pan out.

After talking with Laura Johnson and taking her statement, Rhonda Jackson returned to Fort Payne and stopped by Builders Supply to pick up Headrick's personnel records. His records from Earthgrains were not compiled for pickup yet, but Earthgrains management assured her that the records would be mailed to her at the sheriff's department as soon as possible.

Investigator Mike James, who wanted to arrange another interview with Randy Headrick, got in touch with Headrick's attorney, Bob French, who said that if James would submit a written list of questions, he would screen the questions and then let his client answer those he approved. James agreed, but discussed the matter with his contacts at the Alabama Bureau of Investigation. Some cooperation, they agreed, was better than none, and James began preparing his list of questions he hoped Headrick would answer.

On the following day, Rhonda Jackson took Donnie Watkins, the man who saw the red truck leaving the murder scene, to Forsyth, Georgia, for another try at hypnosis, this time by Dr. Gene Smuckler. This go-round, the attempt was successful. Under hypnosis and while being videotaped, Watkins confirmed that the truck he saw that day was a red Ford Ranger with a "28" tag, the prefix for a tag issued in DeKalb County.

More tips were received at the sheriff's department during the coming days, with several people coming forward offering new information that just might prove to be important. A woman who knew Headrick called Rhonda Jackson and said she had seen him, accompanied by Red Crow, at the Scottsboro Wal-Mart store on Friday night, August 4, attempting to purchase a gun in the store's sporting-goods department. She said he was also trying to buy some ammunition that had been discontinued. Jackson called the store manager, who said he would check with the salesclerk on duty that night in the sporting-goods department, and would return her call.

A short time later, the salesclerk called back and told Jackson that on the night in question, two men who fit the description of Headrick and Red Crow were indeed in the store. One man, she said, was an "Indian type," with long gray hair in a ponytail, and the other man was of a medium build and, she thought, had a beard.

"The guy with the ponytail asked what kind of guns we had, and I showed them the display case," the clerk said. "He was interested in a thirty-thirty rifle, and asked what he needed to do to buy a gun."

The clerk told the man he needed a driver's license, and he would have to fill out the proper paperwork. He asked her what the charge was to put a gun on layaway, and she told him a 10 percent down payment was required. He did not decide to go ahead and buy or lay away a gun at that time, but the clerk said she would recognize him if she saw him again.

After talking with the Wal-Mart clerk, Jackson spoke with the Bakers Union supervisor in reference to one of the insurance policies Headrick had on Carolyn through his job at Earthgrains. On contacting the insurance company, the union supervisor had been told that when someone was terminated or was no longer a member of the union, the insurance policy they obtained through the union was no longer in effect. The company had not been notified that Headrick had been terminated from Earthgrains until that day, when the supervisor called them.

On August 8, Jimmy Phillips and Rhonda Jackson interviewed another Builders Supply employee, whom they had not yet spoken with. He said that he had spent time with Randy Headrick on the day of the murders, and the investigators asked him for a detailed account of their activities together on July 7.

"I saw him around seven A.M. in the hallway," he told them, "and I saw him again around eleven-thirty A.M. when he called in a lunch order for him and me, and I went to pick it up. I brought it back and we ate together in my office."

The man told the investigators that Headrick "acted normal" that day. "He didn't act any different from any other day," he said. "I saw a white Ford CF-seven thousand flatbed truck sitting down at warehouse number two next to the creek that afternoon," he added. "It doesn't normally sit down there, is the reason I remembered."

The investigators asked Headrick's coworker what kind of conversations they usually had, and the man said that Headrick talked to him about military weapons and told him that he had been in the Vietnam War.

"He talked in general terms about being able to have someone knocked off," the man said. "He didn't say anything specific."

Headrick had given him a spear two or three months earlier, he said, to give to his son.

"It's a bamboo shaft with a feather, with a screwdriver point," he told the investigators. "He used to get me to cut out some things with the torch for his spears and stuff after work.

"Randy talked a lot," the man said, "but I didn't pay much attention to him."

That same day, a large file arrived for Investigator Mike James from the Texas Department of Public Safety with detailed information concerning Headrick's federal firearms conviction in Texas, and other materials, which the department had compiled at that time, that might be of interest to the DeKalb County investigators.

James was particularly interested in the man who was convicted along with Headrick in the pipe bomb incident, and had asked the Texas officers if they could locate the man and question him about his association with Headrick, and to verify his whereabouts on the afternoon of July 7. The man's current address had been determined, and his house was staked out for a few nights to confirm his identity and the vehicle he usually drove. Then, on August 1, the officers interviewed the man whom they described as cooperative, noting that he seemed genuinely surprised when told of the murder investigation in which Headrick was the prime suspect. He told them he hadn't had any kind of contact with Headrick in over eight years, and would "run if I was to see him coming."

When the man's alibi for the week of the murders was

checked out at his place of employment, his time cards and the statements of his coworkers and supervisors proved beyond a doubt that he was present every day on the job throughout that week. He was officially cleared of any suspicion of involvement in the case.

In checking out Headrick's former codefendant in the pipe bomb case, a great deal of other details about the incident came to light. On November 7, 1986, a pipe bomb damaged a trailer occupied by two women in Grand Prairie, Texas, doing an estimated $4,000 in damages. The next day, one of the women told investigators she had been threatened by Headrick, and told them that Headrick and his codefendant had built bombs in the past, and that Headrick had amounts of smokeless powder, a low explosive, stashed at his home in Fort Worth.

On November 9, the investigators learned through an informant that Headrick and his friend were in possession of a large pipe bomb, which probably was going to be used against the same location. The trailer was placed under surveillance, and on November 10, around 1:00 A.M., Headrick and his friend were spotted circling the trailer in a pickup truck, driving slowly in a suspicious manner. They were stopped by police at the Waffle House restaurant in Arlington, Texas, and gave written consent for the search of Headrick's home, garage and the pickup truck.

When the truck was searched, agents found a quantity of explosive materials, a silencer and a large functional pipe bomb. Headrick's friend also had a .25-caliber automatic pistol in the waistband of his pants. The barrel of the pistol was threaded, and it fit the silencer found in the truck. The gun was fully loaded with eight rounds of ammunition. The truck also held three other items described as "destructive devices," which were pipe bombs that had not been fully assembled yet.

The search of Headrick's house and garage revealed three additional destructive devices, also not yet assembled. Both the men were arrested and held without bond. They eventually entered guilty pleas and were sentenced for possession of an unregistered firearm, which referred to the functional pipe bomb found in the truck.

During the course of the investigation of the pipe-bombing incident, a great deal of background information on Randy Headrick had been collected. Investigators had learned that Headrick's involvement with the law began when he was thirteen years old, with referrals to juvenile court in Gadsden, Alabama. Later, at his junior high school, Headrick was suspended for possessing a .22-caliber blank pistol, which he flagrantly displayed, and he told the other students that he planned to use the pistol to shoot a coach and a teacher. His behavior problems eventually led to a stint at the Alabama Boys Industrial School on the basis of his delinquency.

Headrick's adult charges began in 1974, when he was arrested at the age of sixteen for car theft. Much to the amusement of area law enforcement, the car, that he and two friends stole was an Etowah County Sheriff's Department car which belonged to the Etowah County Commission. Headrick was judged to be a youthful offender, and was sentenced in 1975 to serve three years' probation, but was discharged the following year. His only other charge on record, other than the pipe bomb incident, was a forgery charge in 1985, which was dismissed after Headrick made restitution.

In evaluating the background information in the pipe bomb case, investigators noted that at every opportunity, Headrick appeared to be attempting to shift as much of the blame as possible to his codefendant.

CHAPTER 15

For six weeks, the investigation into the murders of Dora Ann Dalton and Carolyn Headrick had continued full-time for Rhonda Jackson and her team. Every bit of information, every tip received, pointed to Randy Headrick as the prime suspect, but his alibi still remained unbroken. Sheriff Reed told the news media that the case remained at the forefront of his department's workload.

"It's still as wide open as a case knife," he said. "We concentrate on it every day; we have a very active interest on it."

Rhonda Jackson's interest in the case was far more than just "very active." It had become highly personal to her, and she felt that securing justice for Carolyn and Dora Ann was her responsibility. She often lay awake at night going over every detail of the case and worrying about what she might be overlooking. On each of those sleepless nights, she prayed for guidance and for the family of the victims.

On August 18, yet another person was interviewed and came forward with a large amount of highly incriminating information about Headrick, a postal worker whose position in the community and unimpeachable reputation made her a highly credible source. Headrick, it seemed, had come into the post office where she worked on many occasions, starting the previous summer, and had talked to her at length about some very unusual topics.

"He told me that he had gotten him some bamboo, and that he was going to build himself a bamboo garden," she said. "He said that he knew where to shoot someone and it would kill them instantly, and that he knew where to stab someone and how to cut their neck to kill them instantly."

After he got the bamboo, she said, Headrick would come in every two or three weeks to fill her in on his progress with the bamboo garden. He would always talk about how he could kill someone, she told Jackson.

"He said he knew how to hurt somebody with bamboo. He would tie them up with their arms outstretched, cut them in either the back or stomach, and insert the bamboo. He said it grows so fast it crowds the heart and lungs and kills them."

Headrick also talked to her about the cow skulls and bones he was accumulating, and how he had started working with the skulls and was going to paint them. He could make good money selling them, he told her. On one occasion, he bragged to the woman that he knew how to do the perfect murder, and said that he would be at work at the time.

"I told him that was easy, that he would just hire someone to murder the person," she said. "He said that he would do it himself, and he would have the perfect alibi.

"He told me that if he did a murder, that he would climb up a tree and act like a monkey and would act crazy, and would not serve a day for the crime, but would be sent to a mental institution."

The investigators were astounded by Headrick's audacity, and how he had bragged about being able to commit a murder and have an unbreakable alibi. But there was more information to come from this witness as she recalled several other occasions when Headrick had talked with her.

"He told me he was having trouble with someone at work, and asked if I knew where he could borrow a

pocket tape recorder," she told Rhonda Jackson. "It was
to booby-trap his locker at Earthgrains to record someone's conversation. He also said he had been in a fight
with somebody, and he said he had been questioned
about a fire that had occurred at the home of a girl who
worked at Earthgrains. He said he didn't do it. He said
he had an alibi. . . . He said he was at work."

The woman also remembered Headrick saying that
he had a lot of life insurance on his wife, and that he could
be in two places at one time for a sum of money. He could
have an alibi, he repeated again.

CHAPTER 16

On Monday, August 21, the *Chattanooga Times* ran an article by reporter Mary Gabel that brought the growing feud between the Dalton family and Randy Headrick out into the open. Billy Jack Dalton, Dora Ann's son and Carolyn's brother, told Gabel that he believed Headrick had both the opportunity and the motive to kill the two women, but he just couldn't prove it.

"At first, I couldn't believe he could have done that," Dalton said. But he claimed Headrick had shown no interest in the investigation and had made statements to his friends and acquaintances that made Dalton suspicious. Dalton said Headrick had not been in touch with police about the progress of the investigation, and had bragged that he was going to get the Dalton home and land.

Headrick vehemently denied his brother-in-law's charges and told Gabel that he believed the murderer, or murderers, had gone to the wrong house and had intended to kill someone else. The murders had been too much for him, he claimed, and he said that he'd had to go on nerve medication.

"I haven't even had time to grieve," he complained. The authorities had been blaming him from the first, he said. "I just want these people found."

Dalton said that he believed Headrick was somehow

able to leave his job long enough to kill the two women, but Headrick said that he did not leave his job and wasn't responsible for the murders.

"I was at work," he said. "You know, there's too many people who seen me there."

Dalton claimed that he grew suspicious when he learned about the large amount of life insurance that had been taken out on his sister by her husband.

"Three hundred and fifty thousand dollars is what got them killed," he told Gabel. "If [Headrick's] not the actual triggerman, he's the one who initiated a deal. We know he's guilty; we just can't put him at the scene."

Sheriff Cecil Reed wouldn't comment to the press on Dalton's allegations against Headrick. "I can't comment on any suspects. [Dalton's] an individual. He can say what he wants to."

Reed said again that his officers worked on the case every day. "It's our number one case. If something comes in on it, we check it out. It's very active."

The reward at that time totaled $21,000, with the community contributing $11,000 to go along with the $10,000 offered by the governor. The community fund would continue to grow.

Kathy Porter, Billy Jack Dalton's sister, told the newspaper that "the community has been wonderful," and said the family was still receiving letters of sympathy almost two months after the murders. Both she and Dalton said they felt the sheriff's department was doing everything possible to solve the crime.

"The piece they need to put the whole thing together, they haven't gotten," Kathy Porter said. "That's the big thing. Nothing's going to bring them back. Maybe once we can find out who did this, we can put it behind us. The not knowing is eating at me."

Kathy Porter would not comment to the press on her brother's allegations against Randy Headrick, but she already had voiced her opinion on the identity of the murderer when she was interviewed by the investigators the day following the killings. At that time, she told them, "I think Randy did it."

When Jimmy Phillips climbed the narrow flight of stairs to the second-floor investigators' offices to report for work on August 22, he handed Rhonda Jackson a clear cellophane envelope that contained a single one-dollar bill. He had received it that morning from Stanley Porter, Kathy Porter's husband. It was given to Stanley by Donald Smith, who found it in the money removed from the automatic car wash at Ider. Written in ink on the bill, across the head of George Washington, were the words "I'm a murderer." Whether or not the dollar had been marked by someone who had any connection to the slayings, it still was a gruesome reminder to the investigative team that the killer was still out there somewhere, waiting to be caught and charged.

That eerie incident was the start of another busy day for Rhonda Jackson and her team. Copies of incident/offense reports were sent to Woodmen of the World Insurance Company, and subpoenas were mailed to the First National Bank of Scottsboro for a record of transactions pertaining to the case.

Later, following up another new lead in the case, Jimmy Phillips, Rhonda Jackson and Mike James stopped by the Fort Payne Wal-Mart Supercenter and spoke with one of their cashiers who had gotten in touch with them about an incident she thought might be in some way related to the Headrick case. The woman told them that two or three weeks earlier, she was working at the store when Randy Headrick came in with a lady and two small children. When Headrick was ready to check out, he came to the woman's register and presented a credit card in Carolyn Headrick's name. The cashier, who was familiar with the case and knew that Carolyn had been murdered, told him that Carolyn would have to be there in order for him to use the card. Headrick then told her, she said, that the woman with him was Carolyn, but she knew that was not true. The cashier called for a supervisor to approve the sale. Unaware of the circumstances surrounding the use of the credit card, the supervisor overruled the cashier and okayed the purchase. Headrick signed his own name to the credit card.

"They bought toys, and I don't remember what else," the cashier told the investigators. "The woman was in her late forties or early fifties, and they left the store through the garden center exit."

This information, of course, provided no hard proof of anything other than another example of suspicious and questionable behavior on Headrick's part. The officers took careful note of the incident, however, and it went into the huge piles of statements about Randy Headrick that were mounting on the desks in the tiny upstairs offices at the sheriff's department.

CHAPTER 17

The following week, Headrick's attorney, Bob French, came to the sheriff's office and picked up the list of questions that had been prepared for his client by Mike James. Two days later, Rhonda Jackson was summoned to French's office and was given Headrick's answers. The questions had been carefully thought out by James and the members of Jackson's team, with the help of investigators from the ABI and FBI. The answers had been just as carefully given by Headrick under the strict guidance of French.

In their first question, the investigators stated they would like to know why Headrick had not been cooperating with them in their efforts to find the killer of Carolyn Headrick and Dora Ann Dalton.

French answered that his client had attempted to solve the murder, but accused the officers of telling him that he was their prime suspect. Headrick could not help, he said, when he was continually being accused of being the murderer.

The detectives then asked if Randy knew of anyone with whom he had problems, who might have been capable of committing the murders.

No one hated him enough to kill his wife and mother-in-law, claimed French, but he went on to say that there were members of both Headrick's family and his wife's family who had enemies who might have killed the women by mistake.

When asked who some of Headrick's friends were while he was in prison, French went into somewhat more detail. He said that Headrick didn't have too many friends in prison because he was frequently transferred from one facility to another. There were two men he made friends with, one man who at that time lived on the Mescalero Apache Reservation in New Mexico, and another man who lived in Quitman, Georgia. The Georgia man's address and phone number, he said, were in one of Headrick's address books that was currently in the possession of the authorities.

French went on to say that Headrick's prison sentence was in his past and that his client had tried to put that behind him. Headrick couldn't remember anyone else he was at all close to during the time he was imprisoned.

The next question from the investigators concerned some of the insurance issues. They said they needed to know if Carolyn Headrick had signed the insurance paper on the $100,000 policy and if Headrick and his wife were having problems of any kind concerning the policy.

Carolyn signed the insurance papers, Headrick claimed. He said she had trouble writing, so he filled out the application, but Carolyn marked the blocks and signed it. They had an agreement on the insurance policies, French said his client told him. The couple had planned to cancel all the policies and take out a joint policy for $250,000. The only disagreement they had, according to Headrick, was that he wanted Carolyn to drop her Woodmen of the World policy and go along with his plan for a joint policy. She wanted to keep the Woodmen policy, he said, because she had been paying on it for such a long time. But finally they agreed on the joint policy, with Carolyn keeping her Woodmen policy while Randy dropped his.

The fifth question posed by the investigators concerned the red pickup seen leaving the murder scene. They asked if Headrick knew anyone who drove a small red pickup truck, maybe a S10 or a Ford Ranger.

There were several such trucks, French said, that traveled past the Headrick home on a regular basis. A few weekends before the murders, Headrick said, a red S10 pulled into the garage of the Headrick home, and Headrick's mother evidently saw the truck from her home across the road and called the Henagar police, but no officers ever came out to check out the call. Headrick went on to say that Dora Ann Dalton had a red S10 which her daughter took after the murders. Other than that, Headrick said, he knew of no one with such a truck.

When the investigators asked if Headrick would be willing to take a polygraph, French answered that he and his client had the polygraph request under consideration and would let them know of their decision within the next few weeks.

When the officers asked why Headrick had made no effort to return to his job at Builders Supply after the murders, French said that Headrick had heard he had been fired because he falsified his initial employment application and failed to admit that he had a criminal record. Since the murders, French said, his client's past had leaked out and a fellow worker told him that he didn't have a job any more. There was no reason to return to work, French said, and be told by his employers that he was fired.

When asked if Headrick had ever tried to hire anyone to do any harm to any of his former girlfriends or their husbands, French said that Headrick had never talked to anyone about any such thing. He had been accused of this in the past, French said, and had taken a polygraph and passed it.

The officers wanted to know where Headrick bought the .22 rifle, and what credit cards he currently held. The rifle, French said, was purchased at the Fort Payne Wal-

Mart prior to Christmas of 1994, and his client had credit cards from Mastercard and Exxon.

The next question on the investigators' list was whether or not Headrick sold his brother-in-law a 9mm pistol and, if so, where he got it.

Headrick said that he did sell his brother-in-law a 9mm pistol which had been bought by one of his relatives at the Gun Shop in Fort Payne. The relative then gave it to Headrick, and later, when he and Carolyn got into a financial bind, he sold both the pistol and a 410 shotgun.

The next question on the list was somewhat unusual; the officers asked if Randy had ever robbed any Indian graves.

The answer was short and succinct:

"No."

When asked where his client was currently living and working, French said he was living and working with his parents.

The next question concerned Headrick's military service, specifically where he served in the Army and what kind of discharge he received.

According to Headrick, he served at Fort Worth, Texas, Fort Wainwright, Alaska, and Fort Benning, Georgia. His discharge from the National Guard was Honorable; the U.S. Army discharged him with Other Than Honorable status.

Then, the investigators casually slipped in a question they were very curious about, since so many rumors were running rampant around the north DeKalb communities near the homes of the Dalton and Headrick families.

Who, they asked, did Headrick think killed his wife and mother-in-law?

His answer, though incredulous, was about what the officers expected. French said that his client believed that the person who killed Carolyn and Dora Ann was someone who had intended to kill another of his relatives, or one of the Dalton family themselves, or someone who had planned to kill one of the Dalton relatives.

Then, the investigators said, they needed to know what life insurance policies Headrick had on Carolyn, and asked French and his client to list the policies he currently had on himself or those he had previously had but which were no longer in effect.

The policies French and Headrick listed for Carolyn were State Farm Insurance for $250,000, Union Privilege Life Insurance for $100,000, and Woodmen of the World for $25,000. On himself, Headrick said, there was a Woodmen of the World policy for $25,000 and a Union Privilege Life Insurance for $25,000. There had also been another policy for $100,000 from an unidentified company, but it had lapsed over two years earlier, Headrick claimed. During the two years prior to the murders, there had been an additional $40,000 on Headrick, perhaps a policy from his employment, and he said maybe there had been some smaller term policies that he could not remember.

Then, as is always the case with investigations, the officers used a questioning method that often produced results. They requested a repeat of information they had already obtained on several earlier occasions. Headrick was asked to account for his whereabouts for 48 hours prior to and after the murders.

On Wednesday morning, he said, he got up at 5:30 A.M., got dressed and went to his job as usual. He worked an eight-hour shift, then went over to Red Crow Snapp's home, loaded some things Red Crow was giving him, carried it back to his own home, unloaded it, ate supper, watched television, talked to his wife, and went to bed.

On Thursday, the early routine was the same. He punched in at work at 6:30 A.M. and finished his shift at 3 P.M. He stopped by home, picked up Carolyn, and went to Red Crow's house. Carolyn helped with some of the packing, and Headrick called another couple to come pick up some scrap metal. Headrick loaded his truck with items he planned to store for Red Crow until the Snapps finished moving to another location. Headrick named five people who were present in addition to him and his wife and the Snapps. He and Carolyn then went home, unloaded the truck and ate a quick supper, and Headrick said he took a bath and went to bed while his wife stayed up watching television.

Then, Headrick's account became somewhat sketchy. The next day, French said, the day of the murders, his client remembered going home and being stopped by law enforcement, frisked, and being told that everyone in the house was dead. Headrick became incoherent, according to French, and sat on the tailgate of a pickup for several hours while investigators questioned him. Then he went to the funeral home and to the hospital, where he was given shots and pills. He went to the funeral the following day, and claimed that was about all he could remember about the two days after the murders.

When asked if Headrick had owned a small caliber pistol, the answer was simply, "No."

Then came another question the investigators were anxious to see answered. They asked what Headrick's relationship was with his mother-in-law.

French's response began with an admission from Headrick that he and Dora Ann Dalton had not talked for almost a year. She would talk to Carolyn, Headrick said, and have Carolyn talk to Headrick, and he said he did the same, claiming they got along better that way. Headrick said he did whatever Dora Ann wanted done, and said she bought him a Father's Day gift, a pair of slippers, and he bought her a Mother's Day present.

French said his client had allowed Dora Ann to use his credit card to purchase a dehumidifier, and that she loaned him money when he was in a financial bind. Likewise, when she needed medicine and was short on cash, Headrick supposedly gave her the money to pay for her prescriptions.

Overall, Headrick claimed, Dora Ann did more for him than she did for her own children, but she talked with her other children and with her minister, telling them that she and her son-in-law didn't speak to each other. Around two years previously, Headrick said, she had tried to order him around and they had a big disagreement. When she was off her medication, he said, she was a terror, becoming irritable and hostile when she wasn't feeling well. He claimed he felt he was better off not speaking to her, and said she felt the same way.

Although it seemed unlikely in view of his refusal to speak to her, Headrick said he helped Dora Ann with her business matters, took her to the hospital when she was ill, and helped her buy money orders. Generally, he said, they got along well, aside from not speaking to "avoid problems." And three weeks prior to the murders, Headrick said he took both his wife and his mother-in-law out to dinner. It was hard for the investigators to imagine such an outing, with relations so strained between Headrick and Dora Ann that they went to a restaurant, seated themselves at the same table and had a meal without even speaking to one another.

When asked the identity of the men in a green pickup truck who were at Headrick's house on the sixth of July, Headrick said he didn't know, but added that it could have been the men who were working on the house and painting the trim. He didn't see their vehicle, he said.

The officers then asked if Headrick would be willing to give blood samples, hair samples and saliva samples.

French answered that blood samples had already been taken, and said his client would agree to give hair and saliva samples.

When the officers asked why Headrick had left his earlier job at Earthgrains bakery, he said he was "discharged for horseplay." And when they asked, "Is Headrick an atheist?" the answer was a simple "No."

Then came another loaded question, more repetition which the officers hoped would eventually result in getting some answers which conflicted with Headrick's earlier statements.

"What was Headrick's relationship with his wife?" they asked.

French answered that Headrick and Carolyn had a great relationship. They kidded each other all the time, he said, and people who weren't well acquainted with them could have gotten the wrong impression. But people who knew them well, he said, knew the pair were very close and loved each other very much. Headrick claimed that at the time of the murders, he and his wife were the happiest they had ever been in their lives.

Headrick went on to say that people continually put Carolyn down, making her believe she couldn't do things, and she began to think something was wrong with her. Through her friendship with the Snapps, he said, she learned that she could do craft work and whatever else she wished. Headrick said he and his wife began to enjoy making things together and having more fun than they had ever had.

Not once, French said, did Headrick and Carolyn ever have serious problems. The most serious marital problem they had, he said, was Headrick's "attempted" affair with his girlfriend at Earthgrains. Headrick said he had confessed this to his wife, and she forgave him and then forgot about it.

"Yeah, right," muttered one of the investigators.

French said his client claimed that he and his wife talked about everything between themselves, and had been planning to make a trip to Mobile on the week following the murders. And they had invited Melva and Red Crow Snapp to dinner on the ninth of July, and both Headrick and Carolyn were looking forward to the evening.

The next question concerned Headrick's financial situation, specifically whether he had taken out any loans at a bank, or any loans at all, within the two or three months prior to the murders. His answer was no, he had not. And when asked if he had hospital insurance on Carolyn, Headrick said that he had hospitalization through his job at Builders Supply.

Then, once again, the investigators asked Headrick to repeat information that he had already given several times during other questioning sessions. They asked Headrick to retrace his steps on the day of the murders, from the time he got up until the time he arrived at the scene after work.

According to French, Headrick said that he woke up at 5:30 A.M. and wasn't feeling well, but he decided to go in to work anyway. Carolyn asked him if he wanted to stay home, but he told her he had to go to work because they had bills to pay; he was going to work.

Headrick said he arrived at work at Builders Supply at 6 A.M. and clocked in at 6:30. He collected his job tickets, got into his truck and went to his first stop of the day, Sola Electric. He unloaded and returned to Builders Supply, where he worked on the yard with a supervisor and two or three of the yard hands until around 11:15 A.M. Headrick saw an acquaintance parked in the yard waiting for her son to pick up her paycheck, and he walked out and talked with her for around ten minutes. Then he walked back over to the maintenance shop and ate lunch there with the mechanic. Another man, a former employee, came in during their lunch break and talked to the two men.

Around noon, Headrick said, he walked back to the break room and told the supervisor he was going to pull his load for the next day. He picked up his tickets, got into his truck and pulled off the lot. Then he noticed a Milan Express truck parked across the road at the warehouse. Headrick said he pulled over there, opened the warehouse, and told the Milan truck driver that he'd walk across the parking lot and get someone to help unload the truck. He told the supervisor about the truck, walked back over to the warehouse, and started unloading the truck, with another employee who was sent to help.

Headrick said he was complaining because he didn't think he would have time to pull his load for the next morning, so the other employee stayed and helped Headrick put away the Milan truck load and then helped him

pull his next day's load. Then the other man left around
2:20 P.M.

Headrick said it took him ten to fifteen minutes to lock
up the warehouse and take his truck back to the main
yard. He walked up to the front of the store and talked
with the other delivery loaders until around 3:00 P.M., then
clocked out, went by the bank on the way home to deposit
his paycheck, and stopped to get gas in his truck. Then
he went home.

The investigators were almost finished, but they
dropped a couple more loaded questions, to which they
already knew the answers, to see what kind of response
they would get. They first asked Headrick if he was seeing
a woman at the present time, and he said no. Then they
wanted to know if he had ever used Carolyn's credit card
since her death.

"Randy does not have Carol's credit card," French
said, adding that his client had made a few purchases on
his own card, but had not seen Carolyn's credit card, nor
anything else from her purse.

The officers wanted to know the whereabouts of Head-
rick's children and his ex-wife, and also his sister, Rhonda
Ruth Gill. Headrick said he thought his daughter was in
Dallas, and his son was supposed to be with his mother,
but said that he did not know where they were at that time.
His sister, he said, lived in Dallas.

And, finally, the last question:

"Does Randy own a gun?"

The answer was no.

The answers to the investigators' questions, carefully
gone over by attorney Bob French before being returned
to Rhonda Jackson, did not provide any new information
from Headrick, but several were in direct conflict with
statements that had been made by other people. The officers had already learned, for example, that Headrick and
his wife had been having problems over the excessive cost

of their high insurance premiums before the murders, and that Carolyn had spoken to several people about her intentions to drop some of the policies. And many others had made statements about Randy's offers to "get rid" of the husbands of potential girlfriends, as well as his attempts to get other people to "mess up" his ex-girlfriend after their breakup.

Officers had reason to believe Headrick was seeing another woman at the time the questions were submitted, and might have possibly been doing so before the murders. And his claim not to have Carolyn's credit card was contrary to the statement of the Wal-Mart clerk, who had told the investigators Headrick had come into the store, along with a woman and two small children, and made purchases on the card after the murders.

His claim not to have tried to purchase a gun might have technically been true, but there was the statement of the Scottsboro Wal-Mart clerk who said he and Red Crow had come into the store looking at guns in the sporting-goods department and inquired about layaway requirements.

Even after receiving Headrick's answers to their long list of questions, there were still many other issues and contradictions that would baffle the investigators for some time to come.

On the last day of August, LaRue Cornelison ran another update of the Headrick/Dalton double homicide in Fort Payne's *Times-Journal*. Sheriff Cecil Reed told her that his department continued to investigate the murders actively, and stressed that the brutal slayings remained on top of the case list for his department. Questioning continued, Reed said, with many out-of-state residents being contacted for information.

Again Headrick's as-yet unbroken alibi was mentioned, but Reed also said that he could not ignore the fact that $350,000 in life insurance policies had been taken out on Carolyn Headrick—policies Headrick claimed were to help take care of Dora Ann Dalton in the event of Carolyn's death.

Billy Jack Dalton once again emphatically stated in print his suspicion that Headrick was to blame for the deaths, either directly or indirectly, but told Cornelison he "just can't prove it."

Headrick, who claimed he loved his wife and would never do such a thing as murder her, said in the interview that he believed whoever killed his wife and mother-in-law "was looking for something or someone and just ended up in the wrong house."

Sheriff Reed told Cornelison that no particular person was being named as a suspect at that time. "Evidence is needed," he said, "and not enough evidence exists to arrest Randy Headrick or anyone else at present."

Cornelison ended her article by asking any of her readers who might have tips or other information about the case to contact the sheriff's department, and gave the appropriate phone numbers. And, as had been the case since the morning following the murders, the tips just kept on coming.

CHAPTER 18

On September 11, a local surveyor contacted Rhonda Jackson and told her about an incident that had occurred around three weeks before the murders, when he had been surveying land on the Dalton estate.

"A nephew of theirs, whose name I don't know, walked down the dirt road from the direction of Dora Ann Dalton's house to the rock house where I was surveying," he said. "The guy was mouthing off about the property. He made some comments about some of the family getting more property than they were supposed to."

The nephew didn't make any threats toward anyone's life or anything of that nature, according to the surveyor, but some of the other people who were standing around watching the surveying got into an argument about the land.

That afternoon, Rhonda Jackson contacted the Texas Department of Child Protective Services and spoke with a caseworker, who was able to give her the address and phone number of Headrick's ex-wife, Bonita, who lived at that time in Arlington, Texas. Rhonda called the number the following day and left a message on the answering machine, asking Bonita to return her call. The next morning, Bonita Headrick returned Rhonda's phone call and asked if she could call her back that afternoon after three o'clock.

There was little or no new information to be learned from Rhonda's conversations with Bonita Headrick, but their talks served to confirm the events that took place in Texas when Headrick and his friend were caught with the pipe bomb that was allegedly intended for Bonita's trailer. The phone conversations also confirmed something else that both of the women firmly believed— Bonita was extremely lucky to have escaped with her life from her marriage to Randy Headrick.

Several people, when calling in tips to the sheriff's department, had mentioned the possibility that the killer was looking for another person with the last name of Dalton, and had mistakenly gone to the wrong house. In mid-September, Rhonda Jackson spoke with the mother of the man who had most often been named in those tips as the possible target. She told Rhonda that she didn't know where her son was, and said he had left the area in May and had only called home two times since he had been gone.

"He owes child support and had a garnishment on his check, and that's why he left," his mother said. "The last time I talked to him was about three or four weeks ago, but when he calls again, I'll have him get in contact with you."

CHAPTER 19

   As time passed and information about the murders continued to trickle slowly in to the investigators, the Dalton/Headrick case remained at the top of their priority list. Despite their efforts to pursue every possible lead, nothing of substance seemed to ever point anywhere except directly toward Randy Headrick. He remained the prime suspect, whether or not they acknowledged it to the media, but his alibi was still holding up, no matter how hard the investigators tried to break it. Rhonda Jackson and her team were frustrated, but their frustration made them work all the harder to obtain any clues that would identify the killer of Carolyn and Dora Ann, whether or not that killer was Randy Headrick.

   On the first of November, Headrick was given a polygraph at the request of his attorney, Bob French. The test was administered by Commercial Polygraph, Inc., a Birmingham, Alabama, firm that held membership in the American Polygraph Association and the Alabama Association of Polygraph Examiners. The examiner reported to French that his client, during the pretest interview, gave his vital statistics, personal background and previous arrest record. Headrick told the examiner that he'd had nothing to do with either of the killings, and went on to say that he did not know who committed the murders, but said that he strongly suspected his brother-in-law, Billy Jack Dalton. This suspicion of his, coincidentally, seemed to have begun around the time that Dalton started publicly announcing that he believed Headrick was responsible for murdering his mother and sister.

The examiner asked Headrick if he planned to lie about any of his questions, then asked if he had told the whole truth about the murders. He then asked if Headrick had ever caused someone to die; if he'd ever hired anyone to kill a person; if he was trying to withhold any information about the murders; if he knew for sure who killed his wife and mother-in-law. To all the questions, Headrick answered no.

In the second phase of the testing, Headrick was asked if he knew Carolyn was going to be killed; if he asked anyone to kill her; if he killed her himself; if he had anything to do with the deaths; if he had purposely tried to lie to any of the examiner's questions.

Again Headrick answered no to all the questions; then when he was asked if he had told the whole truth since the testing began, he answered yes.

At the end of the test, the examiner prepared his report of the results and stated that it was his conclusion that Headrick had told the truth during the polygraph.

Later that month, an irate Billy Jack Dalton came into the sheriff's department full of questions concerning a report he'd heard that the investigators had received. He had been told someone had claimed he had been hauling drugs back from Texas in an eighteen-wheeler. Rhonda Jackson assured him she had not received such a report, but told him she had heard that the tale had originated from Headrick's attorney. For Billy Jack Dalton, to have such rumors allegedly spread about him by his former brother-in-law, who he was certain had been the person responsible for the deaths of his mother and sister, was more than infuriating. Dalton was already grief-stricken and frustrated, and felt that his entire remaining family had been devastated almost beyond repair by the murders. And now, attempts were being made to undermine his reputation, both within the community and with law enforcement. He was justifiably furious.

Clearly, the feud between the Daltons and the Headricks was in full swing, and it continued to escalate as time passed.

Toward the end of November, Rhonda Jackson again subpoenaed the telephone records from the Fyffe Antique Mall for the period of July 1, 1995, to November. The Headrick family still claimed that Randy's mother had gotten a collect call from the Jackson County Hospital shortly after the murders from a young woman who told her that she had been at a Happy Hollow residence when two men came in claiming they had "done the job." Then they burned their bloody clothes in the yard of the house.

When the subpoenaed phone records were picked up, they showed that no collect calls had been made at any time, from July 1 to November, from the Jackson County Hospital to the Fyffe Antique Mall's number.

As the Christmas season drew near, the DeKalb County officers and investigators found themselves forced to spend much of their time on residential burglaries, shoplifting, domestic violence and all the other holiday traditions that law enforcement must deal with in increasing volume at the time of peace on earth and goodwill toward men. The Headrick/Dalton case, however, remained foremost in the minds of Rhonda Jackson and the other investigators. Rhonda prayed every night for that one little detail that would break the case, and she had faith that in time, her prayers would be answered. She keenly felt the grief of the victims' family, and she was determined that she would never give up until the killer was brought to justice. And the killer, she firmly believed, was Randy Headrick.

On December 8, Rhonda spoke with Bob French to ask whether or not he would allow his client to take a polygraph administered by a law enforcement polygraph examiner. French, ever the wily defense attorney, said he would not let Headrick take such a polygraph unless the investigators gave him a letter saying that if Headrick passed the polygraph, he would be removed from consideration as the prime suspect.

"I advised him we could not do this," Jackson said, not surprised in the least by French's tactics.

The following week, Jackson spoke with a clerk in the DeKalb County Tax Assessor's Office to request another list of vehicle tags, this time on red Ford Rangers registered in the county from 1988 to 1996, broken down by towns or cities. The witnesses' accounts of a small red truck seen leaving the murder scene was still a sticking point. Headrick was driving a full-size red pickup at the time of the crimes, not a smaller model. The investigators were determined to check out every red Ford Ranger in DeKalb County, just in case.

CHAPTER 20

As the calendar rolled over into 1996, tips and rumors about the Headrick case continued to come into the sheriff's office on a slightly less frequent basis than before, but much time was spent carefully following up each one of them. In mid-January, Rhonda Jackson accompanied Investigator Joel York, of the Rainsville Police Department, on a search of a Rainsville woman's house on another case she was assisting the Rainsville department with. While searching the house with the woman's consent, a .22 revolver, EIG model E4, was seized from a man who was also living there at the time. He identified the gun as being his, and told the investigators he had formerly lived with one of Headrick's sisters. Since the gun fit the description of the weapon that possibly could have been used to kill Dora Ann Dalton and Carolyn Headrick, the officers sent it to the Department of Forensic Sciences for ballistics testing.

While the investigation into the Dalton/Headrick murders continued, the insurance companies that had issued the policies on the murder victims were busily conducting their own inquiries into the case. Autopsy reports and other case information was requested; phone calls were made back and forth from the companies to the sheriff's office; representatives of the companies stopped by frequently to check with the investigators on the status of the case.

In early February, an attorney from State Farm Life Insurance came to Rhonda Jackson's office to speak with her about the current status of the investigation.

"I advised him that the investigation was still pending, was still an open file, and that Randy Headrick was still a prime suspect," she said. "I told him that I had the original life insurance policies in my possession."

The following day, Jackson turned over a large file of material to an agent of the Alcohol, Tobacco, and Firearms (ATF) Bureau, which had agreed to take a look at the case and offer any input he might have. Included in the files were firearm transaction records from Wal-Mart and the Gun Center, a copy of Headrick's driver's license, a copy of the questions and answers asked to Headrick and answered through his attorney, a copy of a taped statement from Headrick on the day following the murders, a copy of the case summary and the name, address and phone number of a Headrick relative who had bought a 9mm pistol from Headrick. The investigators welcomed the input of the ATF agent. They eagerly sought assistance from any other agencies that might spot that tiny, overlooked detail that could break the case.

On Valentine's Day, a young woman came into the sheriff's department to make a statement concerning some things she had overheard at her place of employment, Sola Electric, the week following the murders.

"I was in the restroom at work at Sola," she said. "Two other women were in there talking about Randy Headrick coming in to Sola and delivering skids. They said he gave one of his Indian artifacts to a guy in the shipping department and told him to go and put it in his truck and not be seen with it. He told the guy somebody was after him."

Rhonda Jackson, who was conducting the interview, asked the woman to try to recall what else the two women were saying.

"As best as I can remember, they were saying Randy told

the guy he was supposed to make a bunch of stuff for 'them' and that there would be a bloody massacre," the woman told a startled Jackson.

"I don't remember the guy's name, but he worked in shipping. This happened the day of the murders."

Although this hearsay evidence could not be put to use, it was astounding to think that Headrick might have had this conversation with someone at Sola Electric, his first delivery of the morning, on the very day that the murders were committed.

On February 23, Rhonda Jackson spoke with an FBI agent in the Birmingham, Alabama, field office, talking with him about the possibility of obtaining an FBI psychological profile of the killer in the Dalton/Headrick case. Jackson felt this might help the investigation, and hoped for assistance from the FBI. After she gave the agent the facts of the case, he said he would contact headquarters at Quantico that afternoon and get in touch with her about the requirements for the profile. A few days later, Jackson received a Violent Criminal Apprehension Program (ViCAP) form to fill out on Carolyn Headrick and mail back to Quantico, and another form was sent for Dora Ann Dalton. Hopefully, the expertise of FBI profilers would provide some help in the search for the killer, or give some confirmation of the investigators' suspicions.

In early March, some disappointing test results were received on the EIG .22 revolver that had been sent earlier to the Department of Forensic Sciences after being seized during the search that Rhonda Jackson had assisted with in Rainsville.

"The weapon was test fired for comparison with the bullets from the bodies of the subjects," the report stated. "It was determined that the bullets were not fired by the weapon due to a difference in general rifling characteristics."

During the first week of April, a Dalton relative called Rhonda Jackson and told her that a man had gotten in touch with some of her family members saying he had information on a small red pickup that he saw the day of the murders. Rhonda immediately called the man and set up an interview with him for the following day.

The caller had also told Rhonda that Carolyn and Randy Headrick had gone to another relative's home in Chattanooga twice in May and June before the murders, and both times Headrick left the home and stayed gone for about an hour, refusing to let anyone accompany him.

"When he got back, Carolyn asked him where he had been. He said he went and withdrew money from the ATM machine, went to the store, and went to a little bead shop."

When the informant came in to be interviewed about the small red pickup, he told the investigators the truck was at that time located in Chattanooga. A few days later, Mike James and Rhonda Jackson traveled to the Chattanooga Police Department and met with Sergeant Rodney Bowman, who took them to the address listed on the tag number, which was given to them by the informant.

When they arrived at the address, they found that the house was vacant. They went next door to a small grocery and learned that the lady who owned the house was now in a nursing home in Fort Oglethorpe, Georgia. It didn't appear that this particular red pickup truck was going to figure in the investigation in any way, and James and Jackson returned to Alabama empty-handed.

The next day brought a payoff so big that the countless disappointments of the previous weeks were forgotten. Jill Shrader called to tell Rhonda Jackson that she had some important information on the murders and was now ready to talk. Rhonda and Mike James immediately made arrangements to meet Jill, who was living at that time in Brunswick, Georgia, at the King and Prince Inn located on St. Simon's Island, Georgia. Jill and Shane Headrick were still living together. When the investigators arrived at the inn the following day, Jill was already there, waiting for them. And she was very afraid.

CHAPTER 21

After restating the fact that Jill had lived as a common-law wife with Randy Headrick's brother, Shane, for two years, and that Jill had been interviewed by Mike James and Rhonda Jackson previously in regard to the murders of Carolyn Headrick and Dora Ann Dalton, James started his tape recorder and began the conversation. Jill was obviously very nervous, and she seemed to be anxious to tell the investigators what she had learned since her first statement.

"Back a short period of time after the murders, Rhonda and I came to Georgia in the Atlanta area and talked to you and Shane; is that correct?" James asked. "And since then you have developed some information concerning the murders. I'd like you to tell me what you know and have heard."

Jill took a deep breath and began telling her story.

"Well, I think that I was set up from the very start because of the way everything happened the day of the murders, the way Shane's dad called me at work that morning, and he never had done that. And the way I had to call Shane every little while to tell him what time it was, and he had a watch. He told me it was broken, and I later found out that it wasn't.

"I was at work, in downtown Atlanta, that morning. We

got up for me to go to work and I had been driving to work every day in his truck. Well, Shane said, when I started leaving and asked for the keys, he said he was gonna take me to work, which was a good drive from where we were staying. I was surprised about him taking me to work; that was out of the ordinary. I called him at different periods that morning. He kept reminding me to call him; it was real important for me to call him that day."

James asked if that was unusual, and Jill told him it most definitely was.

"He told me that his watch was messed up and that he wouldn't be able to know the time during the day, and for me to call him when I got breaks and stuff," Jill said, "and to call him a couple of hours before time for me to get off from work."

"And he was there at the motel room that day, all day?" asked Rhonda.

"Well, no, there was about a five-hour period that I didn't get ahold of him and I worked between that, and tried to call him," Jill said. "He told me later that I talked to him at lunch, but I didn't, because I remember eating lunch with a nurse and I didn't use the phone at all."

Jill had previously told the investigators that there was about a two-hour period when she wasn't able to contact Shane, but now she said that after she thought about it, she figured it was actually around five hours between the times when she had called him.

"You know, like I said, that's been a pretty good while and I've had a lot on my mind here lately. I could have it wrong, but I think it's long enough till we were wrong about him not having enough time. I didn't talk to him from that morning, about ten, till that afternoon, because he tried to tell me I did, and I didn't."

Mike James asked Jill what she had learned since their first conversation that caused her to call the sheriff's department the previous day.

"I always knew that Randy was, you know, had something to do with it and Shane will tell you that too, but I kept telling myself all this time that Shane didn't have nothing to do with it," Jill said. "But over the months, there's just one thing after another, just one little thing after another, and then he'd say stuff to me. . . ."

Jill was growing increasingly nervous, and Mike James asked her to take her time and try to articulate, one at a time, those little things Shane had told her or implied to her that had led her to believe he was involved in the murders. The information began to spill out, with Jill saying that she wasn't allowed to talk about the murders or she and Shane would have a big fight.

"He'd say stuff to me like, 'You couldn't stand the truth if you knew it; you couldn't deal with the truth,' which is true, you know, and I couldn't stand the thoughts of him having anything to do with it, and it was driving me crazy. But anytime anybody mentioned the murders, like his mom and dad mentioned them all the time, he'd just go off; he'd say stuff like nobody would never be able to figure it out and it wasn't never gonna be solved."

Jill said she had thought about things that had been said to her, and other things that she had overheard.

"I thought about all the stupid stuff they said to me, like Billy Jack did the murders, he had it done and it was drug related, and that he hated his mama. And one day Shane said that Carol had jumped onto him about something. I said, 'You had no reason to hate Carol; why would you have done anything to Carol?' He said Carol wasn't as good as everybody thought she was. I asked him why Randy didn't just leave Carol instead of all this happening, and he said she wouldn't let him go, that she told him she never would; she'd die before she'd leave him, or let him leave."

Jill told the officers that sometimes Shane would agree with some of the things she would say to him.

"I said, 'You know what, the more I think about this, Shane, somebody had to rent a truck or a car or whatever they drove, if they were planning out the perfect crime.' Well, he agreed with that, and when I said 'red truck,' yeah, but then he just gets mad. I can talk to him just a little bit, but if I push it too far, I'm in trouble, big trouble, as in threats and stuff."

Mike James asked Jill what kind of threats Shane had made toward her.

"He told me night before last that I didn't have to worry about Randy killing me, he was going to kill me himself," Jill said. "And he was taking my hair, just yanking it around, and he picked up a sleeper shirt that was lying there on the couch and started trying to tie my hands together. I thought I bought the farm this time, I mean I did.

"And I asked him why he was tying my hands up; what was he gonna do? And you know how I got out of it? Same way as every time, beg and plead and tell him I love him, and he calms down."

"He blames it on you," Rhonda said.

"And it's the same way with all of this," Jill continued. "They don't blame theirselves; they blame Carol and Ann because if they hadn't been like they were, it wouldn't have got to this point."

Rhonda asked Jill if Shane had ever said there were three people involved.

"Yeah, he didn't answer me on that, but I know there was, the way he looked at me. I know there was another man. Rhonda, I know it sounds crazy, and I'm forty-four years old and I've been married before, but I've never faced anything like I faced with him. I can't explain how just the mention of some of that stuff can set him off. I take a big risk every time I do it."

Jill said that Shane had never told her anything directly about the murders, but had just agreed with things she'd said, except he had told her Randy did it.

"What has he told you about Randy?" James asked.

"That Randy is a crazy, psycho son of a bitch, that Randy did it, that nobody else would do that. And he says that until he gets around his dad and them, and then he starts switching."

Jill said that she told Shane, "You know what, I think if they would do a hundred-mile radius and see who rented a red truck that day, they'd get somebody."

Shane then jumped up, she said, and shouted, "I'm tired of this goddamn shit, you better shut up!"

"I hit a mark on that one," Jill said. "I know him well enough to know when I hit a mark, so I got to thinking, the halfway point between Henagar and Atlanta was Rome, Georgia."

Rhonda asked Jill if she thought Shane would have rented a truck, and Jill said neither he nor Randy would have rented a truck in his own name.

"So, you think it would be the third person?" asked Rhonda.

"Yeah, that's the one rented it," Jill said.

Rhonda asked Jill who she thought the third person might be.

"I think it's a good possibility, and this is speculation only, that it might be their cousin. Randy's been living with him for a long time now, and when he wasn't living with him, he was running around with him since the murders."

James asked Jill if she and Randy ever talked to each other.

"Nope," she said, laughing. "Since Randy tried to get me and my son to do what he did, I've not had much to do with Randy."

Jill told again about Randy requesting her and her son to hurt his former girlfriend, marking her face and assaulting her.

"I really thought these people were just bullshitters, you know. I thought they just ran their mouth, watched too much TV, you know; that's really what I thought about these people for so long . . . until the murders."

James asked Jill if she ever had asked Shane a direct question concerning the murders, and got a direct answer.

"When I asked him, did he think Randy did it? Yes, he said yes. When I asked him if he would have participated in the murders, his answer, most of the time, was 'No, hell no, you know I didn't do something like that.' And then it's been, 'You couldn't deal with the truth, Jill, if you knew it.'"

Rhonda asked Jill if she thought she could talk further to Shane and find out what the truth that he was referring to might possibly be. Jill said she could, but she would be afraid for her life. She believed with all her heart, she said, that they could do something to her and she didn't believe anyone would ever find her.

Jill then repeated what she said Shane had told her about the way the murders would have had to be done.

"Their clothes were stripped, from the top of their head to their feet and they were burned; everything they had on would be burned; the vehicle they used, the truck they used, was lined with plastic and paper was put in the floorboard. I'm trying to remember his exact words on stuff. When he tells me stuff like that, he says, 'This is the way you do it,' not like *he* did it or *we* did it. He said that's the way they probably did it."

Jill said that Shane was carrying a gun, and got it out when he grew angry with her.

"It's nothing for me to have a gun in my face," she said. "He'll get a gun and play with it when he's mad, which makes me extremely nervous, but a lot of times, he does things to mess with my head."

Jill said Shane got mad one night while they were having an argument about the murders, and he picked up the phone and called Randy at his parents' home.

"He jumped onto him, and I could hear him talking, and he said, 'Your little deal across the road has fucked up my life. I have to listen to this shit day and night,' and that was it. Randy hung up on Shane because they were on his dad's phone and they think the phones are tapped. But I heard Shane say that to him."

After she finished the interview, Jill told the investigators, "I do think that if you-all can get Shane somewhere and question him real good, you might do better, but I don't know how. I just know that, what he said to me, you know that's not worth anything."

Mike James and Rhonda Jackson, however, felt that what Shane had said to Jill might prove to be worth a great deal.

CHAPTER 22

On the day following Jill's interview, Mike James and Rhonda Jackson had a meeting with an agent of the Georgia Bureau of Investigation. They brought the agent up to speed on the case and discussed the possibility of the GBI's cooperation on areas of the investigation that might fall within their jurisdiction. As was the case with the FBI involvement, Rhonda was glad to have assistance from any other agency willing to help out. More and more strongly every day, she felt that it would only take a small tidbit of the right information to bring down the killer.

As the days passed and Jill Shrader carefully worked toward persuading Shane Headrick to talk once again with the investigators, several new leads on small red pickups began to come in. Rhonda Jackson and Jimmy Phillips spent April 29 and 30 in Dade County, Georgia, to interview several individuals who had trucks meeting that description. Some of those people they spoke with had slightly questionable police records, and others had ties of one sort or another to DeKalb County. But of the seven young men they took statements from, not a single one could be considered to have even a remote possibility of involvement in the killings. All of them had solid alibis for the day of the murders.

In mid-May, Rhonda Jackson got another break she had

been hoping for. Almost a month after Jill Shrader's interview, Shane Headrick finally decided to come forward and talk to the investigators. Jill and Shane arrived in Fort Payne on May 14, and Sheriff Cecil Reed promptly checked them into the Best Western motel so that they could be well-protected during their stay in the county.

Around 2:00 P.M., the couple was brought to the sheriff's department, where they met with Rhonda Jackson and Jimmy Phillips. Although Shane was the primary subject, Jill remained with him during the interview. Rhonda could see that Shane seemed very upset, and he claimed that he wanted to cooperate with the investigators. He and Jill were there, he said, to tell what they knew and what they thought about the murders.

Rhonda started by asking Shane if he wanted to be interviewed without a lawyer present.

"Yes, ma'am," he answered. "I'd like to correct my other statements."

"Have there been any developments since we talked to you before, do you know anything further that you're wishing to tell us today?"

"Yes, ma'am. I did know more," Shane began. "Randy had asked me in November of the previous year to either help him commit or find somebody to commit the murders, and he asked me on two occasions. The first time was in November of '94. He came to get me to go to the grocery store with him so he could make a phone call. On our way back from the store, he started asking me if I would help him or find somebody to help me murder Ann and Carol, and he described how he wanted it done. He wanted them shot, both of them shot twice in the head, their heads cut off and a spear stuck through their bodies; then for me or whoever to go . . . he told me where Ann kept her money, he told me to go and get the money."

"Where did he tell you she kept her money?" Phillips asked.

"It was either in a jewelry box on the nightstand or under the mattress on the bed, and then take what money was in her purse to make it look like a robbery. I told him no, if he wanted away from them, to get a divorce, 'cause I didn't . . . ah . . . That was just too far out there. And then he offered me half of the insurance money."

"Which was how much?" Rhonda asked.

"At that time, to my knowledge, it was one hundred fifty thousand."

"And he offered you seventy-five thousand to help him, or to do it?"

"Yes, and he said that he was wanting to be at work when all this went down. I told him no."

"Okay," Rhonda said, "when was the second time he asked?"

"It was a few days, or maybe two weeks later, he came by and we went to the store again. On the way to the store, he started asking me again, but he got more insistent."

"What did he say this time?"

"He described to me how he wanted them to die again, the same way he had said before. And if I could find somebody to help or to go up and to do it, and I got violent with him, told him I didn't want to have nothing to do with it, that he shouldn't even be thinking of it. He wanted out of there, get a divorce."

Shane then told the investigators how Randy had told him the murders could be committed.

"He wanted whoever—if I didn't do it, whoever was supposed to go in and commit the murders—to act like their car was broke down in front of the house, so they would let them in, let him or them in to use the phone. He had kept asking for a twenty-two pistol, but he quit asking me anything after I got violent with him. He never did say anything again."

"What do you mean, how did you get violent with him, what happened?" Rhonda asked.

"I grabbed him by the scruff of the neck and jerked him up by his shirt and I got in his face and I told him to just leave me alone, that I don't go for that," Shane said.

"Where did this happen?"

"It was outside the Chevron in Henagar, where the pay phone is, at night."

Shane said that ended Randy's requests for help with the murders, but a couple of months later, his brother told him he would get Jill out of jail if she would get him an unregistered .22 pistol that couldn't be traced. Randy did not tell Shane what he wanted the pistol for, he said, and his brother didn't mention using a .22 pistol when he described how he wanted the murders committed.

"A few weeks after the murders," Shane said, "I carried him off by hisself—at the time he looked like he was telling the truth, but I couldn't really tell, he was on medication. . . ."

"What did you ask him?" Phillips asked.

"I asked him directly, 'Did you have anything to do with them murders? Did you do them or did you have anything to do with them?' and he said no."

Then Shane blurted out some astonishing new information.

"We went to see a psychic," he said. "I was not involved in this, Jill was. The psychic didn't know me, my family, nobody involved in it except for Jill, and the psychic went on tape to describe my brother, Randy, the clothes he was wearing, the tattoos on his arm. [She] said the boy that was driving did not know that it was going on until the truck was lined with plastic, but that he was scared right now. The psychic said there were three men, one being one of our cousins, but right off, I couldn't think of anybody that would do it. I don't know of anybody else that's like Randy, that's crazy enough to do it."

"Shane, why are you here now?" asked an exasperated Phillips. "Why didn't you tell me this to start with? Why are you here now?"

"'Cause I was in fear of what Randy might do to me or Jill or both of us for knowing too much."

Shane said that he had not talked to his brother recently, but was still afraid of him and the other men who he believed were involved, and he agreed to take a polygraph. Phillips asked him if he had been coerced or threatened in any way to come forward and tell what he knew.

"No," Shane said, visibly upset, "it's my own mental state, the way I was feeling. I didn't know who to talk to."

"But why are you so upset if you're not involved?" Rhonda asked.

"Because I asked my mother; I hadn't said nothing to my daddy, but I asked my mother two days ago. I told her the same thing I'm telling you-all, and she just acted like she didn't want to hear it. It's eating me up inside, 'cause I knew it and I could have done something to help then, but I was just too scared to do it then."

"Are you saying before they were killed you knew something about him trying to hire you, and you could have stopped it?" Rhonda asked. "Is that why you're so upset?"

Shane, miserable and racked with guilt, hung his head. "Yes."

The investigators moved the questioning in a different direction, asking Shane if he knew of anyone Randy hung out with at the time of the murders.

"Only ones I know of is the man he was riding back and forth to work with and a man called Red Crow. I believe Randy's working with him now in Chattanooga. And he had sent a man to my house in November—I didn't know the man, I hadn't never seen him before. All he said was that he was in prison with Randy and Randy told him to come to my house because he was having problems with his wife and didn't want her to see him."

Shane said he gave the man directions to get to Dora Ann's house, and described the man as being in his mid- to late-thirties, with salt-and-pepper hair and a scraggly beard. This happened a short time after Randy had asked Shane to help with the murders of Carolyn and Dora Ann, and Shane said he had never seen the man before or since that day.

Rhonda then asked Shane if he and Randy got along with one another at the present time.

"We tolerate one another, that was it; and being my brother, I had to tolerate him and he had to tolerate me."

"Did he ever say anything before he asked you to kill them, about killing them or let you know he wanted them dead, or anything like that? Why did he tell you he wanted them killed, Shane?" Rhonda asked.

"'Cause they was just on him all the time, wouldn't leave him alone. From what I, ah . . . I knew he was sleeping around on Carol, and he was unfaithful to her, and that's why they were like they were toward him."

"Did you know who the girl was?" Phillips asked.

"Not at that time, but I do now. Her name's Tonya."

"Do you know her last name?"

"Headrick, now," Shane said.

"See, I'm a little behind now. Is he married now?" Phillips asked.

"Yes, he got married last month and we didn't know about it till yesterday, and he's living in Tennessee now."

The investigators turned the questions toward Shane's knowledge of his brother's relationship with Red Crow.

"Let's talk about Red Crow a minute," Phillips said. "You know him?"

"I've seen him one time, but I didn't talk to him. Randy said Red Crow was moving and he was helping him move a lot."

"Did he tell you that Red Crow was getting him started in these Indian artifacts, and when he told you how he wanted them killed, he told you that he wanted a spear drove through them, right?"

"Yes," Shane said. "He started doing the Indian artifacts after he talked to me in November, and got real heavy into the spears and blades. He hadn't started making spears before then."

"Was he familiar with spears?" Rhonda asked.

"As far as I know, he was," Shane said. "He was involved with Indian organizations he's been with and trying to learn stuff from."

"And most of that was through Red Crow, right?"

"Yes."

"I mean, bottom line, Red Crow . . ."

"Helped him out," Shane answered.

"Thinks he's an Indian," Phillips remarked.

"Yeah," Shane said.

CHAPTER 23

Shane Headrick's interview with Jackson and Phillips entered another phase of questioning as it continued into the afternoon. There were many conflicting areas concerning Shane's whereabouts on the day of the murder, and the investigators took the opportunity to find out as much as they could while the time was right and Shane was talking. Shane had answered many questions about Randy, and now the spotlight was about to be turned around onto him.

"Let's go back to you," Rhonda said, "you said you were in Atlanta on the day of the murders, and you took Jill to work that morning, which was unusual. And you wanted her to call you during the day and let you know what time it was; is that right?"

"I told her when I dropped her off, 'Call me when it's time for you to go so I can come get you.' Then my father called that morning, and she called on her own a couple of more times during the day."

Shane said he was in the motel complex, either out at the pool or in the apartment, when Jill had called. He talked to her three times that day, he said, and his father had called and talked to Jill.

"Did you tell Jill that your watch was broken?" Rhonda asked.

"Yeah, it was broke when she left that morning."

"Was it, was it in fact broken?" Rhonda asked.

"Yes," Shane answered hesitantly.

"Was it running?"

"No."

"Wasn't running," Rhonda repeated. "Did it start running later?"

For the first time during the interview, Shane found himself with nothing to say.

"It didn't," Rhonda said. "Shane, you need to think about that because I think the watch did start running."

"Which watch was it?" Shane asked.

Jill had been sitting quietly, listening, saying nothing. But she broke in, telling Shane, "The one that was in the truck glove compartment. It was running when I got in."

Jimmy Phillips looked Shane in the eye. "You need to think about this," he advised.

"Well, the watch I had at that time, it had a tendency to just quit; then a day or two later, it'd start back again," Shane claimed.

Rhonda was skeptical. "Well, that's kind of weird," she said.

Phillips, who had known Shane for some time, was aware of Shane's ongoing drug problems, and could see the young man was wrestling with guilt and confusion about the murders.

"Shane, I'm gonna be blunt, okay? That's the only way I know to be. I'm gonna ask you straight up. Did you have anything to do with this—in any way, shape, form or fashion—I'm talking about anything?"

The room was silent for a moment; then Shane answered, "Yes. I knew about it."

"You knew it was gonna happen, right?" asked Phillips.

"I didn't know, I thought that he was just running his mouth," Shane said miserably. "I didn't know that he was actually gonna go through with it."

"Shane, you didn't kill them, did you? You weren't there. Were you in Alabama the day they were killed?"

"No, sir, I was in Georgia that day."

Rhonda asked Shane if he knew that the murders were going to happen that day.

"No, ma'am, I didn't, I didn't know. I thought it just went as far as him asking me and then it got dropped."

Phillips then zeroed in on another area of interest.

"After your dad called that morning, on July seventh, he called another person that day, or that morning," Phillips told Shane. "I'm not going to say who it was, we've talked to them. That particular gentleman called you, or tried to call you, all day that day and he never got hold of you. He called the desk; he called your room; he called just about everywhere he could call. He was trying to help your dad find you. If you'd have been there, and I'm not saying you weren't there, but if you had been, some of those people would probably have known you were there, wouldn't they? At the motel?"

"Yeah," said Shane.

"And they would have probably got you to the phone. You see what I'm saying. . . ."

"Yeah, well, I was at—"

"You see the problem that I'm having and Rhonda's having with that day," Phillips said. "This person tried to call you all day long and nobody knew where you were at that day."

"W-well, I was right there," Shane stammered, "if I wasn't next to the phone, I was out at the pool. I didn't stay at the pool but about an hour before I came back in."

"This person told me he called you probably fifteen times that day, or called your room and called the motel 'cause he was trying to help your dad find you," Phillips told him.

"Well, I never did know, the only calls to come in were from Jill and James Bethune. James called late that afternoon and told me that . . . ah . . . the police were looking for me and that's when we contacted you-all."

"So, you didn't talk to Randy, or any of your family, on July seventh, other than your dad?"

"I didn't even talk to my daddy. Jill talked to him and she relayed the message."

"All right," Phillips said, "then when did you hear about the murders?"

Shane claimed that he'd learned about the murders that afternoon, Friday, or the next day.

"It was Sunday," Jill reminded him, and he quickly agreed with her.

Rhonda found it suspicious that someone had called Shane on Friday and told him the police were looking for him. She asked what the man had said.

"He just said that . . . ah . . . I needed to get in touch with somebody 'cause I—I was being looked for, for questioning. I didn't know about what then."

"He didn't tell you about the murders?" asked Phillips.

"No," Shane claimed.

Jill was clearly surprised by this news. "Found out Friday," she said. "Why didn't you tell me?"

"I did," Shane protested.

Jill turned to the investigators. "We didn't know about the murders till Sunday," she told them.

Shane went on to claim that he thought the reason that the police were looking for him might have been for something he'd been involved in previously, having to do with drugs or being in jail. He couldn't remember who had told him about the murders, or when.

"I don't remember," he said. "I think it was my dad. I know somebody called and told us."

Jill's mother had called on Sunday while Jill had been at a friend's house in Atlanta, and Shane said she had called her there and told her.

"And your parents, your family, didn't call you and tell you what had happened?" Rhonda asked Shane.

"Not that I know of. Not that I can remember. I don't believe they did."

"Well, did you call them then, after you heard it?"

Shane said he had called home to find out what had happened, and talked to his father, who told him that

Law enforcement from several communities in rural Alabama rushed to this quiet road following a July 7, 1995, emergency call. *(Author photo)*

Family members found the bodies of Carolyn Headrick and her mother, Dora Ann Dalton, in their home. *(Photo courtesy of the DeKalb County Sheriff's Department)*

Carolyn Dalton Headrick was shot, stabbed with a large knife, and impaled with a long Indian spear. *(Photo courtesy of Olan Mills Studios)*

Dora Ann Dalton was shot and stabbed with an Indian spear as she sat at her kitchen table. *(Photo courtesy of Olan Mills Studios)*

Jars of freshly canned sauerkraut sat on the kitchen counter and green beans were steaming on the stove when the victims' bodies were discovered. *(Photo courtesy of the DeKalb County Sheriff's Department)*

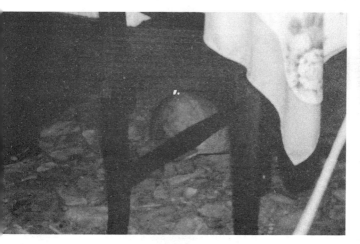

Half of a watermelon, which Dora Ann Dalton planned to eat for lunch, lay on the kitchen floor beside her body. *(Photo courtesy of the DeKalb County Sheriff's Department)*

The two Indian spears, handcrafted by Randy Headrick, which impaled the bodies of Carolyn and Dora Ann. *(Photo courtesy of the DeKalb County Sheriff's Department)*

There was no sign of forced entry at any of the doors of the house. *(Photo courtesy of the DeKalb County Sheriff's Department)*

This arrowhead display was part of Randy Headrick's collection of Indian artifacts.
(Photo courtesy of the DeKalb County Sheriff's Department)

Autopsy results determined that the victims were stabbed with the knife and spears after they had died from gunshot wounds.
(Photo courtesy of the DeKalb County Sheriff's Department)

Randy Headrick had an airtight alibi for his whereabouts at the time of the murders. *(Photo courtesy of the DeKalb County Sheriff's Department)*

Headrick's Ford F-150 pickup truck. *(Photo courtesy of the DeKalb County Sheriff's Department)*

Randy Headrick, moments after he was told of the murders. *(Photo courtesy of Stephen V. Smith)*

Sheriff Cecil Reed told the press Headrick had an iron-clad alibi, but he still considered him the prime suspect. *(Photo courtesy of the DeKalb County Sheriff's Department)*

Lead Investigator Rhonda Jackson documented and supervised every detail of the Headrick case for five years. *(Author photo)*

Investigator Mike James conducted countless interviews in search of leads in the case. *(Photo courtesy of the DeKalb County Sheriff's Department)*

Investigator Jimmy Phillips had many useful connections that eventually helped break Headrick's alibi. *(Author photo)*

Investigator Clay Simpson interviewed dozens of Headrick's friends, relatives, and co-workers. *(Author photo)*

Headrick set up a tent beside the Dalton house to store items given to him by his friend, Red Crow. *(Photo courtesy of the DeKalb County Sheriff's Department)*

A bookshelf holds Carolyn Headrick's romance novels and her husband's thrillers, horror stories and murder mysteries. *(Photo courtesy of the DeKalb County Sheriff's Department)*

The Ider Church of God, where Carolyn and Dora Ann were beloved members of the congregation. *(Author photo)*

Family members rushed to the nearby Cabbage Bowl Family Restaurant to get help when the bodies were discovered. *(Author photo)*

Sheriff Reed talks to reporters from a Chattanooga, Tennessee, television station. *(Photo courtesy of LaRue Hardinger)*

An aerial view of Shady Lane, with the Dalton house at the right and the bridge over the creek at the lower left. *(Photo courtesy of the DeKalb County Sheriff's Department)*

Headrick's coworkers confirmed he was at work at Builders Supply in Fort Payne, Alabama, on the day of the murders. *(Author photo)*

Phone records were subpoenaed for the Fyffe **Antique** Mall, owned and operated by Headrick's family. *(Author photo)*

William Randall Headrick pled guilty after being indicted by a grand jury for the murders of his wife and mother-in-law. *(Photo courtesy of the DeKalb County Sheriff's Department)*

Waylon Shane Headrick was also indicted, but the case against him was dropped. *(Photo courtesy of the DeKalb County Sheriff's Department)*

Dora Ann Dalton rests in a rural Jackson County, Alabama, cemetery beside her husband, D.L. Dalton. *(Author photo)*

Carolyn Dalton is buried beside her parents. The family chose not to use the Headrick name on her gravestone. *(Author photo)*

Ten years after the murders, the house on Shady Lane sits empty and forlorn. *(Author photo)*

BLESSED ARE THE PURE IN HEART,
FOR THEY SHALL SEE GOD.

These words on the back of Carolyn Dalton's gravestone continue to bring a measure of comfort to her family. *(Author photo)*

Dora Ann and Carolyn had been murdered, but didn't give him any details.

Jill disagreed with this, and the couple began to argue.

"Shane, you had to have been told by somebody because you called me at my friend's house and told me on the phone. . . ."

"No, I didn't. Your mother called you."

"No, she didn't. You called me and then I called Mother at home and Mother told me; you told me on the phone."

Shane seemed to grow even more confused.

"Well, I didn't know about it, I just called you and told you your mother had called."

"You told me about the murders. I said, 'What's wrong?'"

"Well, somebody called," Shane said resignedly. "I don't know who it was."

Jimmy Phillips decided it was time to break in and calm things down.

"Okay, all right, just think about that, maybe you'll remember," he told them. "I mean, I know it's hard to remember a year ago but, you know, if it hadn't of been for these murders, I wouldn't have known what I was doing on July 7, 1995, but I know where I was at that day because of this. But just, just relax and think about it for a minute because, you know, it's important. It may not look like it's important, but it's important that we know who contacted you about it."

In spite of Phillips's efforts, the disagreement was still on.

"Jill's mother had called looking for her," Shane said, "and Jill called and said she was going to be just a little bit late getting in, so I told her that her mother was looking for her. That's when I found out, when Jill got home."

"But none of that is right," Jill stated flatly.

Shane glared at her. "I believe it is."

"No, it's not," Jill said.

"'Cause you called your mother and she told you and you was all tore up, you could barely drive—"

"But I called you," Jill claimed. "I called you to tell you

I was gonna be later and I kept saying, 'What's wrong, Shane?' And you said, 'Something real bad's happened, Jill,' and I said, 'Well, tell me,' and you said, 'No, I'll wait till you get here.' And I said, 'No, I got to know now, I ain't driving on—'"

Shane broke in. "Well, can you remember who told me?"

"Mother, so you said," Jill told him.

"Well, Mother, your mother, told me then. Some-fucking-body told me."

Shane was upset and aggravated by his apparent inability to remember how he had learned of the murders, and by his argument with Jill.

"You said my mother told you," Jill continued, "and when I hung up talking to you, I called my mother. I was tore all to pieces and Mother started telling me how they was killed. You just told me they was killed; Mother told me how they was killed."

"I didn't think I told you they was killed, because it would tear you up," Shane claimed.

"Well, you did, 'cause you kept saying, 'I'll wait till you get here.'"

Phillips interrupted the argument again. "So, Jill's mother told you about them being killed, you think?" he asked Shane.

"I think," Shane answered hesitantly.

Phillips was doing his best to try to help Shane remember, but it seemed to be a losing battle.

"James Bethune didn't call on Friday; he called on Sunday," Shane offered.

"Well, I'm gonna beg to differ with you there," Phillips said, "because I talked to James."

"He called on Friday?" Shane asked.

Phillips assured Shane that Bethune had indeed called on Friday.

"Okay, well, I know there was just phone calls coming in and all," Shane mumbled.

Rhonda Jackson asked him, "Were you messed up on drugs or anything else?"

When Shane claimed that he wasn't high at the time, Rhonda asked him if he knew that for sure. He replied that he was sure; he was too broke to afford drugs.

"Were you working?" Rhonda asked him.

"Not then," he answered. "I was looking for work. I found work about two weeks later."

Phillips steered the conversation back to how and when Shane learned of the murders of Carolyn and Dora Ann.

"Okay, all right; needless to say you found out somehow or other that they were dead," Phillips stated.

"Yeah," Shane said, "I can't remember right now how, who called."

"Okay, you found out they were dead. What did you do then? You called your parents, right?"

"I'm not for sure," Shane said. "I think I may have waited till Jill got in."

"And then you called who?" Phillips continued, patiently picking information from Shane, bit by bit.

"I would have called my daddy," Shane told him.

"All right. Do you remember what your daddy told you?"

"He was tore up and said they was killed. He didn't give any detail how they were killed and we didn't find any details out till we got back here and found a newspaper."

Now we're getting somewhere, Phillips thought.

"And you, when your daddy told you they were killed, what did you think, Shane?"

Without hesitating, Shane replied, "Randy."

"Right off the bat, you thought Randy did it, right? And why didn't you tell anybody then?"

"I was scared because of what I know," Shane said. "Whenever I got back here to Henagar, I had a feeling like he was watching me, Randy was watching me, waiting for me to say something."

Phillips just wasn't buying Shane's excuse for not telling of his suspicions that Randy had committed a double homicide.

"Well, let me say something right here, Shane. You're

bigger than Randy, and you grabbed him by that shirt and you threatened him that one time, right? So you wasn't really scared of him that day, were you? I mean, I know you and you know me, but you weren't scared of him that day."

Shane was quick to answer. "At that point, he hadn't of murdered two women then," he said.

"But you knew he did it then, right off the bat, you knew he did it," Phillips said. "Didn't know how, but you knew it because he'd asked you to do it."

Shane agreed.

"But he's never told you that he did it?" Rhonda asked.

Shane said Randy had never said he did the murders, or had them done.

"I've asked him one time, and I got the response of no," Shane said.

Phillips asked Shane if he knew how the victims were killed, and how he found out.

"From people talking, family members, the newspapers," Shane said. "But Randy will not talk about it; he wouldn't talk about it at that time."

Jimmy Phillips was, by nature, a very patient man, but his patience with Shane's inability to remember several important details was beginning to wear thin.

"I know it's a year ago, and I'm trying to clear you here," he told Shane. "I know it sounds like I'm not believing what you're telling me, but I have trouble with that day because of the fact everybody tried to get ahold of you that day and nobody got ahold of you. If you were there at that motel, looks like somebody would have said, 'He's here, he's out by the pool; we'll go get him,' and you would have talked to somebody."

"Well, they didn't," Shane said. "The people in the office didn't know I was at the pool, they figured I was just at the room. The office was hidden from the pool."

Jill spoke up, telling Phillips the motel went through an automatic operator when no one was at the desk.

"If they weren't there, it would pick up and say this is such and such Buford Lodge, and you dial the room you want."

"It's in the computer," Shane said. "They got a readout of all the calls that come in."

Phillips decided to pursue another route of questioning.

"All right," he said, "you talked to your mother. You told her everything you've told us, and your mother's response was—"

"Just don't say anything, he'll get caught, let somebody else do it," Shane said.

"And she told you to get rid of the tape from the psychic also?" Rhonda asked.

Shane told the investigators his mother had told him to tell Jill to just destroy the tape, without saying why; then she ended the conversation abruptly.

"Do you think your mother knows about it?" Phillips asked.

"I believe she knows that Randy did it," Shane said, "but that's her boy and she's not gonna believe it until somebody proves it to her."

Shane went on to answer questions about a relative who lived out of state, describing a blue truck the man owned; then he was asked what he knew about another Headrick relative.

"I know he's a violent drunk, and greedy," he said. "He's come over there and I heard Carol and Ann talking about him getting drunk and being mean to his wife. And whenever this come up about property being divided, it wasn't none of his business, but he was wanting to have both feet in there showing them what he wanted out of it."

Shane said the man and Randy had started hanging around together, and then the man stole some tools from Randy and that ended it.

"Now they were having something to do with each other before the murders," Jill spoke up, "because Randy and Carol went up there and spent the night with him and they went camping or something."

The investigators told Shane and Jill that they had learned the relative had taken Randy and Carol to Indian powwows, and that he was the person who first introduced Randy to Red Crow.

"Do you know that Randy sold [the man] a gun?" Rhonda asked.

"What kind of gun? I didn't know about a gun," Shane said.

When he was told it was a 9mm pistol, Shane remembered that it was a gun Carolyn had bought for her husband, about a year before the murders.

Jimmy Phillips had known Shane Headrick for quite some time—knew of his long-term drug problems and knew quite a bit about his background. He decided to shoot straight with the troubled young man.

"Well, I'm gonna be honest with you, Shane, I thought you did it."

"So did everybody else," Shane replied.

"I'm telling you straight up, I thought you did it or you knew who did it, and you wouldn't tell us."

"And I'm sorry for that," Shane told him.

"But I still got a little bit of a problem because I know you, number one, and I don't think you're capable of killing anybody; I hope you're not."

"If I did," Shane said, "I couldn't handle it—"

"I know that you've got a temper," Phillips told him, "and I know you can't control that temper. And I know probably that you are not afraid of Randy. I believe you could whip Randy all over the place."

"Randy by hisself, that's one thing," Shane said, "but when there's somebody might be coming at your back too, that's another thing."

"I'm trying to ease my mind just a bit," Phillips said, "because I think basically if he asked you to do it and then after it was done you only asked him one time about this, just knowing you the way I do, that just don't sound right to me."

"Well," Shane answered, "he's on prescription medication, he's on Xanax, and for the time he was on them, there wasn't no need of trying to get anything from him."

"Let me ask you something," Rhonda said. "Did he ever tell you not to tell anybody what he asked you to do?"

"He told me the night, those two nights he asked me, he said, 'Well, let's just keep this between us then.'"

"You see what our problem is, Shane," Phillips told him. "Whoever did it, [Randy] had to know them, he had to know that they wouldn't tell. He had to be a hundred percent sure they wouldn't tell, and those women had to know them. And they knew you, right? And I don't know if they knew Red Crow or not, they probably did, and they knew [the relatives we talked about]. And you've never talked to Randy by phone or anything about [the murders]? Randy has never contacted you about this anytime?"

"No," Shane said, "but I contacted him. We was in Brunswick and it was eating me up and Jill was on me, and I called him on the phone. I started getting onto him, 'cause I knew he had something to do with it."

"What did you tell him?" asked Phillips.

"I told him he was a sorry motherfucker," Shane said. "He said, 'For what?' I said, 'For that deal across the street,' and that's when he said, 'Momma, he's crazy.'"

Randy was living at his mother's house at that time, and he refused to talk to Shane anymore after that, Shane said, and Randy got off the phone.

"After you called him a sorry motherfucker, is that all you said to him?" Phillips asked. "I mean, did you-all talk any before that?"

"There wasn't time," Shane said. "He picked up the phone and I started in soon as he picked up the phone."

Shane went on to talk about his feelings of guilt for not coming forward sooner with his suspicions about the murders. Rhonda asked him why he had decided to come in and talk to them that day.

"'Cause it's eating me up inside, just me knowing it, and I don't want nothing to happen to Jill for what I know," he said. Shane added that he didn't have anything to do with the murders: "Except for the fact that I knew he was planning something, but I didn't think he was gonna go through with it."

Shane told the investigators that Randy had mentioned

to him several times that he was good at killing, and said it was training that he had gotten in the army. Randy bragged that he could kill someone and no one would be able to trace it back to him.

"In other words, he's probably telling you that he knew how to do the perfect murder and nobody would know about it? Did he use those words?"

"Yes," Shane said.

The long interview with the troubled young man and his common-law wife ended, leaving a tangled knot of questions and answers that would not be sorted out any time soon. But in the meantime, Shane Headrick had agreed to take a voluntary polygraph examination. It was arranged for the test to be administered on May 17 by an agent of the Tennessee Bureau of Investigation (TBI) at their office in Chattanooga. Hopefully, the polygraph would provide some answers that were more definitive and clear-cut than the ones Shane had been able to give during his interview.

CHAPTER 24

On May 16, Shane Headrick and Jill Shrader returned to the sheriff's department to meet Rhonda Jackson and Jimmy Phillips, who accompanied Shane and Jill to the office of then-Assistant District Attorney (ADA) Mike O'Dell. O'Dell spoke with the couple about their cooperation in the case, and Jackson told him that Shane was willing to take a voluntary polygraph test the following day at the Tennessee Bureau of Investigation's Chattanooga office.

At 10:15 A.M. on May 17, Shane arrived at the TBI office to begin his testing. The examiner had been briefed thoroughly on the case and on the statements Shane had given in his previous interviews, including the fact that, so far, Shane had not been able to provide an alibi for the time frame of the murder. Once again, Shane waived his right to legal counsel and signed a statement that he was undergoing the polygraph voluntarily.

Unfortunately, the polygraph results turned out not to be what Shane had obviously hoped for. The examiner concluded that Shane's answers indicated that he was practicing deception when answering the relevant questions he was asked during the test:

Did you help anyone kill those women?
Did you shoot either of those women?

*Were you present when either of those women were killed?
Has anyone told you they killed those women?*

To all the above questions, Shane answered no, but his polygraph readings indicated that he wasn't being truthful. After the testing equipment was removed, Shane continued to deny he had any involvement or knowledge of the murders, and finally asked to conclude the interview. The test results, as he would later learn, left him in an even worse position than before.

Shane and Jill were still staying at the Fort Payne Best Western, with Sheriff Cecil Reed picking up the tab, when Rhonda Jackson called Jill and asked her and Shane to come in to her office on May 19. Jill agreed to an appointment at 2:00 P.M., and she and Shane showed up around forty-five minutes late.

Jill said she wanted to talk to Rhonda about something Shane had told her the night before at the motel, when she asked him if he could remember anyone else being at the motel pool on the day of the murders, other than the Mexicans he had previously mentioned.

"Was there anyone else that could prove you were there?" she asked him.

He then told her that there had been a white girl with a black baby at the pool, and he didn't tell Jill about it before because she was jealous.

"I knew the girl," Jill told him, "she was there at the pool on Saturday, the day after the murders, and I talked to her."

The girl had told Jill her name and said that she was moving.

"She told me where she was moving to, but I can't remember now," Jill said.

Jill told Rhonda that she had told Shane she would get hypnotized to be able to bring out the girl's name and where she was moving to, and also to remember whether or not Shane's bathing suit was wet when she got home from work, so that would prove his alibi.

When she brought this up, Jill said, Shane had become very enraged, and she became very scared of him.

"Why did you react that way?" Rhonda asked him.

"I offered to be hypnotized myself," he said, "and y'all hadn't wanted me to, so I couldn't understand why Jill was so special to try and get one done."

The investigators then separated the couple, with Shane remaining in Rhonda's office and Jill going with Mike James to his office. Once she was away from Shane, Jill quickly seized the opportunity to tell James that she was afraid for her life and wanted to go to a women's shelter. James took her to the Etowah County Sheriff's Department, and it was arranged for her to go to a well-established domestic violence shelter in the Gadsden area, where she would be protected in a secure location.

While Jill was being removed to a safe place in the adjoining county, Shane remained in Rhonda Jackson's office for another two hours for a lengthy interview. They discussed several incidents from his childhood and his early relationship with Randy. His home life was pretty good when he was growing up, he said, and he got most of what he wanted. But he said that when he was ten years old, he had killed a little boy accidentally.

"He had got my mama's gun and was playing with it," Shane said. "I knew it was loaded, but he didn't, so I tried to take it away from him. The gun went off, and it killed him."

Shane said he'd had problems dealing with the accident all his life.

Randy apparently had spent much time bullying Shane when they were children. Shane told Rhonda that Randy had hit him in the face with his fist when Shane was six years old, resulting in a broken nose for the younger boy. Randy also used to tie him up in the hammock, he said, and then abandon him, leaving him hanging there for hours.

During the interview, Shane admitted that he'd had an AMT .22 Magnum semiautomatic pistol, with a damaged firing pin, which had been stolen from his trailer in March

1995. He didn't, however, report the theft. He also said he just couldn't explain why he'd failed the polygraph.

"If I did it," he said, "I can't remember it. I don't think I have it inside me to kill two innocent women. If I could think of some way to bring it out, if it's inside of me and is blocked out, I would, but I can't see myself killing those women."

During the interview following his polygraph, the examiner had told Shane to close his eyes and see if he could visualize the crime scene, and how the victims were positioned. Rhonda later showed him some of the pictures from the scene, and he showed no emotion or reaction to the graphic photographs. He did say that was not the way he had imagined them.

Until his own interview was finished, Shane had no idea that Jill had left the sheriff's department and already had been taken out of the county to a women's shelter. He was saddened, but not surprised. There had been a great deal of friction between the couple for some time, and since the murders, their disagreements had increased dramatically. Shane told the investigators that since Jill was gone, he would stay on in DeKalb County, either with his parents or with other relatives. He told the officers that he still wanted to help them in any way he could. Although the young man seemed sincere, some of his behavior and his failure of the polygraph test still cast a heavy shadow of doubt on his innocence. He remained a key person of interest in the murders of Carolyn and Dora Ann.

CHAPTER 25

Over the course of the next several days, Rhonda Jackson and Mike James remained busy with the details of the ongoing Headrick investigation. They paid the bill for Shane and Jill at Best Western, a total of $303.96 for six nights, and traveled to Chattanooga to get some additional information on the people that Randy Headrick and his new wife were currently staying with.

Special Agent (SA) Bill Fleming, from the Birmingham, Alabama, FBI field office, came up to the sheriff's department and met with investigators Jackson, Simpson and Phillips, who took him to the Ider/Henagar area to visit the crime scene on Shady Lane. Fleming photographed the outside of the house, and enlisted an FBI pilot to fly over the property and take several aerial photos of the neighborhood. The photos showed Highway 75, with Shady Lane turning off to the east side of the highway, and the Dalton and Headrick homes situated on either side of the dirt road. They were the first two houses on the road, and a small wooden bridge spanned the little creek that ran across the road a short distance past the houses. In the aerial photos, it was plain to see that there were at least two possible routes the killer or killers could have taken when first leaving the scene of the crime: either back out onto Highway 75, or traveling in the opposite direction on Shady Lane. Since witnesses had spotted a red pickup "fishtailing" from the direction of the Dalton driveway and then crossing over the bridge, it was likely that the driver of the red pickup had sped down the short length of Shady Lane and turned onto the paved road where Shady Lane ended. From that location, there were several different routes that could have been taken back to Builders Supply in Fort Payne, if a person coincidentally happened to be headed in that direction.

A few days later, Rhonda Jackson traveled with Phillips and ADA O'Dell to the Department of Forensic Sciences in Huntsville to look at the crime scene photos that were taken by their personnel on the evening of the murder. The investigators requested and were given copies of most of the slides to add to their file.

A few days later, a young man was interviewed who told the officers that he had been friends with Shane Headrick since high school and had worked with him in a Henagar supermarket for around two years.

"I started running with Shane in 1995 when he was living on Highway seventy-five at Ider," the man said. "When I was hanging out there, it was more or less a drug hangout. Before then, I worked with Randy at Kmart in Fort Payne for about three weeks. During this time, Randy told me that he had smuggled guns and that is why he spent time in prison. He also told me how to make a bomb out of pizza pans, gunpowder and BBs. He also told me that he knew some drug dealers, that he was going to break in and kill them and take their money, and no one would care. He said he could kill people with certain kinds of holds and hitting them in certain places.

"When I worked with Randy, he was single, as far as I know. He also told me that he was in the service, but not what branch of the service he was in. I didn't know anybody that Randy ran around with; I didn't know him that well.

"When I heard about the murders, I was in a halfway house. My mother told me that Randy was married to one of the ladies that had been killed. She told me that the law thought that Randy had killed them."

On June 12, Phillips asked the TBI to request an interview with Roy Stephens, the cousin with whom Randy Headrick and his new wife were staying. The man agreed, and the meeting was set up to take place on the following day in Chattanooga.

When Stephens arrived at 10:00 A.M. to give his statement, it was obvious that he sincerely believed Headrick had nothing to do with the murders of his wife and mother-in-law. He told the officers that he'd had no contact with Randy before the murders except maybe once, at a family reunion two years prior to the murders. Randy had started coming around approximately two weeks to a month after the murders, he said, staying over a night or two at a time. Then he started coming more frequently, and moved in with him in October 1995.

In February of the following year, Randy married Tonya Grim, a young woman he had met at Red Crow's shop in Chattanooga. Stephens said that Randy had counseled her on a drug problem she had, and his expert counseling apparently led to marriage, although the investigators had previously been told that Headrick was seeing someone, possibly Tonya, prior to the murders.

Both Headrick and Tonya continued to live with Stephens, who supported them both since neither worked. Stephens said they sometimes made Indian jewelry and sold it at flea markets.

According to Stephens, he and his father had been sowing grass at his residence on Signal Mountain, Tennessee, on the day of the murders. He was told that Headrick's wife and mother-in-law had been killed when his mother called him to let him know what had happened. She told him she had learned of the murders when she received a phone call from one of her relatives in the Henagar area.

Stephens admitted to having several guns at his residence: a .22 Ruger semiautomatic that belonged to his sister, a Browning 30.06 automatic, a Remington twelve gauge, a .45 auto army-issue, a .22 rifle and a .22 H&R semiautomatic that belonged to his wife's father. He told the investigators they could check the ballistics on those weapons, and said he would take a polygraph and give consent to search his residence.

Stephens remained firm in his belief that Headrick just couldn't have been responsible for the killings. He had been told by some of his other relatives, he said, that the murders were a mob hit to send a message to someone who owed $80,000 for drugs, and that several psychics had said that was the reason for the murders.

Stephens and his wife, Anita, had been living separately for around two-and-a-half years. In the afternoon, following their interview with Stephens, his wife came to the TBI office and gave her statement.

Anita Stephens told the officers she was concerned about her estranged husband because he was extremely gullible and believed everything that Headrick told him. She backed up Stephens's statement about the increase in the frequency of Headrick's visits following the murders, and said that Headrick's parents urged Stephens to help their son out by giving him a place to stay. Randy's parents allegedly feared for his safety if he remained in DeKalb County.

Following the interviews, Phillips and Jackson stopped by Red Crow's gallery and craft supply store, Native American Connection. Red Crow was there that day, and said that Headrick had been helping him out at the store up until around mid-May. Headrick also had put some of his craft work in the store to sell. However, he and one of the co-owners of the store didn't get along too well, Red Crow said, so Headrick had pulled his things out of the store and Red Crow hadn't seen or talked to him since then.

Ever the starry-eyed mystic, Red Crow made it a point to tell the investigators that he still firmly believed that Headrick had nothing to do with his wife's death. And as he had stated repeatedly, even if he did know anything about the murders, he wouldn't tell the authorities.

In late June, the investigators decided to try and trace some of Headrick's acquaintances from his prison years. Rhonda Jackson started by calling the Federal Bureau of Prisons in Atlanta, and obtaining a list of prisons Headrick had been in during his period of incarceration.

The list was relatively long for a period of less than four years; Headrick had been moved around quite a bit. He had started serving his time in 1987 in Latuna, Texas; then in 1988, he was transferred to Oakdale, Louisiana. In 1989, he was moved to Segoville, Texas, and in 1990, he served time in Fort Worth, Texas, followed by El Reno, Oklahoma, and Texarkana, Texas. Checking out his associates among his fellow prisoners in that many facilities would take time, but Jackson was determined to get it done. Several people had mentioned a man who came through the area before the murders, looking for Headrick and saying he was a friend from prison. It was a lead well worth pursuing.

While Jackson waited on Headrick's prison information, she received another tip and went to a residence in the Henagar area to speak to a woman there.

"I was visiting my in-laws one night when Shane Headrick came by," she said. "When the murders were brought up, Shane said he knew his brother done it because he had tried to cut his first wife's head off in Texas."

The woman said Shane claimed that Randy had tried to enlist him to decapitate his first wife.

"Shane said the reason Randy's mother-in-law and wife were killed was because his wife was closing in on him because he was having an affair. He said he knew that she would kick him out if she found out. Shane said several times that he knew Randy done it. He said Randy tried to pin it on him, and that was why he left town."

Shane's credibility was not exactly being reinforced by some of the information that was beginning to come to light. He was starting to look a lot more like a suspect than an informant, and the investigators kept a close eye on him and constantly tracked his whereabouts while they sought more information on his activities around the time of the murders.

CHAPTER 26

As the one-year anniversary of the murders drew near, a television station, Channel 3 from Chattanooga, and the DeKalb County Sheriff's Department made plans to collaborate on a reenactment of the Headrick/Dalton murders for the station's Channel 3-TV *Crimestoppers* program. On July 8, cameraman Kim Norwitz filmed a reenactment of the murders re-created in careful detail. The reenactment aired on July 10, 1996, on the station's 6:00 and 11:00 P.M. news broadcasts. Rhonda Jackson had hopes that this renewed media attention might flush out additional tips, but nothing of importance surfaced—only more obvious falsehoods, finger-pointing and unsubstantiated rumors.

For the next few months, most of the work on the Headrick/Dalton murder case slowed dramatically due to a series of legal proceedings brought about in connection with the Woodmen of the World and State Farm life insurance policies that Randy Headrick had purchased on Carolyn. Headrick was demanding that the policies be paid to him, and Carolyn's family was contesting his demand on the grounds that even though no arrest had been made, he was the prime suspect in her murder. As a result, he should not receive the money. The Daltons understandably found it intolerable that the man who they

were convinced had slaughtered their mother and sister
was now actually attempting to get paid for doing so.
Countless hours were spent taking depositions and
making affidavits for the court case, and mountains of paperwork were generated by the attorneys for all of the parties in the proceedings. Feelings ran high, feuding
between the families increased, and even some of the
members of the supposedly close-knit Headrick clan
began readily to turn on one another, shifting blame
for the murders from Shane to Randy, and back again.

One of the members of the Dalton family gave the following statement about their knowledge of the Headricks'
relationship:

"I was very close to Carolyn, and talked with or saw her
daily. The first year of her marriage to Headrick, they were
happy and he was good to Carolyn and her mother. After
the first year, things steadily changed. He refused to help
around the house, refused to take Carolyn anywhere
and saw another woman. He even had a child with this
other woman.

"At the time of Carolyn's death, Headrick showed no
remorse or emotion. He even refused to help the family
pay for the funeral flowers and the tombstone. He only
asked for Carolyn's checkbook and two silver ingots he
gave her. He never asked for any other personal items, not
even her wedding band. Neither he nor any of his family
made any contribution toward the reward money for information about her death."

Another Dalton family member had this to say:

"Carolyn and Headrick had been married about four
years, and he and I did not get along. Approximately three
weeks before the murders, Headrick asked me to come
over to their home. When I arrived, he showed me a collection of spears, swords and axes. Several of these items
were razor sharp. He started acquiring these weapons
about six months before the murders. At the time I saw
these items, I began to fear that Dora Ann and Carolyn

were in danger. I even told some friends that I was afraid Headrick would kill them.

"Headrick has made threats toward me, and I now fear for the safety of myself, my children and my entire family.

"During the marriage, Headrick took out three life insurance policies on Carolyn. She never worked and rarely even left the house more than once or twice a month."

Jill Shrader's affidavit stated that she and Shane had once again resumed living together after her flight to the safety of the women's shelter, and they had stayed together until August 4, 1996. On that date, she said, Shane disappeared from their home and she had not seen or heard from him since.

Jill repeated the allegations that she had made during her interviews with the investigators, and added that when he left on August 4, Shane had threatened to harm her father. Other Headrick family members told her, she said, that they knew that she and Shane had been lying and that they would no longer help Shane or have anything to do with either Shane or Jill.

"They told me we were both going to get it over this," Jill said. "I now fear for the safety of myself, my child and my entire family."

Then came a Headrick family member, a person who supposedly had always loved and cared for both Shane and Randy, but now seemed ready and eager to throw Shane to the wolves.

"For the past four years, Shane, who is twenty-three years old, has been living with a forty-five-year-old woman, Jill Shrader. Unfortunately, he is hopelessly addicted to drugs. He has a very difficult time holding a steady job. At the present time, I do not have any idea where he is living, nor what he is doing. I do know that Shane is hiding from Jill Shrader, who has children older than him.

"After the murders, Jill and Shane came up with the idea that they could solve the murders and get the reward money. These addicts believed that Randy Headrick hired the murders to be done. They approached many people in the family and neighborhood in an effort to obtain help in proving that Randy was guilty of the murders.

"There was never a more devoted couple than Randy and Carol. If you saw one, you usually saw the other, if Randy was not at work. They worked around the house together; they traveled together and generally appeared to be a very devoted married couple. The fact that Randy allowed his mother-in-law to live in the house with them showed how close-knit the family was."

That Randy had moved into his mother-in-law's house when he married Carolyn, and the fact that the house was Dora Ann Dalton's and not his, seemed somehow to have escaped the attention of this close relative, who was extolling Randy's virtues.

"The statements Shane and Jill gave are totally unreliable. First, they were doped up most of the time and rarely knew what was going on around them. Second, they wanted to get the reward money and move to Australia and homestead some land. Third, knowing Shane, not one member of the family would trust him with any valuable information. Shane is very slow. Everyone who knows him knows that he does not have the ability to keep a secret. Shane would tell a secret almost by the time he heard it. If he were a normal person, Jill Shrader would not have the hold on him that she has had for the past several years. Once, Shane told me that Jill turned him on to dope and sex, and he liked them both."

Another close relative of both Randy and Shane Headrick's was completely prepared to betray Shane in order to make things look better for Randy, and some shocking allegations were made in that relative's affidavit regarding the statements that Shane and Jill had given to the investigators.

"Jill and Shane came to me and asked me to go with them to Rhonda Jackson and confirm the stories they were going to tell. They had decided to tell her that Randy had asked Shane to kill his wife and mother-in-law, and both of them, Shane and Jill, admitted to me that this was a lie. This is why they needed me to lie to confirm what they were going to tell. They said they would split the money with me and I would be able to get on my feet. I refused and told them that they should not do it, but they did it anyway.

"Jill told me that she was going to see to it that Randy did not get any insurance money, and she was going to see to it that he was fried. She has gone to great lengths to convince me that what she and Shane told was the truth. She constantly tells me that I know it is the truth, when I know that it was all a lie from its inception when she concocted the lie that was told to investigators. I was there when she and Shane made up the entire story."

It appeared that many more accusations and allegations were continuing to surface in the fight for the insurance money than had previously come to light in the investigation of the murder of two innocent women. Greed, jealousy and family infighting had left the Headrick relatives betraying their own blood kin at every opportunity.

CHAPTER 27

On February 5, 1996, a complaint and interpleader action was filed with the Circuit Court of DeKalb County on the behalf of State Farm Life Insurance by Jack Livingston of the firm, of Livingston, Porter and Paulk, P.C., of Scottsboro, Alabama. At the same time, State Farm Life Insurance's assistant counsel David N. Koth submitted a check in full settlement of all claims under the policy on Carolyn Headrick. The check, payable in the amount of $201,762.31, was made payable to Jimmy Lindsey, clerk of the Circuit Court of DeKalb County, to be held until such time as the rightful recipient of the payment was determined in court.

State Farm Life Insurance Company submitted its complaint, beginning by identifying itself as doing business in DeKalb County, Alabama.

The defendant, William R. Headrick, they stated, was over the age of nineteen years and was a resident of DeKalb County.

The complaint then said that the Estate of Carolyn J. Headrick, deceased, was an interested party to the action, and to State Farm's knowledge, no person had qualified at that time as the personal representative of the estate. Carolyn, according to the complaint, was survived by no children but was survived by one brother and two sisters.

If none of them qualified as the personal representative of the estate, then the DeKalb County Sheriff, acting as the General Administrator for the County according to the provisions of the Code of Alabama, would be authorized to act as the personal representative of the estate until such time as a personal representative was appointed. And, the complaint said, to the knowledge of State Farm Life Insurance Company, Carolyn Headrick died without leaving a will.

The subject of the interpleaded action in the case was the proceeds of a life insurance policy on the life of Carolyn J. Headrick, which was issued on or about March 28, 1984. The policy, which insured her life for $200,000, named Randy Headrick the primary or first beneficiary, and Dora Ann Dalton was listed as the successor beneficiary.

A copy of the policy was attached to the complaint, and was made a part of the complaint by reference as Exhibit A.

On July 7, 1995, the complaint stated, both the insured, Carolyn J. Headrick, and the alternative beneficiary, Dora Ann Dalton, were killed by an unknown party and each met a violent death by shooting and stabbing. State Farm noted that the company had been informed that Randy Headrick, the primary beneficiary of the policy, was a prime suspect in the murders. No formal charges had been made at that time, the complaint said, and the authorities continued to pursue the investigation of Randy Headrick as a person who perpetrated the murders.

If Randy Headrick was found to have feloniously and intentionally killed the insured party, his wife, Carolyn, he would then forfeit his right to recover the proceeds from the policy. And if he was found guilty of the murders, forfeiting his right to the policy proceeds, and since Dora Ann, the successor beneficiary, had also been murdered, the proceeds of the policy would be payable to the estate of Carolyn J. Headrick.

The complaint then stated that it had tendered into the Court, at the time of filing the action, the sum of $201,762.31, in the form of a check made payable to the

Clerk of the Court. Kerby Funeral Home had been paid the sum of $4037.00, and a letter of explanation was attached to the check explaining the amount of interest calculation on the policy as of the day of filing. Copies of the check and letter were attached to the complaint as Exhibits B and C.

State Farm, which identified itself as merely a stakeholder, stated that it was paying the money to the Court as the proceeds of the policy, and requested that upon filing, the Court would enter whatever orders necessary to require the defendants to file claim for the proceeds via the Court. Then, State Farm requested, the company could be discharged by the Court from further responsibility in the case.

The complaint and interpleaded action concluded by formally requesting that the Court take jurisdiction of the matter and issue orders to be served on Randy Headrick, on one of Carolyn Headrick's siblings, and on the DeKalb County Sheriff as the General Administrator of the County on behalf of Carolyn's estate (with a personal representative to be named at a later date and substituted for the General Administrator). The order of the Court would direct each of those parties with interest in the proceeds of the insurance policy to file whatever claims they felt were appropriate on the money paid to the Court. Then, State Farm requested, the Court would discharge and relieve State Farm of all liability of all kinds on account of the issuance of the policy against the claims of all persons.

"State Farm prays for general relief," the complaint concluded.

On February 16, the Claim of William R. Headrick was filed with the circuit court, containing his claim of entitlement to the insurance proceeds. The claim was presented by his attorney, Bob French, who began the claim by offering Headrick's affidavit and verifying that his client had appeared before him and was sworn in prior to giving his statement.

Headrick identified himself and said he was thirty-eight years old and a resident of Henagar, Alabama. He said he was the widower of the late Carolyn J. Headrick and was the primary beneficiary of the State Farm life insurance policy.

Carolyn was murdered on July 7, 1995, Headrick said, in their home in Henagar, and her mother was murdered during the same incident. He claimed he had been initially informed that the murders occurred between 2:00 P.M. and 2:30 P.M., but said he had been informed and believed that the local authorities who were investigating the case had narrowed the actual time of the murders down to a 15-minute time frame.

At the time of the murders, Headrick stated, he was working at his regular job in Fort Payne, which he claimed was twenty-two miles from his home where the murders took place. He was working with witnesses, he claimed, and could not possibly have killed his wife and mother-in-law as the authorities seemed to suspect. One person working with him, he said, was a cousin of his wife and mother-in-law. In addition, Headrick said he had submitted to a polygraph examination by one of Alabama's foremost polygraphers. He had passed the test, he said, which constituted proof that he was not involved by any manner or means with the deaths of his wife and mother-in-law.

Headrick then identified himself as the primary or first beneficiary named in the insurance policy and, as such, he was entitled to the proceeds from the policy which had been paid into court. He did not feloniously and intentionally kill his wife, he said, nor anyone else. Therefore, he formally made claim to the funds paid into court by State Farm, and requested that the funds held by the court be paid directly to him with "all deliberate speed."

On February 27, Winfred B. "Rocky" Watson of the Fort Payne law firm Watson, Gillis and Carver, P.C., identified himself as attorney of record for Carolyn Headrick's brother and sisters. At the same time, Watson filed an answer to Headrick's complaint. It confirmed that on Feb-

ruary 20, Carolyn's sister, Kathy Porter, had applied to
qualify as personal representative of the estate. The
answer also claimed that the proceeds of the insurance
policy should be ordered to be paid to the estate, and that
Randy Headrick should be disqualified from taking any
of the proceeds.

On the following day, Bob French entered a motion to
invest the court-held insurance proceeds in an interest-
bearing account until the lawful beneficiary was decided.
French moved the court to require the clerk to invest the
funds being held in the case, in excess of $20,000, at in-
terest. He based his motion on the grounds that invest-
ment of the funds was in the best interests of all parties
involved.

Interest income during the pendency of the case, he
stated, would be substantial and would add to the funds
eventually awarded to the successful claimant. A large
loss would be suffered by his client, Randy Headrick, if he
should be awarded the funds because of the loss of interest on the money while the matter was tied up in litigation.

When this motion was received by Circuit Court Judge
David A. Rains, he was in favor of French's suggestion. He
called the motion "well taken," and on March 19, 1996,
ordered Circuit Clerk Jimmy Lindsey, at his discretion, to
invest the proceeds paid into court at the highest and
safest available rate of interest.

Since State Farm Life Insurance Company was the
plaintiff in the case, Judge Rains also issued a separate
order which stated that State Farm had interplead the
money in question and sought a determination as to the
correct party entitled to receive the funds, in addition to
discharging State Farm from any liability on account of
the issuance of the policy.

Rains ordered the court clerk to invest the money as
described, subject to withdrawal on thirty days notice. The
funds, he ordered, would not be disbursed by the clerk
until further orders of the court indicated who would be
the rightful claimant to receive the money.

Rains also ordered anyone claiming an interest in the funds to file their claims within thirty days from the date of his order. Unless an objection was received within those thirty days, Rains ordered, State Farm would be deemed a mere stakeholder, and having paid the policy proceeds into court with an explanation of the source and amount of the money, the company would then be discharged from all liability for any and all claims against the proceeds of Carolyn J. Headrick's life insurance policy.

Much to the company's relief, State Farm was officially relieved from further responsibility in the case unless Headrick or his wife's family objected.

CHAPTER 28

On April 22, Jack Livingston, of the Livingston, Porter and Paulk, P.C. law firm, representing State Farm, notified Judge Rains that no objection had been received from either party to the dismissal of State Farm as a party to the lawsuit. Judge Rains then issued the following order:

This is an interpleaded action commenced by State Farm Life Insurance Company. All parties are now represented by counsel. The policy proceeds have been paid into Court and are now in possession of the Clerk.

More than 30 days have transpired from the date of the previous order and no objections have been filed. Therefore it is ordered as follows:

1. State Farm Life Insurance Company has interplead the proceeds of the subject life insurance policy on Carolyn J. Headrick, deceased.

2. All parties in interest have appeared by counsel.

3. State Farm is no longer a necessary party in the case, as the issue for this court to decide is the proper party or parties to whom the insurance proceeds should be paid.

4. State Farm is hereby dismissed as a party to this action, and is relieved of all liability of all kinds on account of the issuance of policy number LF-1348-7958, dated March 28, 1994, insuring the life of Carolyn J. Headrick, now deceased.

5. There being no just reason for delay, this judgment is expressly made final pursuant to the provisions of Rule 54(b), Rules of Civil Procedure in Alabama.

Done and ordered this 15th day of May, 1996.

While the dispute over the State Farm policy was moving through the DeKalb County Circuit Court, a similar suit involving the Woodmen of the World Life Insurance Society's policy on Carolyn Headrick was being heard in the United States District Court for the Northern District of Alabama, Middle Division.

Headrick's attorney, Bob French, had filed a reply to his motion for summary judgment in the case of *Woodmen of the World* v. *William Randall Headrick and Carolyn Headrick's Family Members,* with Headrick claiming he was entitled to receive the money from the life insurance policy. Carolyn's other heirs, her two sisters and a brother, were the nonmovants in the case, and were represented by their attorneys in the Fort Payne law firm of Watson, Gillis and Carver. The case was heard in the United States District Court for the Northern District of Alabama, Middle Division, with the initial complaint filed on March 1, 1996, by Woodmen of the World Life Insurance Society. At that time, Woodmen of the World deposited $25,000 in proceeds from the life insurance policy with the Clerk of the United States District Court for the Northern District of Alabama, to be held by the Court, as with the State Farm proceeds, until the case could be resolved.

On March 13, 1996, Woodmen of the World deposited an additional amount of $968.15 in interest that the policy had accumulated since Carolyn Headrick's death on July 7, 1995, until the time of the complaint in interpleader, March 1, 1996.

Bob French, in preparing his client's reply brief, presented his usual brilliantly thought-out arguments for a judgment in favor of Headrick. He pointed out every possible detail in support of Headrick's alibi, his claim to have had a happy marriage, and his continued insistence that he did not kill his wife and mother-in-law. French stated that the investigation of the murders had been ongoing for over a year:

"Notwithstanding the lengthy and exhaustive investigation, there has been no indictment. Similarly, a sizable $21,000 cash reward has resulted in no indictment. Finally, Headrick has passed a polygraph examination concerning involvement in the homicides."

French stated, "The highly speculative and biased circumstantial evidence offered by the nonmovants does not present a preponderance of evidence that Headrick committed any crime. Indeed, a review of the nonmovants' evidence demonstrates that there exists no evidence that Headrick was involved in the homicide of the deceased."

French went on to review Jill Shrader's claims that Randy Headrick had asked her to hurt his former girlfriend and to find him a .22 pistol. He then stated the claims of the Headrick relatives who said that Shane Headrick had drug problems and that he and Jill had concocted their stories about Randy Headrick in order to obtain the reward money, offering to split the reward in exchange for verification of their stories.

As for the affidavits presented by the Dalton family, French claimed that Randy Headrick's interest in Indian artifacts did not present any evidence that he committed any crime, nor did his purchase of the insurance policies. French said the Daltons who had given affidavits for the case were entitled to a portion of the estate of Carolyn Headrick and would achieve financial gain if Carolyn Headrick's life insurance fell into the estate.

French tore into Investigator Rhonda Jackson's deposition with relish, calling it "double hearsay-ridden" and "narrowly focused." He summarized the brief, saying the nonmovants' accusations against his client relied heavily on the statements of Shane Headrick and Jill Shrader, whom he referred to as "the drug-addicted couple."

"Additionally, they have offered the deposition of a DeKalb County Investigator, which only points out the narrow focus of the fruitless investigation.

"The nonmovants have not offered substantial evidence in support of their position. The nonmovants have not presented a *preponderance of the evidence* that William Randall Headrick was involved in any crime. The facts are undisputed and movant William Randall Headrick is entitled to judgment as a matter of law."

CHAPTER 29

One of the attorneys for the Dalton family, Sheri W. Carver, was also a skilled defense attorney who went on to become a judge. At that time, Carver was a partner in the prestigious law firm of Watson, Gillis and Carver. She and her partner Winfred B. "Rocky" Watson did the majority of preparation of the case materials, and Sheri Carver was not in the least intimidated by the prospect of going head-to-head with Bob French. She was confident and well-prepared as she submitted the brief of her clients in opposition of a summary judgment in favor of Randy Headrick: "The only issue before the Court is whether or not there is a genuine issue of material fact as to whether or not William Randall Headrick feloniously and intentionally murdered Carolyn J. Headrick. In the present case, the evidence presented establishes that a genuine issue of material fact does exist."

Carver went on to point out that the beneficiary in a life insurance policy, who murders or feloniously causes the death of the insured, automatically forfeits all rights he or she may have in or under the policy.

"This rule is based on sound public policy and the principle that no one shall be allowed to benefit from his own wrong."

Carver summarized the details and history of the case,

noting that although no arrest had been made, the investigation was ongoing and Headrick had been and still remained the prime suspect. She stated that Headrick's regular job at Builders Supply was in the door department inside the main building, but on the day of the murders, he was working in the block yard in an isolated area, approximately one block away from the main building.

"It is inconsistent that someone who was planning a murder would volunteer to work at a time when he was normally scheduled to be on vacation and volunteer to work in an isolated area where his coming and going would likely go unnoticed."

Carver stated that the Headrick/Dalton residence was located seventeen miles from Builders Supply, and that investigators had timed the shortest route in normal traffic traveling at the speed limit and found that it took twenty-two minutes to drive from Builders Supply to the residence.

"Shortly before the murders took place, Headrick told an unidentified witness that he knew how to commit the perfect murder; that he would be at work, but he would do it himself. This statement, coupled with the change in his normal work routine, indicates that he possessed an intent to murder his wife."

The brief detailed how each of the victims had been killed, saying that they had appeared to be engaging in normal everyday activities at the time they were killed. There was no evidence that they had been startled or surprised by an unknown intruder, and no sign of any forced entry had been found at the crime scene. Since the victims, at the time they had been killed, had been in areas of the home where they would have been able to see an intruder, Carver's brief said that those facts, along with other evidence, established that the victims likely knew the intruder and were clearly not alarmed by that person's presence. They undoubtedly were accustomed to that individual entering the residence unannounced.

Also mentioned in the brief were the findings of an

investigation of Headrick's background, namely his conviction in the Federal Court of the State of Texas for unauthorized possession of a firearm. This referred to the well-documented incident when Headrick and a companion had been arrested for the possession of several pipe bombs, and the two men had earlier thrown a pipe bomb and blown up the end of the trailer where Headrick's ex-wife was living at that time.

Carver then restated Headrick's several alleged attempted solicitations of his brother, Shane, to murder Carolyn and Dora Ann, or to get someone to do it, and how he wanted the murders committed. Headrick's attempt to get Jill Shrader and her son to assault his former girlfriend was also described, with Shrader's claim that Headrick told her he wanted the woman tied up, her legs broken and her face cut and scarred for life. Shortly after that request was made and turned down by Jill and her son, the woman's home had been broken into and her wedding rings were stolen; following that, her house was burned. After the house burned, the ex-girlfriend's wedding rings had been returned to her anonymously in the mail.

The brief described Headrick's statement to Jill Shrader that he hated both Carolyn and Dora Ann and wanted their lying tongues cut out and something jabbed through their evil hearts, and when Shrader asked why he didn't just divorce his wife, he told her that he couldn't.

Carver stated that during the marriage, Headrick purchased three life insurance policies on Carolyn's life, one in the amount of $200,000. Shortly before the murders, Carolyn had told a family member that when the policy was due to be renewed in late July, she planned to cancel it due to the couple's financial difficulties. However, despite their money problems, at the time of the murders, Headrick was leasing a new full-size pickup and had recently bought a cellular phone.

"It is clear that at the time of the murders, Headrick was living well above his means. He clearly expected to collect the life insurance policy proceeds to finance his lifestyle. Had Carolyn Headrick lived three more weeks, there would have been no proceeds from the largest life insurance policy held in Carolyn's name.

"Based on the foregoing brief and supporting documents, it is clear that there exists a genuine issue of material facts indicating that Headrick feloniously and intentionally caused the death of his wife. Therefore, Headrick's motion for summary judgment should be denied and he should not be allowed to receive the proceeds from the life insurance policy insuring the life of Carolyn J. Headrick."

CHAPTER 30

On May 13, 1996, the United States District Court awarded the attorneys for Woodmen of the World Life Insurance Society a fee of $1,198.50 and a $148.28 reimbursement of court costs for a total of $1,346.78. The remainder of the funds deposited with the court remained in the court's possession awaiting a settlement.

The case in DeKalb County Circuit Court, still filed as *State Farm Life Insurance Company* v. *William R. Headrick*, despite State Farm's dismissal from the action, was set for pretrial on September 13, 1996, at 1:30 P.M., but was postponed until January 13, 1997. However, before time for that scheduled court appearance, attorneys for both parties involved in both cases notified Judge Propst and Judge Rains of developments that would put the need for further court appearances to an end.

Judge Robert B. Propst, senior judge of the United States District Court, received a letter on December 26, 1996, from Bob French advising him that the parties in the case had reached an agreement.

French informed Judge Propst that, along with a settlement agreement, he was enclosing two proposed orders in the case for the judge's choice. One was brief, he said, and the other was somewhat wordier. Since all issues in the case had been resolved, he said, the judge's attention to the matter would be appreciated. He closed his letter in typical Bob French style, wishing the judge, "Happy New Year!"

At first glance, the settlement agreement French forwarded to the judge appears to be in Randy Headrick's favor, but on closer inspection there were major concessions made on Headrick's part that awarded the Dalton family those things which meant the most to them.

The settlement agreement, including both the Woodmen of the World and the State Farm cases, was entered into on December 20, 1996, by Randy Headrick, Kathy Porter, Billy Jack Dalton and Diane Smith.

The funds had been interplead by Woodmen of the World Insurance Company and State Farm Life Insurance Company, and it was the position of Randy Headrick that he did not feloniously or otherwise take Carolyn Headrick's life. But it was the position of Carolyn's siblings that he did indeed intentionally kill her, the settlement said.

Since the siblings had no proof or evidence at that time to support a finding, based on a preponderance of the evidence, that Headrick had intentionally murdered his wife, the parties had negotiated a settlement of the distribution of the funds being held by the court, as well as certain other issues.

French's settlement agreement stated that all parties agreed to an order being entered in the case of Woodmen of the World Life Insurance Society against William R. Headrick and Carolyn's brother and sisters, ordering that the money currently held by the United States District Court for the Northern Alabama Middle Division be paid to French's client, William R. Headrick.

In the State Farm case, French requested that an order be entered specifying payment to Billy Jack Dalton, Kathy Porter and Diane Smith in the amount of $92,500.00. Randy Headrick would receive the balance of all funds held by the Circuit Court of DeKalb County.

At the execution of the agreement, French said, his

client would issue a quit claim deed to Carolyn Headrick's siblings the real estate owned by Carolyn at the time of her death. In return, her brother and sisters would release any and all right, title and interest in insurance proceeds or any other funds payable to Headrick by the Union Labor Life Insurance Company as a result of Carolyn's death. The siblings would also release and discharge any and all claims that they might have, existing "from the beginning of time until the present date," against Headrick, whether or not the claims were currently known or unknown. Headrick also agreed to release accordingly any and all claims against them.

The settlement agreement also specified that Kathy Porter would immediately submit her resignation as administrator of the estate of her sister Carolyn, and it was agreed that she would be released from those duties without accounting, appraisal or reporting to the court of any nature.

And that, French stated, was the entire agreement between the parties, with all negotiations included, executed on December 20, 1996. The settlement agreement was accompanied with the notarized signatures of all four parties involved in the dispute.

On December 23, Judge David A. Rains issued his final order concerning the State Farm case in DeKalb County Circuit Court. After the settlement agreement was received by the court, Judge Rains ordered the payment to Watson, Gillis and Carver, attorneys for Carolyn's siblings, the sum of $92,500. Payment was ordered to Bob French, as Headrick's attorney, the balance of any funds held at that time. The balance totaled $113,985.59. Then, Rains discharged State Farm from any further liability, as requested. A similar order was issued in the Woodmen of the World case on December 31, 1996, by Robert B. Propst, Senior United States District Court Judge, saying that the court had now been informed that the parties had settled all issues between them and had compromised their claims to the funds in question, as manifested by the settlement agreement attached to and made a part of the order.

The dispute over the proceeds from Carolyn Headrick's life insurance policies had finally been settled, and although it might have seemed that Randy Headrick had won out, that was not necessarily the case. Monetarily, he had been awarded a far greater portion of the settlement than Carolyn's siblings, but to them, money was the least important aspect of the case. They had succeeded in protecting their mother and sister's home and land, and Randy Headrick, having signed off on any rights to it for perpetuity, had forfeited any claim to it. The final slap in the face to Carolyn and Dora Ann's survivors would have been for the man they believed to be the murderer of their mother and sister ultimately to live in their home and own their property. Now the real estate would remain secure in the hands of the Dalton family members, exactly where Carolyn and Dora Ann would have wanted it to stay.

CHAPTER 31

While attorneys for the Headricks, the Daltons, State Farm and Woodmen of the World were presenting their cases to the courts to determine the true beneficiary of Carolyn Headrick's life insurance policies, Investigator Rhonda Jackson and her team had been poring over Randy Headrick's alibi yet again, hoping to find a weak spot that might have been previously overlooked. The coworker who had vouched for Headrick, the man who said he had worked with him from 12:45 until 3:00 P.M. on July 7, 1995, was asked and had agreed voluntarily to take a polygraph exam at the TBI office in Chattanooga. On September 30, 1996, he went with investigators Jackson and Phillips to the office, where he made a written statement prior to the test. The man waived his right to legal counsel and confirmed that he was undergoing the polygraph voluntarily. He also verbally answered the three key questions that he would later be asked during the test:

1. Was Randy with you on July 7, 1995, from 12:45 until 3:00 P.M.? The man answered, "Yes."

2. Has Randy ever told you that he committed these murders? The answer was, "No."

3. Are you withholding any information concerning these murders? The man answered that he was not, but

then added something that he had forgotten to tell the investigators when he was first questioned.

"On the day of the murders, while Randy and I were loading the truck, Randy told me that he was fixing to come into enough money to retire on," the man said. "I told him I knew where he worked and he wasn't going to be able to do it from there. Randy looked kinda funny and didn't say any more about it. The reason I didn't tell you about this when I was interviewed the first time was that I didn't remember it."

The man then took the polygraph test, after which the examiner concluded that he was telling the truth and was not practicing deception when answering the relevant questions. It was also determined that he had not lied in any of the statements he had given to the DeKalb County sheriff's investigators. His truthfulness had been verified, and his willingness to cooperate was proven, but nothing else had been brought forward that could help to put Headrick's alibi in doubt.

As had been the case in the previous year, the holiday season brought a much-increased workload for the investigators, as well as all the sheriff's personnel. Home burglaries, domestic violence, house fires and intoxicated drivers kept the Headrick case temporarily moved to the back burner during the holiday season, which, unfortunately, seemed to be less joyous for some than for others. But Carolyn and Dora Ann remained in the forefront of Rhonda Jackson's thoughts every day, and in her prayers each night. She was determined never to give up until she could prove beyond a shadow of a doubt that Headrick was guilty of their murders. She was certain in her heart that he was responsible for the deaths of his wife and mother-in-law, and she believed that eventually God would provide that vital, key piece of evidence that would bring justice for his two victims.

CHAPTER 32

Once the holidays were past, Rhonda Jackson was able again to devote most of her time to the Headrick case. On January 17, 1997, she took part in a conference call with two FBI agents from the FBI's headquarters in Quantico, Virginia, and the FBI agent from the Birmingham, Alabama, field office who had previously offered his advice on the case. The agents suggested that Jackson try to locate Shane Headrick and develop a background on him. They also suggested that Jackson should obtain the current phone records of Randy Headrick and his parents, as well as another subpoena for motel phone and registration records on the motel in Georgia where Jill Shrader and Shane Headrick were staying at the time of the murders. Jackson started the process to obtain the records as suggested, and began working up the information on Shane Headrick into a comprehensive file. Jackson's record keeping was an amazingly painstaking process; she carefully logged every phone call, every scrap of information and every interview in writing—no matter how irrelevant it might seem—with times, dates and parties present. This careful detailing of events was very important to her, with the Headrick case being her first as lead investigator. She had a lot to prove, both to herself and to her coworkers, and she was determined to do the job and do it well. Her meticulous attention to detail would prove to be invaluable in the coming months of the investigation.

In April, Rhonda Jackson was called back to the residence of John Boggie, the gun-loving taxidermist she had questioned following the murders. Boggie had been involved in a situation a couple of weeks earlier, and was ready to make another statement about what he had heard at that time.

"I was at this guy's residence just off Highway forty about two or three weeks ago," he said. "Another guy was there too, and we were all drinking, and two women and another fellow were there too. One of the guys was drinking whiskey; I saw him drink a quart, sitting at the table. He threatened me and one of the women while he was sitting there. He said he had killed other people before and he didn't care to kill us either."

The taxidermist said he later took the man to the store at Dutton, a nearby town, and that the man had told him, while they were in the car alone, that he killed the two women at Henagar and had killed two other people.

"I didn't ask him any questions, and he didn't go into any detail," Boggie said. "He mentioned something about Indian artifacts when he said that he killed the women, but I don't remember exactly what he said. I haven't seen him anymore since then."

The investigators checked this story out thoroughly, but it proved to be yet another one of those tales that had flourished in the remote northern areas of DeKalb and Jackson Counties on so many weekends since the murders. After several hours of drinking, quite a number of men had claimed to be the killer in an effort to scare their wives or girlfriends into obedience, or to impress and intimidate their drinking buddies.

In early May, Rhonda Jackson received a tip that Randy Headrick and his current wife, Tonya, no longer lived with Headrick's relative and had moved back to Chattanooga. Three days later, she received a call from a reserve officer with the Hamilton County, Tennessee, Sheriff's Department in Chattanooga. The officer had heard about the case under investigation and told Rhonda that Randy Headrick had opened a Native American store on Highway 153. When he visited the store, the officer said, Red Crow was cleaning and polishing a bayonet for Headrick, and the officer asked Headrick what he needed with it, or what he was going to use it for.

"Headrick looked at me and said, 'You never know what you can use something like this for.' I got an awful feeling when he said that."

The officer also said that Headrick was going to give him a large bowie knife, but he couldn't bring himself to take it.

"I told him I didn't have any use for something like that," the man said. "I know it's an insult in the Native American culture to turn down a gift, but I just couldn't accept it."

Headrick had told the man that he "didn't fool with guns; if he needed a weapon, he would use a knife." He let the man know that he was good with knives; he never mentioned owning any guns, but a twelve-gauge riot shotgun lay on a back counter in the store. When the man saw it and commented on it, Headrick stepped in front of the shotgun to block his view of the weapon.

Headrick never mentioned the murders of his wife and mother-in-law to the reserve officer, but told him that he'd been a U.S. Ranger in Vietnam.

"He tried sucking up to me," the man said. "He wanted officers in the store because it looked good."

CHAPTER 33

On Monday, May 19, 1997, Sheriff Cecil Reed received a phone call that sent his department into frenzied action. A funeral director from Kerby Funeral Home in Henagar, the funeral home that had conducted the services for Carolyn Headrick and Dora Ann Dalton, called the sheriff and told him that Randy Headrick had called the funeral home that morning and said that he wanted them to exhume Carolyn Headrick's body and have it cremated on Wednesday, May 21. The sheriff immediately contacted newly-elected DA Mike O'Dell, who took office after Richard Igou's retirement. A court order was issued to stop the exhumation temporarily. O'Dell then received a memo from the state medical examiner that enabled the exhumation to be prevented entirely:

The memo stated that the medical examiner had been informed that there was an impending exhumation and cremation request on Carolyn Jean Headrick. The medical examiner said that while he foresaw no missed features in regard to the original autopsy at that time, the case was a homicide with an ongoing investigation. He strongly recommended that a request for cremation be denied in the event that exhumation might be required and further examinations of the body would be necessary.

The medical examiner went on to say that in his many

years as an examiner for the states of Alabama, Florida and New Mexico, he had never seen an exhumation/ cremation order granted on an unsolved homicide.

"I feel that this would be a dangerous precedent to establish," he stated.

Whatever Randy Headrick's intent had been by wanting to have his deceased wife's body exhumed and cremated, his plan had been effectively foiled by the quick action of the authorities and the funeral home.

On June 5, Rhonda Jackson received a call from Jill Shrader, who told her that a couple of Shane and Randy's relatives had gone to Texas, to the home of another Headrick relative, about four or five weeks previously.

"They told the woman that if anyone came to her asking her anything about a truck driver, not to tell them anything," Jill said. "She asked them why they didn't just call her about it, and they told her they thought all their phones were tapped. She said they only stayed about thirty minutes, then left. It was about a fourteen-hour drive from Alabama to where she lives in Texas."

Jill also said Shane had gotten upset with her for calling Rhonda the previous week.

"I told him, 'Well, you told me I could call her.' He said, 'Well, you're not the one going to prison.' He got real mad and said if the investigators pull up out there, he's not talking and he'll ask for a lawyer."

Shane must have felt the noose tightening, and was evidently becoming very nervous at the amount of attention he was getting from the investigators. His nervousness was beginning to look justified; five days after Jill's phone call, Jackson and Phillips spoke again with the man who had earlier told Phillips that he had tried repeatedly to call Shane at the motel on the day of the murders and had gotten no answer.

"On July 7, 1995, Shane Headrick's father called me about six-thirty or seven A.M. and said he was trying to get in touch with Jill and Shane. He wanted to know if I had talked to them, and I told him I hadn't. He told me he had talked to Jill earlier at work and she told him Shane was at the motel, and he had called and didn't get an answer. He wanted me to call and see if I could get in touch with him."

The man said Headrick's father gave him the phone number of the motel.

"I called and couldn't get an answer, and called Mr. Headrick back and told him that I didn't get an answer either. He didn't say what he wanted, but he said that he just needed to talk to Shane. I tried four or five times to call again before lunch and didn't get an answer. Jimmy Phillips called me after three P.M. and told me Mrs. Dalton and Mrs. Headrick had been killed, and he wanted to know if I knew where Jill and Shane were. I told him I had been calling all day to try to get in touch with Shane for his dad, and couldn't get an answer."

The man said he called again, and that time, he contacted Jill at the motel.

"I told her the law was hunting them, that they needed to talk to Shane," he said. "I didn't tell her what had happened. I told her I had been trying to call all day. She told me Shane was supposed to be at the motel, that she had been trying to call him too and hadn't got an answer."

On July 3, 1997, Rhonda Jackson took a copy of a list of questions for a voice analysis–structured interview that she hoped Randy Headrick would agree to answer. They were delivered to attorney Bob French's office, and on July 8, Jimmy Phillips told Rhonda that Bob French had told him that Randy wasn't going to answer the questions and that he had helped the investigators all he was going to. This came as no surprise; the officers had felt it was doubtful that Headrick and French would agree to the voice analysis, but they thought it was worth a try. After two years of tirelessly working the case, they weren't about to pass up any chances, no matter how slim.

CHAPTER 34

Jill Shrader called Rhonda Jackson again, on July 25, with another bit of information that cast even more suspicion on Shane Headrick. She told Rhonda that around three weeks earlier, Shane had told her that the last time Randy asked him to do the murders was on the Sunday before Carolyn and Dora Ann were killed on Friday. This contradicted Shane's earlier claims to the investigators that the last time Randy had asked him to kill the two women was in February 1995, prior to the murders in July.

Things were not looking good for Shane Headrick. The young man's story kept changing, whether from drug-induced confusion or from intentional deception. Shane was growing more and more afraid that he was going to be blamed for the killings, and as a result, his behavior became even more volatile and unpredictable than ever.

On August 1, a letter arrived at the sheriff's office that astounded Rhonda Jackson and her team. It was from one of the county's best-known citizens, a high-placed public official whose credibility absolutely could not be questioned. The information he provided was via a third party and could only be categorized as hearsay, but the letter was nonetheless riveting.

The man had been told by a person whose name he said he could not reveal that "Jill Shrader's boyfriend, which [*sic*] is now in Texas and whose name is Shane," had told the person that he threw clothes out over the bridge off Highway 117, and stated that "he was wearing these clothes when he killed them."

The person then gave the exact location of the bridge in question, and said that the clothes would be in a garbage bag that was thrown from the bridge, and they would be under the bridge.

"Shane is on acid drugs and my source stated that he is very dangerous," the letter said. The man stated that Shane was now living in Texas, and that his source was afraid that Shane would come back and kill him if he found out that he had told anyone.

Needless to say, the officers sprang into action. The area under and around the bridge on Highway 117 was searched immediately and thoroughly. But after two years, if there had ever been a garbage bag full of bloody clothing thrown underneath the bridge, it was now long gone.

A month later, another amazing tip surfaced, courtesy of a local medical professional. Rhonda Jackson met with the person at their office, and was told that a client had given some information on the murders. The client had said that he knew that Headrick was in debt to drug dealers in New York and claimed that Headrick had hired his brother and possibly two others to commit the murders, and that one of the persons that was there at the scene of the murders might be a "weak link." That weak link, the client said, didn't actually shoot the two women, but was present when the murders occurred and was afraid that if he talked, the others would take his life.

The client told the medical professional that the reason the two women were killed was to collect the insurance money to pay the drug dealers. The client said that he had been in the Headrick/Dalton residence and had seen Randy Headrick's Indian artifacts. He said the mutilation of the bodies with the artifacts was done after the victims were killed.

The medical professional said the client might possibly be willing to cooperate by going to the other person described as the "weak link," but was not willing to talk to law enforcement.

After checking out this third-party information as well as possible, and learning no further details, it was determined that this, like so many other tips received in the long-running case, was unsubstantiated hearsay and would be of no use to the investigation.

It was a disappointment to the officers, but they continued to pursue the hard evidence they needed to put Randy Headrick, and very likely his brother, Shane, behind bars for murder.

CHAPTER 35

Yet another busy holiday season came and went, with very few new developments in the Headrick/Dalton double-homicide case. Several persons were interviewed and their statements were taken after the start of the new year, but as usual, nothing surfaced that provided any valid evidence—only more useless third-party rumors and hearsay.

In April 1998, one of the Dalton relatives contacted Rhonda Jackson, saying he had heard that Headrick's alibi "was tired of lying for him, that he wasn't going to lie for Randy anymore."

Investigator Mike James reinterviewed the man, Headrick's coworker who earlier had passed a polygraph test, which indicated he was being honest and truthful and was telling the authorities everything he knew about Headrick's whereabouts the day of the murders. The man told James that he had told the truth from the beginning, which the investigators believed, and said that he had not told anyone that he wasn't going to alibi Randy Headrick anymore.

A young man came forward in mid-June to make a statement that interested both the DeKalb County investigators and the ATF. The young man stated that he and his brother had gone to Fort Payne with Randy Headrick in

Headrick's truck around five years earlier to look for Indian relics. On the way, he said, Headrick asked him to get something for him out of the glove compartment. The young man saw what he thought to be a blue steel semi-automatic pistol in a black nylon holster in the glove compartment. He pulled it out and was looking at it, and Headrick said that it belonged to him.

The young man stated that he had seen Headrick with at least ten guns. He told the officers he saw Headrick shoot at a snake in the creek behind the house with a .22 rifle. He said he also saw several long guns in a gun rack in the bedroom of the Headrick/Dalton home. He described them as one or two 12-gauge shotguns, a high-powered rifle, possibly a 30.06 or a 30.30, and a .22 rifle. Headrick showed him a blue steel pistol in a black box that appeared to look like a 9mm, and Headrick told the young man that all these guns were his. This was of considerable interest to the ATF, since Headrick was a convicted felon, who was not supposed to be in possession of a single firearm, much less a personal arsenal. They had an investigation of their own in progress, and Randy Headrick would soon find himself subject to some serious charges other than those the DeKalb County authorities were pursuing.

On August 5, 1998, Headrick was arrested in Chattanooga by ATF officials and Chattanooga police. He had been indicted by a grand jury on five counts of federal firearms violations, including possession of several firearms and falsifying an application to purchase a firearm after having been convicted on federal charges. After his arrest, Headrick was sent to the Etowah County Jail in Gadsden, Alabama, a holding facility for federal inmates, where he was held without bond. At last, he was in custody. But the DeKalb County investigators would not feel any true satisfaction until they could arrest Headrick, and any accomplices he might prove to have had, for the murders of his wife and mother-in-law.

CHAPTER 36

The three-year anniversary of the murders had come and gone with little progress made toward solving the case. There was the satisfaction of knowing that Headrick was now sitting in jail on the federal firearms charges, but the DeKalb County investigators desperately wanted to bring charges of their own against him for Carolyn and Dora Ann's deaths. As usual, a wealth of unsubstantiated rumors, false leads and hearsay had flooded the sheriff's department during that time, and much of it involved people and situations that were located out of state. Rhonda Jackson decided it was time for a road trip. In August 1998, she and Jimmy Phillips traveled to Texas for a number of interviews with several people who might be able to provide that key piece of evidence they continued to hope for.

Shane Headrick had moved to Arlington, Texas, where he was living with his new, and very pregnant, girlfriend, and Jill Shrader lived in Fort Worth with her new boyfriend. Shane and Jill had split up about a year earlier when, according to Jill, he had beaten her up and shot at her.

When Jackson and Phillips arrived in Texas, their first stop was at ATF headquarters, where they met with two ATF agents who put them in touch with a detective in the

Arlington Police Department. The two Alabama investigators brought their Texas colleague up to speed on the
case and explained their interest in Shane Headrick.
The following day, the three officers met at the Arlington
Police Department, where Shane Headrick was brought
in to be reinterviewed. He was willing to talk, and even
seemed relieved to give his statement.

After first claiming he didn't know anything else other
than what he had told the investigators already, he was told
that Randy was currently in jail. He wasn't aware of that,
he said, and was very glad Randy was in jail without bond
because "I won't have to look over my shoulder anymore."

The last contact he'd had with Randy, he said, was
around two years earlier when he had questioned him
about the murders at the investigators' request. When he
asked Randy if he'd done it, Shane said that Randy just
stared at him and said no, he didn't do it. This, Shane said,
took place at their parents' home on the back porch.

Shane said that Randy found out that he'd told the officers that Randy tried to hire him to kill Carolyn and Dora
Ann, and Shane had been afraid that Randy would try to
do something to him in retaliation. Shane said Randy had
asked him twice, about a week or two before the murders,
to kill the two women, or to get someone to do it.

"I suggested that he talk to this guy he worked with at
Kmart, when they both worked there cleaning floors,
but I don't think the guy would be capable of something
like this," Shane said. "Randy hung around with a guy
from Flat Rock and rode to work with him, but I don't
know who he is."

Phillips then handed Shane some reading material—
the statement that claimed he had told someone he
threw the bloody clothes and a gun off the bridge. When
Shane read it, his face turned red and he asked the officers if they had found anything.

"I didn't throw anything off the bridge; I was in
Atlanta," he said.

Shane told the investigators that he was currently living

with his girlfriend, who was six months pregnant with his baby.

"I'm just trying to get my life back together," he said.

Following the inverview, the Arlington officers took investigators Jackson and Phillips to the home of one of the Headrick relatives who also lived in Arlington. She gave a brief statement and told the officers that Shane had not told her anything about the murders. Another relative that Rhonda Jackson would very much have liked to question had unfortunately passed away in October of the previous year. Rhonda attempted to speak to the deceased woman's daughter, leaving two messages on her answering machine, but the calls were never returned.

That evening, Rhonda called Jill Shrader and asked her if she could meet with her and Phillips the next morning. Jill agreed, and came over to the motel where the officers were staying, the LaQuinta Inn in Grand Prairie, Texas. They took Jill to breakfast at the Denny's restaurant adjoining the motel and reinterviewed her. Since she and Shane were no longer together, and she did not feel threatened by the prospect of telling what she knew and suspected, Jill was willing to disclose some additional information about the case.

Jill told the officers that two men she and Shane knew had come to Texas in the summer of 1994 and had gotten drugs from one of Shane's relatives there. Shane had set it up, she said, and Jill and Shane were supposed to receive some of the drugs as payment for Shane's trouble. When the deal was done, Shane was not given anything, and he was upset about it.

In the spring of 1997, Jill said, she and Shane were at the relative's mother's home, and she told them at that time that two of the Alabama Headrick clan had driven to Fort Worth from Alabama, evidently just to tell her that if anyone asked her who it was that had come to her house to buy drugs in 1994, she was to tell them it had been Billy Jack Dalton. The woman told Jill that she didn't know why the men traveled all the way to Texas just to tell her that, and then immediately turned around and drove back to Alabama; they didn't want anyone to know they had come to Texas. The woman didn't know who the man was that they wanted her to say had bought the drugs, and she was upset with the men for telling her what they expected her to do without any explanation or a reason.

Jill also provided some additional information about Randy's former girlfriend, saying that both Shane and Randy had told her that the woman had had a baby by Randy, and that the woman had told Carolyn about it. After their breakup, Randy wanted the girlfriend to be paid back for screwing up his life.

Shane gave Jill a pinkie ring one day after he left Randy's house, she said, a specially made ring. Jill wore the ring for several months until a girl came to her house with a friend of Jill's, and she told Jill that she had seen the ring before, but couldn't remember where. Jill told Shane what the girl had said, and Jill's ring came up missing that very night, never to be seen again. Jill described the ring as being gold, with a heart and tiny diamonds.

Jill also said that Shane had told her that Randy wanted him to help burn down the former girlfriend's house, but Shane refused to help him. He also told Jill that Randy allegedly stole a safe from the house that had jewelry and drugs in it, and Shane said the safe was buried somewhere in the woods.

CHAPTER 37

Following Jill's interview, the officers left on their way back home to Alabama, where they promptly scheduled a meeting with Headrick's former girlfriend and her husband. The statements they gave provided an up-close and personal look at the many hazards of extramarital affairs. Revenge, jealousy, obsession, betrayal—their story had it all.

The ex-girlfriend said that she and Headrick worked together at Earthgrains in Fort Payne, and had a relationship from October 1993 until January 1994. Her home was burned down the following April. Headrick was also seeing another girl, she said, a small girl with long blond hair. He "took care" of all the women on the production line, and had a reputation around the plant as a real ladies' man.

During their relationship, Headrick told the woman that he hated his mother-in-law, and told her that he had taken out an insurance policy from Woodmen of the World on Carolyn because he planned to get rid of her, his mother-in-law and the ex-girlfriend's long-suffering husband. Headrick told her this a couple of times, although she didn't take it seriously at the time. He also tried to get her to take out insurance on her husband, but she refused.

On one occasion, Headrick put a greeting card on the woman's car at work. It said that if he could get rid of his wife, his mother-in-law and the girlfriend's husband, he would have what he wanted. The card, she said, had been turned over to an investigator with the sheriff's department in adjoining Jackson County, the county where she lived and where her house had been burned.

After she decided to end the relationship with Headrick, she said, he had threatened her several times, saying he would sneak up and get her. He would come up to her in the locker room at work, or in the men's bathroom when she was cleaning it, and corner her and tell her he was going to get her. She said he would tell her he was "coming over some night soon," and threatened to call her husband.

When the subject of her pregnancy was brought up, the woman said there was a distinct possibility that the son she gave birth to was Headrick's child.

"I don't know for sure, and I don't want to know," she said. She denied calling Carolyn and telling her she'd had a relationship with her husband, and said that Headrick was the one who had told his wife about it. A fireproof box was taken from her house when it burned, she said, and inside the box was an agreement she and Headrick had drawn up saying that if the baby was indeed Headrick's, he agreed to relinquish all parental rights. She and Headrick each had a copy, she said.

Also stolen at the time of the fire, according to the woman, was a special ring: a gold band with two interlocked hearts in silver, and with a small diamond. The description was an exact match for the ring Jill had described to the officers, the ring that Shane had given her and that had come up missing after someone recognized it as one they had seen somewhere before.

One night after the woman ended the relationship with Headrick, but before her house burned, she and her husband came out of a Fort Payne grocery store and found Randy and Shane Headrick sitting on the hood of the couple's car. Later, Headrick called the husband's mother and told her that she'd better tell her son to shut his mouth or she was going to get some insurance money. The ex-girlfriend said she had seen Randy and Shane together a lot, at the Krystal drive-in and at Wal-Mart, and said that Headrick had told her on several occasions that he could do anything he wanted to and get away with it.

The woman's husband, apparently an extraordinarily forgiving man, chimed in and said that at the time of the house fire, he had told the Jackson County investigator that someone better keep their eyes on Headrick's wife and mother-in-law, because Headrick had threatened to kill them.

On a parting note, the woman told the investigators the name of the man who she claimed was Headrick's best friend on the job at Earthgrains, a man from the Lookout Mountain area with long gray hair and tattoos.

Within five days, the tattooed, gray-haired man was sitting in a chair at the Valley Head Police Department, giving his statement to the investigators. He was eager to make it very clear that he had no part whatsoever in the murders, and told them that he had worked with Headrick at Earthgrains for about six to seven months. He was the leadman on the line that Headrick had worked on, and during the time they worked together, he and Headrick became friends.

The man had been to Headrick's home a number of times, he said, and had met Randy's wife and mother-in-law. "They were nice people, and always treated me nice," he said. He had been aware of Headrick's affair, and said that Headrick had told him that the woman was pregnant with his child. Everyone knew about the affair. "It was the talk of the plant," he said.

The man described Headrick as a "loafer" at work and said he read science-fiction books during break time very often. Headrick also told him that he was a veteran and had served in the U.S. Army. He had seen Shane once, he said, when he was with Randy, and that was before the murders happened.

After Headrick lost his job at Earthgrains, the man went to get lumber at Builders Supply and saw him working there. Headrick asked him to help put a water line in at Dora Ann's house in Henagar.

"Randy never asked me for a gun and didn't ask me to help him commit the murders," he said. "The only person that still talks about the murders at Earthgrains is a cousin of Randy's. Randy also told me that he was a bodyguard in Texas, and that he had got into trouble because he was with a man and the police stopped them. He said the man had something in his trunk, but he didn't say what it was, and he was arrested and served time due to this.

"I didn't help Randy commit these murders."

As usual, the officers intended to check out this man's story thoroughly, although they believed he was telling them the truth, and telling them everything that he knew about Headrick. Nothing new was learned during the interview; nothing that would lead to an arrest. But the very next day, Investigator Jimmy Phillips got a phone call that finally blew the Headrick/Dalton murder case wide open. At long last, Rhonda Jackson's prayers had been answered. The vital missing piece of the puzzle had landed squarely onto the board, and it fit perfectly into place.

CHAPTER 38

A husky, quiet young man sat in an office at the DeKalb County Sheriff's Department at 8:34 P.M. on August 20, 1998, waiting to talk to Jimmy Phillips, Rhonda Jackson and Deputy District Attorney Ben Baxley. Terry Durham was a steady, responsible fellow who, earlier that day, had heard his wife and sister-in-law talking about Headrick's arrest on firearms charges and the murders of Carolyn Headrick and Dora Ann Dalton. When he heard them talking about the details of the murders, Durham realized that he had to tell the authorities what he knew, and had to tell them quickly.

When the investigators and Baxley were ready to begin the interview with Durham, Rhonda Jackson turned on her tape recorder and began asking about Durham's current address, his marital status, how many children he had and his current place of employment. He worked with Metropolitan Security in Chattanooga, at the Marriott hotel, where he had come in contact with a man named Randy Headrick, who worked in the hotel's maintenance department on the first shift. Durham said that he worked as a security guard on second shift and often doubled over into third shift, and he and Headrick would sometimes speak to one another in the mornings when their paths crossed during shift changes.

Durham had been stationed at the Marriott for around two months, and Headrick was already working there at the time that Durham started his job. The men had casual conversations, Durham said, and would occasionally go on calls together.

"What kind of calls?" Rhonda asked.

"Well, if something broke down, I'd have to go secure the area and make sure nobody came in it . . . just normal stuff."

Durham said he had no idea what Headrick's job description was.

"They have seven different ones that work different jobs. Some work air conditioning, some work plumbing—"

"Okay," Rhonda said, "during this time that you've been working with him or around him, has he told you anything about any homicides in DeKalb County?" Rhonda held her breath, waiting for the answer that she knew was coming.

"He mentioned to me on August first, he asked me if I knew of any murders, especially the ones in the Henagar/Ider area, and I told him that I didn't, and he started going into details about it, and all this and that."

"Tell me what kind of details he gave you," Rhonda said.

"At first, he told me that they never would catch who done it because they didn't have no proof who it was that done it. And then we just kinda talked around a little bit, and he finally looked at me, and looked at me straight in the face, and said, 'The reason they won't never catch who done it is because I'm standing right here; I'm the one who done it and they ain't caught me yet.'"

Rhonda's heart was pounding. She had waited, hoped and prayed for three years that this case would finally break, and here sat Terry Durham, telling her that Randy Headrick had not only freely admitted to murdering Carolyn and Dora Ann, but had practically bragged about it. She was almost too excited to continue her questioning, but she composed herself and asked Durham what kind of details Headrick had given him.

"He went into some details about the murder as far as using an authentic, I guess it was an authentic, Native American spear. He said it was six foot long, that's all, and I didn't believe him at the time; I mean, who would confess, you know?"

"Did he say anything else?"

"He never really went into details, except for he started mentioning stuff like one woman was eating watermelon, and then I just kinda not paid attention to him for a little bit, and then I caught back up with his talking about burning some clothes in a barn. I have no idea what kind of clothes they were, and he also mentioned wrapping the truck seats in plastic. At least the interior, he said the interior, so I took it as the truck seat . . . car seat . . . I don't know."

"And he mentioned, what did you say about burning clothes in a barn?" Rhonda asked.

"That him and his brother burned clothes in a barn," Durham answered.

Jimmy Phillips broke in, asking, "Did he say where the barn was that they burned. . . . Anything about it?"

"From what I gathered, it was his father's."

"Did he give you any more details?" Rhonda asked.

"Nothing real specific," said Durham. "Like I said, I didn't believe him. Why, you know, why would he come out . . ."

Phillips asked if Headrick told Durham what each of the victims was doing at the time of the murders.

"Just that one of them was eating watermelon."

"And the other one was, what did he tell you what she was doing?"

"I thought he said vacuuming, sweeping, mopping or something, some sort of that nature."

"All right," Phillips said, "and then you said he burned some clothes in the barn, how did that come up?"

"We was talking about it and he said, this is where we got into this 'They won't catch me because they don't have fingerprints,' all this and that, and 'They don't have no evidence.' He said, 'They don't have no evidence 'cause we burned the clothes.'"

Phillips asked if Headrick had told Durham that Headrick and his brother had burned the clothes, and Durham said yes, but said that Headrick did not mention his brother by name.

The investigators asked Durham how many times he'd talked to Headrick, and he said at least once a day, sometimes only a casual "Hello, how you doing?" He said Headrick had never mentioned anything even remotely like his admission of murder in any of their conversations before August 1.

"The only thing he ever mentioned was that he had a twenty-two pistol. I have a thirty-eight Special and he had seen it and was looking at it, and I asked him, 'Do you own one?' And he said, 'Yeah, I've got a twenty-two pistol,' and that's all he ever said. I never saw the pistol, just what he said."

Durham told the officers that Headrick didn't say what kind of pistol it was, or whether he had it at home or kept it somewhere else. Headrick, he said, had told him about the pistol around two weeks after Durham started working at the Marriott, because Headrick was trying to get him to buy a pen that held a concealed knife. Headrick told Durham that he owned a store where he sold items of that sort.

The investigators asked Durham several questions to pin down exactly when he first began talking to Headrick at work, and what time the August 1 conversation took place. Durham told them that he and Headrick spoke that day for around an hour, from about 6:00 to 7:00 A.M., Eastern time.

"Did he ever mention why he killed those people?" Phillips asked.

"He just said something about he felt like his wife was cheating on him, and the mother knew it."

Rhonda Jackson, having come to know the Daltons so

well during the course of the investigation, was flabbergasted to hear that statement.

"And the mother what?" she asked.

"Knew that was happening, and that's why he done it."

Rhonda shook her head in disgust. The very idea of Carolyn cheating on her husband, or of Dora Ann condoning it, was beyond ludicrous.

Phillips asked Durham if Headrick ever mentioned anything about insurance money.

"Yeah," Durham said, "he said that he had some odd amount of insurance and that he couldn't get it all back. I think he said around three hundred thousand, I don't know."

Phillips asked if Headrick had said he collected some of the money, but didn't get it all.

"I don't believe he told me he collected any of it," Durham said.

Rhonda asked if Headrick had said anything about living in Tennessee and not being able to come back to Alabama.

"He said he couldn't come back to Henagar or Ider because of an ongoing investigation with him involved," Durham answered. "He said that if he come back, that he'd be arrested for homicide, murder, whatever."

"Was anybody else around when he told you this?" Rhonda asked.

"Not when he told me, but right before I left, we was outside talking and another security employee come to relieve me from my shift. He seen me speaking with Randy."

Rhonda asked Durham if Headrick had said whether or not he'd ever told anybody else what he had told Durham that morning.

"No, like I said, I didn't believe him when he told me, so I didn't really ask him any questions."

"Well, Terry, what made you come to us today?" asked Rhonda.

"My sister-in-law was talking to me and she mentioned

Randy being arrested in Chattanooga or somewhere, and when she said his name, it just made me think, and I said, 'Yeah, I know him; he used to work engineering at the Marriott, but they told me that he quit because he got into an altercation with an employee.' One of the second-shift engineers told me that they got in a cuss fight sometime last week."

"Okay," Rhonda said, "at what point, did you start believing what Randy Headrick told you?"

"Whenever I started mentioning it to my sister-in-law what I knew, she told me I needed to come talk with Jimmy Phillips."

Durham said that the conversation between him, his wife and his sister-in-law had taken place earlier that day, around 2:00 P.M.

"And you said that she was saying something about Randy getting arrested on firearms charges in Chattanooga, and then you recognized the name as the man who was working with you and remembered what he told you?" Rhonda asked.

"I said what he had told me."

Durham told the investigators that he hadn't told anyone else about what Randy had admitted to him, because he didn't believe him.

"Not until today, not until all this started going together. I found out today that this was actually true."

Durham said he wasn't familiar with the murders and didn't know about them at all at the time they had happened.

"That's why I didn't believe him when he told me, because I didn't know nothing about this."

"You didn't read anything in the paper about any of this murder or anything?" asked Phillips. "I mean, it was well publicized in the paper and on TV, and I just thought you—"

"I never even heard of them," said Durham.

"So you didn't know anything about the two women that got killed at Ider?" Phillips asked.

"No, that's why when he told me, I didn't believe him,

you know, because I didn't know of anything like that ever happening, 'cause you know how stuff circulates around about that."

Phillips asked Durham, "When he told you this, you said that he looked at you in a strange way?"

"When he told me that he killed them, he just got that glare, like you can just look through somebody, and just turned his head sort of up in the air, over his shoulder."

The investigators looked at each other. This was what they had waited and hoped for: an admission of guilt loaded with enough detailed information, from Headrick himself, to lead to an arrest. And likely more than one arrest, since Headrick had also implicated his brother, Shane, as an accomplice. It was almost too good to be true, and they knew they had to proceed carefully to make sure no loopholes were left in their questioning.

Jimmy Phillips wanted to know if Headrick had told Durham anything about his past, and what sort of other claims he had made. As he had previously claimed to so many people, he told Durham that he was a Vietnam veteran. He also told the young man that he had been a branch manager for Pinkerton in Texas.

"This took place over a period of time, just in casual meetings, you know, like he'd come in and ask me how I liked working for Metropolitan, and stuff like that, and he would tell me about Pinkerton and all that. My office is right where they clock out, so he'd clock out and come in and say, 'I'm going home, see you later,' you know. And like in the morning when I'd work overtime, he would come in maybe ten or fifteen minutes early."

Durham told the investigators that Headrick had also told him about working at Builders Supply in Fort Payne.

"He told me there was fifty-five minutes to an hour that y'all couldn't account for, for where he was for that time."

"Did he say anything much more about his brother?" asked Rhonda.

"Just that he's the one, he accused him of doing it, but

he never said his name. He just said, 'I pointed a finger to my brother as the triggerman.'"

Phillips wanted more about the murders, and he asked Durham if Headrick went into any detail about how the two women were killed, other than what he already had stated.

"He never did come out and say he shot them," Durham said, "but he did say he used the spear. He was telling me how good of a marksman he was with a spear."

Rhonda asked, "Did he tell you about any weapons other than the spears, and what did you say about them being shot? What was his exact words, if you can remember?"

"I believe most of the stuff that happened, as far as the cutting, was after he killed them or whoever killed them, after they were dead or dying. Basically that they were shot, and he speared them."

Phillips wanted to know if Headrick ever told Durham how he got away from work, and Durham repeated what Headrick had said about how there was forty-five minutes to an hour during which the investigators couldn't account for his whereabouts.

"Do you know of anybody else he's talked to about this, or if he had anybody that he hung around much that works up there, that he was friends with?" Rhonda asked.

"Yeah, there was one of the engineers. I don't have no idea what his last name was. If he's still there. You seen them together all the time." Durham told the investigators the engineer's first name, and they knew, with that information, that they would be able to locate the man and question him.

Phillips went back to the conversation on August 1, when Headrick had made his seemingly unbelievable admission of guilt.

"When he told you this, you didn't believe him, right? At the time, you thought he was just more or less running his mouth. Is that what you were thinking?"

"I thought he was just kidding, you know?" Durham told

him. "At the time he told me, I didn't believe him. I mean, why would anybody say that they done it?"

Durham said he had no idea why Headrick had told him he was guilty, especially since he didn't know him that well.

"I was just there when he said it to me. It was just me and him on the back dock until the other man came to relieve me."

Durham said Headrick had never mentioned trying to hire somebody to kill the two women.

"So, basically he told you that he was under investigation for murder in Alabama," Phillips said. "He couldn't come back to Alabama because he was still under investigation, and if he came back down here, he'd be arrested for murder, and that we would never catch him because we didn't have enough evidence?"

"You didn't have no physical evidence was his last words. Nothing that would hold up in court. He mentioned there was no fingerprints found."

Phillips asked if Headrick had told him the location of the barn where he claimed he and Shane had burned some clothes, and asked him to try and repeat exactly what Headrick had said to him about the incident.

"That him and his brother burnt clothes in there. He never said his brother's name; I didn't know his brother's name until you mentioned it. He just said him and his brother put shit in the barn and burnt it."

"Did he ever say, like, clothes, other than 'we put shit in the barn and burned it'?" Phillips asked. "Can you remember distinctly if he said clothes?"

"He said clothes. I don't know what kind of clothes; he just said clothes."

The officers spent some time questioning Durham about the exact time he came to work on August 1, and when he spoke with Headrick, and how long. Durham told them he didn't have any further contact with Headrick after they talked about the murders, and had seen him on a few occasions since their conversation, but they didn't speak any further about the murders or anything else. Durham didn't know Headrick had been arrested; he thought he had quit his job at the Marriott because of the altercation he'd had with another employee. He had first learned about the arrest that day, he said, when he heard it from his sister-in-law.

CHAPTER 39

Deputy District Attorney Ben Baxley had sat quietly, listening to Durham providing a wealth of information about Headrick's admission of guilt. But it was time to move on to other questions that concerned the potential prosecution of Headrick for murder. Baxley knew Durham's credibility would have to be well-established in order for his testimony to hold up in court. He told Durham he wanted to know every person that he had told about Headrick's admissions.

"Just my wife and sister-in-law," Durham said. "I didn't tell anybody at work. I didn't believe it; I thought, yeah, whatever, you know. I just didn't pay attention to him. I told my wife that day when I got home, though."

Baxley asked if Headrick had ever told any other stories that Durham thought were far-fetched.

"Nothing, except for that he was some marksman with a spear, that he could throw a spear sixty yards or something. . . ."

"Did you ever have any other conversations, about family, kids . . . ?" asked Baxley.

"We got in a conversation on where I lived, you know, when I first started there, and when I told him I lived in Ider, he started telling me people he knew, which I don't remember their names. And he said that he has a house up here that he can't go back to. Because of this."

Baxley told the young man that he wanted to get some more background information about him, and questioned him about where he went to school, all the places he had worked, his ex-wife and their three-year-old daughter and his current wife, with whom he also had a child.

Durham told Baxley the details of his divorce and his subsequent marriage to his wife, Holly, and their eight-month-old son. He named all the places where he had worked, and how long he had worked for each of them, and when he started at Metropolitan Security. After the long questioning session, Baxley determined that Durham had nothing on his record other than divorce-related matters and a single speeding ticket. He was satisfied with the young man's credibility.

"When did you first meet Randy?" Baxley asked.

"Sometime my first week when I started at the Marriott. I transferred from the Chattanooga Choo Choo to the Marriott. The supervisor at the Marriott was needing a couple of days off. They brought me over there for two days a week and I did that for about three weeks; then they booted me up for full-time [work]."

Durham said that Headrick had told him he came to work early on August 1 because someone had tried to rob his store and said that he'd been over there guarding the business all night, and then had come straight to work that morning. He told Durham that he sold Indian artifacts in the store: spears, hatchets and the like.

"Did he ever tell you anything about having any firearms in that store?" Rhonda asked.

"Not in the store, but he told me he could get me a stun gun, a Taser."

Baxley had some further questions about whether Durham had told anyone else about Headrick's confession, and the young man said he only told his wife when he got home the morning of August 1.

"Just like I said, she didn't believe me and I didn't

believe it either. I just come in and I said, 'You'll never believe what this crazy son of a bitch I work with said,' and I
told her he said he killed his wife and some other woman."

Baxley questioned Durham again, in detail, about exactly when he came and went from work that day, and
asked if he'd had any contact with Headrick since then
about the conversation they'd had.

"No, I saw him one day the next week when he was
clocking out. He didn't say anything to me, just waved at
me as he was going out the door." Durham said Headrick
hadn't mentioned their conversation at all, but had
seemed to be more distant since then.

"He used to come in the office and say, 'I'm going
home, see you later,' and now he waves and goes home.
Well, he did . . . he's not there anymore. Last week, I asked
the second-shift engineer where Randy was, and he told
me that he left because of an altercation. I was just won-
dering what was up."

Baxley again questioned Durham about his background, just for good measure. This was too valuable a
witness to be discredited by the wily Bob French if Durham
ended up on the witness stand. He asked Durham if he
had ever had any mental problems, if he was on any type
of medication or if he had any physical or medical problems. He asked how Durham was doing financially and if
he was caught up on all his bills, and the young man said
that, actually, he was two months ahead on his bills. Once
again, Baxley felt reassured that he had a credible witness,
and Rhonda Jackson and Jimmy Phillips once again
brought the questioning back to Headrick's admission of
guilt.

Durham repeated what he had told the investigators
about Headrick's claim that he had killed the two women.
He never said he was the person who shot them, Durham
said, but he told him that they had been shot. Then
Headrick had said that he was the one who had speared
both of them, and claimed that the truck had been lined
with plastic on the inside.

"He'd told me, you know, like there's this unsolved murder case and all this and that, no witnesses, stuff like that, no prints or anything."

"In other words, it was a perfect murder," Phillips said.

"Yeah, because he said the only questionable thing that he had was the hour that nobody could account for, fifty minutes to an hour that nobody could account for."

"Then after that, then he goes on and tells you that he and his brother burned some shit in the barn," Phillips said.

"I just kinda looked at him, you know, like why would you burn shit in a barn, and then he just said 'clothes,' you know."

Phillips asked if Headrick had ever said anything to Durham about his wife and his mother-in-law, and how their relationship was.

"The only thing he ever mentioned was that his father didn't like his wife."

Durham said that Headrick had told him he had a large amount of insurance on his wife, but Durham didn't question him about why he had taken out so much insurance on her.

"It didn't make no difference to me, because I didn't think he did; I thought he was lying. I didn't know anything about what he was talking about."

Headrick claimed that his brother was in Texas, Durham said, but he never mentioned his brother's girlfriend, or said where his brother was living at the time of the murders.

Baxley asked Durham how the conversation about Headrick had come up that morning, and he said his sister-in-law was talking about Headrick's firearms arrest.

"When she said his name, it just struck me, and I said, 'Yeah, I know him, I worked with him at the Marriott, and I know some stuff that they'd probably like to know,' and just kinda mentioned a little bit of what I knew. She remembered the murders. And she looked at me and told me that she needed to call Jimmy and told me to come talk to him. The first words out of her mouth was 'Come talk to Jimmy.' She called him, and she come back and told me that Jimmy wanted me down here today to talk to him."

As the interview ended and Rhonda left her office to go home, she felt as if a great weight had been lifted from her shoulders after three long years of hard work. Finally she had what she needed to pursue the arrest and conviction of the man who she had always known in her heart was responsible for the murders of Carolyn and Dora Ann. That evening, she fervently thanked God for sending that vital missing piece of the puzzle that she had prayed for, for so many nights.

CHAPTER 40

The following days brought a flurry of activity in the small, cramped upstairs offices of the sheriff's investigators. Thanks to Terry Durham's statement, a host of other people now needed to be located and interviewed. The first order of business was making arrangements to take the statements of Durham's wife, Holly, and his sister-in-law.

Holly Durham came in first and told the investigators what had happened when her husband came home from work on August 1.

"Terry told me that I wouldn't believe what this stupid son of a bitch told him at work. He told him that he had killed some people up around here; he was talking about around where we live. Terry told me that the man told him that he speared them and that one of them was eating watermelon in the kitchen and the other one was vacuuming. Terry told me that the guy that he worked with was the one who had done the murders, and he worked in maintenance at the Marriott in Chattanooga. This is all that Terry told me."

The sister-in-law's statement, taken next, corroborated both Durham's statement and his wife's.

Later that day, Jimmy Phillips received a page from Terry Durham wanting him to return his call as soon as possible. Phillips immediately called him. When Durham got to work that day, he said, one of the men on the job confronted him about coming to the sheriff's department to talk. Durham was unnerved; he didn't know how the man had found out, but he wanted Phillips to know. That confrontation would soon turn out to be the least of Terry Durham's problems in respect to his involvement in the case against Randy Headrick.

On August 23, one of the deputies reported a conversation with a police officer who worked at the Henagar Police Department in 1994. The officer had told the deputy that Headrick would come by the department and sit around talking. Headrick talked about being arrested in Texas for explosives, and said how stupid the law was in Texas, because if he wanted to do something he could do it and be somewhere else when it happened. He also said that he could kill someone and be in another state when it happened. The officer said Headrick was always talking about explosives and killing; and like so many other people Headrick had bragged to, the officer paid little attention to what he was told.

The next day, subpoenas were issued for the time cards and personnel records on Headrick during his employment at the Marriott. Terry Durham's time cards from Metropolitan Security were also subpoenaed.

On August 25, the investigators set up a series of interviews with employees at the Marriott in Chattanooga. One interview in particular was of interest. It was a man who said that he and Headrick were friends, and that he had shopped at Headrick's Native American store.

"He told me sometime the last of July that his wife and mother-in-law were murdered by being shot and stabbed with a spear," he said. "Randy was acting as if something was bothering him, and he told me that they have never caught the murderer. Randy helped get me my job at the Marriott, and we'd been friends for around five months.

"He told me that a fellow called 'Red Bear' had sold him a gun, a pistol, and Randy said he wasn't going to pay Red

Bear for the gun because Red Bear owed him money. Randy said that Red Bear told him that he would get him.

"Randy told me that when his wife and mother-in-law were murdered, he came home at noon for lunch and found his wife shot and a spear stabbed through her throat. Randy said that he found his mother-in-law shot and speared in the bathroom. When I tried to console him, he told me to leave him alone and let him deal with it himself."

The man then told the officers that Headrick told him that he had gone to the TNT plant on Bonnie Oaks Drive and had taken some hand grenades, as well as other explosives.

"I told Randy that it was a federal crime to go inside the TNT plant," he said. Headrick later told him that the TNT plant was like a small city, and that it had fire trucks, missiles and grenades, all kinds of explosives, just for the taking.

Headrick also told the man around sixty days prior to his arrest by the Bureau of Alcohol, Tobacco, and Firearms that the ATF was watching him.

Shane Headrick had now become a prime suspect in the murders, along with his brother, Randy. Rhonda Jackson contacted the Chamblee, Georgia, Police Department and faxed subpoenas to them to be delivered to the Lodge on Buford, where Shane and Jill were staying at the time of the murders. Again, the subpoenas were for any phone records and registrations that might enable the investigators to pin down Shane's whereabouts more closely on the day of the murders, since there had been so many phone calls to his motel room that day that had gone unanswered.

The subpoenas were delivered, and the officer who delivered them reported that the motel was cooperating fully and would search for the documents, if they still existed.

* * *

Rhonda Jackson and Jimmy Phillips were in Chattanooga again the next day at the Chattanooga Police Department, where one of the officers took them to interview Red Bear and another Headrick acquaintance who called himself "Red Hawk." Unlike Headrick's uncooperative friend Red Crow, these two men were not at all hesitant to tell the officers what they knew about Headrick.

Red Bear, a competent craft worker, said that he had met Headrick through Red Hawk in the summer of 1997, when Headrick and his wife, Tonya, had opened a Native American store on Highway 153. Red Bear went to the store and asked Headrick if he would be interested in letting him put some of his craft work in the store on consignment, which he did.

"That's how we got to know him," he said. "During the next few months, Randy made statements about the murders. He told me that his wife and mother-in-law had been killed, and said he was a suspect in the murders. He asked me if I thought he did it, and I told him that I hadn't known him long enough to make that judgment about him.

"Randy has threatened a lot of people at his store. I have heard him tell people that he had a five-gallon can of gas for that person. Randy has said that to me."

Red Bear said that he had seen a gun at Headrick's house, a .22 rifle, and Headrick told him that he had a .22 pistol, a Ruger, but Red Bear said he never saw that particular gun.

"Randy told me that his wife and mother-in-law were shot and their throats were cut; this was the only time Randy told me how they were killed. He told me that he thought it was his wife's cousin that did it and that it was drug related. He also told me that his own brother had accused him of doing the murders, and if he found him, he was going to kill his brother.

"Randy said that he knew martial arts and knew how to kill people with his hands. He asked me to go to North

Carolina with him to get his guns; we were going to kick the door in, and he said, 'If I have to, I will kill them.' Randy told me that when he was at work, that he could leave anytime he wanted and no one would know. He told me that he went into the military when he was thirteen years old, that his parents had lied about his age to get him in."

Red Bear said that Headrick never told him that he committed the murders, "but he never told me that he didn't. Randy told me that he was arrested, and told me that if they came back that he was going to take some of them out. Randy has threatened just about every crafter that I know, and I did see bruises on Tonya's face at the store, but she told me that she ran into a door."

Next up for an interview was Red Hawk, who said he met Headrick at the Native American Connection, Red Crow's store, in the fall of 1994.

"I didn't see him anymore after that for about two years, when I saw him at a gun show at the Trade Center in Chattanooga. He was buying guns. He had bought a Desert Eagle three fifty-seven Magnum. He invited me and my wife to his house for dinner."

Red Hawk said he got Headrick a job at the place where he worked.

"Randy was at a lady's house one day installing a shower door. Randy got ill because he couldn't fix it. I was going by there and stopped to check on him. Randy was cussing and throwing stuff. He threatened to 'kill the bitch.' I got him calmed down and took him outside.

"His favorite phrase was 'I've got a five-gallon can of gas with your name on it, and I know where you live.' He would say that to anyone that he got into it with."

Red Hawk said that he, Red Bear, Headrick and their wives were sitting beside the pool one evening at the apartments where Headrick lived.

"There were some Mexican men there making some lewd remarks about our wives in Spanish. Randy said he would fix that. He went upstairs and brought down a

Taurus nine-millimeter and a tomahawk and laid them down on the table. He didn't make any remarks, just plopped them down where they could see them." Since there were some children present, Red Hawk told the officers that he later covered the weapons with a towel.

Red Hawk said that Headrick had told him previously that he had put an SKS bayonet through his apartment wall because of the noise that some Mexicans were making in the apartment next door. He also bragged about his bomb-making abilities.

"We were driving one day on the job and Randy pulled out a circuit board from a garage door opener and a remote control, and asked me if I knew what he could do with them. I told him I didn't even want to hear about it. He told me he was a ranger instructor in Vietnam and was an instructor in demolition. He gave me a smoke grenade one time. I was with him about a year ago when he bought one hundred twenty or one hundred thirty dollars in nine-millimeter and three fifty-seven Magnum ammo with his credit card."

Red Hawk said that Headrick had told him he had artillery simulators and a smoke grenade, all of which were nonarmy issue, which he had more than likely obtained from mercenary magazines.

On one occasion, Red Hawk brought a friend of his, a man who was a combat veteran, to Headrick's store. The friend, after meeting Headrick and listening to him brag about his exploits, told Red Hawk in no uncertain terms that Headrick was "full of shit."

CHAPTER 41

After interviewing the two Reds, Bear and Hawk respectively, investigators Jackson and Phillips stopped by Metropolitan Security and spoke to the manager, obtaining records on all his employees who had been stationed at the Marriott. They also received Headrick's time sheet from the Marriott for the hours he worked on August 1. As they were leaving Chattanooga for the day, Jimmy Phillips and Rhonda Jackson stopped by the TBI office and made arrangements to schedule a polygraph for Terry Durham. The young man readily had agreed to take the test during his earlier statement, and the investigators wanted to leave no loose ends for attorney French to grab hold of in the courtroom, because grab them he would.

Later in the week, Jimmy Phillips and Clay Simpson returned to Chattanooga to interview a woman who had met Headrick while they were both working at the Marriott. She occasionally had talked to Headrick, she said, and he had told her that he had been married three times. When she asked him what happened to his other marriages, he said they didn't get along, so they split up. He told her that he and his current wife, Tonya, were about to break up because they didn't get along either.

"Randy was always bragging that he was rich and that he only worked to pass the time," the woman said. "He told me that he could make me a lot of money by investing in real estate with him, and he said that if someone bothered me, he would take care of them. He was always talking about throwing someone down the elevator shaft."

The woman said that she had been to Headrick's store.

"He had all kinds of guns, and he kept trying to get me to hold a pistol, and when I didn't want to, he tried to force me to hold the gun. He said that he traded merchandise for guns and traded guns all the time. He also said that if my boyfriend ever hurt me, that he would kill him."

Earlier in the investigation, a noted community leader had given a tip, saying a third party had told him about bloody clothes that had been thrown off a bridge. Rhonda Jackson wanted to know who it was that had given the man the information, so she could talk with him herself, so she and Jimmy Phillips urged the civic leader to give them the name of his informant. He agreed, providing the man's name and even drawing the officers a map to his home. It turned out to be a wasted effort, for when they arrived, the man stated flatly that he didn't know anything about the murders and then clammed up, refusing to talk to them any further.

Headrick's best alibi from Builders Supply—the worker who helped him unload his truck on July 7, 1995—was feeling the pressure of the rapidly building investigation. Officers heard a rumor that the man had told someone that the investigators hadn't asked him the right questions about everything that happened that day, so Jimmy Phillips set out to talk to him again.

The man told Phillips he didn't know anything else about the murders, other than what he had already told the investigators, and denied saying anything to anyone about having not been asked the right questions.

"I've told you everything that I know concerning this case," he said. "I didn't see Randy from about ten-thirty A.M. until around one P.M. The thing that struck me was that Randy didn't need any help with the truck. I talked to Randy and he told me that he loved his wife and mother-in-law, and then he just changed the subject.

"I can say for a fact that it was after one P.M. on Friday when I saw Randy Headrick."

CHAPTER 42

The investigators on the Headrick case were surprised to hear from Terry Durham again, on September 9, 1998, when he called the sheriff's department and told them he needed to speak to them again because he had left some information out of his previous statement. This struck the officers as not only odd, but potentially disastrous; so, they wasted no time arranging a meeting in Chattanooga, convenient to Durham's work site. Durham arrived at the TBI office that day at 2:30 P.M., and once again sat down at the table across from Rhonda Jackson and Jimmy Phillips. It had been a month since he had given them his first statement, and the stress of that month showed plainly on the young man.

"Okay, you have told us that you want to talk to us a little bit more about this case," Phillips said. "Is that true?"

Durham said it was true.

"Okay, if you would tell us what you forgot to tell us, we need to know everything that Headrick told you that morning."

Unsettled and uneasy, Durham gave the only answer he felt he could give and still be totally honest with the officers.

"I didn't *forget* to tell you anything," he said.

"You said you didn't forget to tell us anything, but you

didn't tell us all of it," Jackson said. "Can you tell us why you didn't tell us all of it the first time?"

"Because I realized, when I told y'all the first time, how much I knew that I shouldn't know, and I didn't like being in that situation," Durham answered.

"Do you feel bad about leaving this out?"

Durham, dejected and humbled, said that he did. The officers then asked him to go back over his entire conversation with Headrick, starting from the very beginning on the day it happened.

"It was a Saturday morning when I got off work," Durham said. "He came in an hour early because he'd been sitting at his store all night. Someone had tried to break into the store and he said he just decided to come on in to work. We carried on a conversation for a little bit, just small talk, and I got a call to escort a vagrant off of the sixteenth floor at the hotel. He went on the call with me to help me escort the man off the floor, and we came back down to the back dock and were standing outside talking. Then he got to talking about this murder case in Alabama.

"He asked me if I ever heard about the murders in Ider, and I said no, because I didn't know what he was talking about. He went on into a little bit of details about what had happened, and then he looked at me and he told me, 'They'll never catch who done it,' and I said why, and he said, 'Because he's standing in front of you now.'"

Phillips asked Durham to tell him exactly what kind of details Headrick went into as he talked about the murders.

"About the spears being stabbed in them and a woman being pinned to the floor or the wall, and one of them was eating watermelon, and the other one was in the bedroom, house cleaning, you know, maybe vacuuming and fixing the bed or something."

Durham said Headrick told him that the woman who was sitting eating watermelon had her back turned to the door where a person would come into the house, or into that room, and that she had been shot and speared, and the other woman was shot and speared and stabbed.

"Did he tell you who killed them?" Phillips asked.

"He told me his brother, Shane," said Durham. Headrick had told him that Shane killed Carolyn, Durham said, and that he, Headrick, had killed his mother-in-law.

"Did he tell you anything about how he got there to the house?" Phillips asked.

"He told me that he was on a run and he worked at Builders Supply, so the run, I figured, was like a delivery. But he never went there or never came back from there or something."

"Now, I don't understand what you mean," Jackson said. "He said he was supposed to be on a run or a delivery?"

"That's what they thought he was on, was a run, a delivery. He didn't have one."

Phillips asked if Headrick had told Durham where he hooked up with Shane.

"I can't remember if his brother was already at the house or if he picked his brother up; I don't really think he ever said that."

"But he never told you that he went and picked Shane up and they went there together?" asked Phillips.

"No," Durham said, "I know they left together."

Phillips asked what kind of vehicle they left in, and Durham said he thought, when Headrick told him that he had worked for Builders Supply, that he meant a ton truck or delivery truck.

"That's what I thought he was talking about, was a truck, because you can't haul stuff in the back of a car."

Durham said Headrick didn't tell him an exact time as to how long he and Shane had stayed at the house, but told him that the murders took place around 12:30 P.M.

"He told you that?" Phillips asked.

"Around twelve-thirty," Durham repeated.

Phillips asked if Headrick had mentioned anything about why he thought there was no evidence that could link him to the murders.

"He burnt all the clothes that they had on and he had plastic in the seat and all that," Durham said.

"Did he tell you one of the things that we couldn't prove is that he was at work all day?" asked Phillips.

"He said he had an hour, one hour, that y'all couldn't account for where he was at," Durham said, "but the rest of that he said he had an alibi for."

Durham told the officers that Headrick had told him that the time he couldn't be accounted for was from about 11:55 A.M. until 12:55 P.M.

"Did he say there was anybody else involved?" Jackson asked.

"Him and his brother, and that his dad is the one that told them to burn the stuff. To burn the clothes in a barn."

"And that's Randy's dad, right?" asked Phillips.

"As far as I know," Durham answered. "I mean, he said 'Dad.' Yeah."

The officers asked Durham if he was certain that he never saw anything about the murders at the time they happened, on television or in the newspapers.

"The reason I asked you that is because I need to know if you've read anything or seen anything on TV. This was a highly publicized case—it was in the paper; it was on TV; it was an everyday thing there for a while."

Durham said he couldn't remember seeing or hearing about the case.

"I'll be honest with you," he said, "at the time y'all said this happened in '95, I had just got married; I wasn't reading no newspaper, you know?"

CHAPTER 43

Once again, Terry Durham patiently explained how he came to contact the investigators for the first time after his sister-in-law told him about the murders and said that he needed to get in touch with them. His sister-in-law was at his house, he said, and they were talking about the issue of sin.

"She asked me if I thought you could be forgiven for sin if you went out and killed somebody, and I said, 'No.' I said I didn't think that if you went out and killed somebody in cold blood, that you'd be forgiven for it. So, then she had said something about a murder at Ider."

When his sister-in-law mentioned Headrick's name, Durham said that at first he didn't know the person she was talking about.

"I didn't know him as Headrick, I knew him as Randy, because I never knew his last name. I started telling what I knew about it; you know, I told her, 'Well, yeah, he done this, he done that,' and she said, 'You need to go talk to Jimmy.' So, I volunteered to come talk with y'all."

"And now we're back up here in Chattanooga talking to you again," Phillips said, "and you intentionally left some details out for a reason."

"I left some of it out," Durham said, "because I'm getting to the point where I'm not trusting people. I trust y'all, but I'm at the point to where I know too much, and don't want to know this much."

"From my understanding, by talking to you," Jackson said, "you said that people are harassing you at work about different things and that sort of thing, right?"

"Yeah," Durham said. "They won't leave me alone about wanting to know what I said to y'all, and some of them, you know, just kinda joke around about it. It don't bother me, but people keep going, 'What have you said to them? What have you said to them?' And, you know, I don't like it. It's come to the point to where the man over where I work, he's going to get rid of me."

Jackson mentioned to Durham that he had told her before the interview began that there was more to his conversation about the .22 pistol than he had told the officers to start with.

"He asked me if I wanted to buy a twenty-two pistol. I told him I didn't have no use for a twenty-two pistol, and he said it was unmarked or unregistered, no serial numbers on it. And I told him I didn't have no use for it, and he said he could sell it to me cheap, and I told him again that I didn't need it."

This, he said, had taken place prior to their conversation about the murders.

"Did he say anything about where that pistol was, or where he had it, or anything?" Jackson asked.

"Not that I can remember. The only thing he ever told me he had at his store was Tasers and stuff like that, you know."

"Did he tell you he dealt in guns at the store?" Phillips asked.

"He told me he could; if I wanted one, he could get one. He gave me a book that morning, a surplus book; anything in it, he said he could get, that I wanted. He said he could get me police issues, Tasers and all kinds of stuff."

"Let's go back to what he told you about the actual murders," Jackson said. "He told you that his brother,

Shane, helped him, and that Shane was the one who killed his wife?"

"That's what he told me," Durham said. "She was in the bedroom cleaning, and she ran to the bathroom, and she was killed in the bathroom. I believe she's the one that was . . . ah . . . stuck to the floor or the wall, one of the two."

"Did he tell you who they killed first?" Phillips asked.

"The only thing he ever said was the lady at the table was sitting; if you walked into the room, she was sitting with her back kinda toward you, and he said he speared the lady at the table and the lady in the bathroom."

"And he told you he did that," Jackson said.

"Yes, that he speared them."

Phillips spoke up and asked Durham why, if Headrick thought he had committed the perfect murder, would he have told someone whom he didn't know all that well about it?

"I don't know," Durham said. "I honestly think he's crazy. I mean, he's always had one of those strange looks on his face."

"The reason why I asked that," Phillips said, "is because a guy that's committed two murders; you know, it just doesn't make any sense for him to go out and just pick somebody to tell about these murders."

Durham thought for a moment. "The best thing I can figure out is that he knew what I did at work, he knew I let people slide with stuff; he probably thought I wouldn't say nothing. I just came off, I guess, as a person at work where—"

"Don't screw me and I won't screw you?" said Phillips.

"Yeah, yeah."

The investigators asked Durham if there was anything else he had left out about Headrick, and he told them he didn't think he'd left anything else out, but said he'd like to think about it and write everything down so he could keep up with what he had said. He also told them again that he'd been having problems at work and at his home because of his involvement.

"It's just right now I've got so many people at work bothering me that I'm getting to the point to where I don't want to say nothing to nobody. I try to keep my mouth shut; I'm in it too deep and I want out of it."

"Do you feel like you're in danger by talking to us?" Jackson asked.

"Yeah," Durham said. "There's people already where I work; they don't know that I've come and give statements and stuff, but they know I'm the one that's talking."

Phillips asked if Durham had been threatened at work in any manner.

"Physical threats, no. But as far as people calling just wanting to know if I'm at work, what time I'm getting off, hanging up, coming to the house beating on the door and leaving, and people hanging around the house."

Phillips asked if those incidents had just started since the time Durham had given his first statement, up until that day.

"Well, the phone calls came about a week before I talked to y'all. It's getting to the point to where I can't get no sleep at the house. I'm having to stay up two or three hours a night just to watch for people. My landlords know some strange things are going on at my house."

"Let me ask you one more thing," Jackson said. "Let's go back to what Randy told you about Shane helping him, and you said that his wife ran to the bathroom. Did he say why she ran to the bathroom?"

"No, I don't know," Durham said. "I'd run to the bathroom too, I guess. I'd be scared or something, but all I know is that she run to the bathroom to hide. That's all he said, was she run to the bathroom to hide."

"And then he told you Shane went in and killed her and then he came in and speared her."

Durham said yes, that was what he had been told.

The investigators asked again if there was anything else Durham could think of that he also might have left out of his initial statement, and he promised to be in touch if he remembered any more details of what he had

been told. The interview ended, but before it could be
transcribed and copied, news came into the sheriff's
office that a barn located behind Dora Ann Dalton's
house had burned.

CHAPTER 44

It had been a while since Rhonda Jackson had made the trip up to Shady Lane. Besides the pile of burned timbers that lay smoldering in the woods behind the house, where Carolyn and Dora Ann had been murdered, little had changed. The neighbors were able to tell her what they had seen on the night the barn burned. Fire trucks responded to the fire, they said, and one woman said she didn't know the barn was burning until the fire trucks started pulling in. They thought the barn might not have burned accidentally, but there was no proof the fire had been intentional. The barn was now owned by a couple from the Chattanooga area, and they were expected to be at the property on Labor Day, September 7, so Jackson asked the neighbors to have them call her.

Jackson got some interesting information by coincidence when a man she was talking to about the burned barn told her that he went by Headrick's parents' home about a month after the murders and saw Headrick digging a hole in the backyard. Around two weeks later, the man said, Headrick put up a pup tent over the hole.

Rhonda Jackson also spoke to one of the Dalton relatives while she was there, and told the young man that she had heard he was still very upset and scared about the murders. He told her he wasn't having problems with it now, but said that he did when it first happened because he had heard that it was intended to be his mother who would be killed.

On Labor Day, 1998, the owner of the burned barn called Rhonda at home and told her that her son-in-law had cleaned up the barn in October 1997. He buried part of the stuff, she said, and piled the rest up in a pile. Whatever evidence, if any, might have possibly still been in the barn was now reduced to ashes.

Over the Labor Day weekend, while reading over a stack of some of the early statements from witnesses, an idea came to Rhonda and she pursued it immediately when she got back to work on Tuesday morning. She called Donnie Watkins, the man who, along with his wife, had seen the red pickup truck leaving the Dalton home at a high rate of speed on the day of the murders.

"Do you folks go by 'fast time' or 'slow time?'" she asked him. The Alabama/Georgia state line is the boundary between the Eastern and Central time zones, and some residents of north DeKalb County who live very near the state line often go by Eastern time, especially if they work, do most of their business, or go to school just over the state line into Georgia.

Watkins told Rhonda that he went by "fast time," meaning that the time frame he and his wife had given for when they saw the red truck was in Eastern time. This made their estimate of the time frame within which they saw the red truck an hour later than the time it actually was in the Central time zone, and placed the possible time of the murders an hour earlier than the authorities' previous estimate. Watkins also said that he and his wife had talked about the truck they saw leaving that day. They had driven by the residence the day after the murders, and said the truck that was sitting under the carport looked just like the one they saw leaving the house the day before.

Another area Rhonda Jackson readdressed was the fire that burned Headrick's ex-girlfriend's home and the investigation of that incident, which had been conducted by Investigator Tommy Holt, of the Jackson County Sheriff's Department. Jackson and Jimmy Phillips looked through Holt's file on the case and made copies of forensic reports, and Holt let them have the originals of a card, an envelope and a sheet of paper that contained the ring that was mailed to the former girlfriend after the fire. Phillips called the fire marshal who had worked the case, and he arranged to meet with him the following day to let the DeKalb officers look at his file on the arson case.

September 14 was a busy day for all the investigators on the Headrick case, packed with interviews, phone calls and errands. Rhonda Jackson began her day by serving a subpoena on a local tax and bookkeeping service for their records on some business they had done for Headrick and his former girlfriend. She was able to obtain copies of an agreement signed by Headrick and the woman, with Headrick waiving all parental rights to the woman's unborn child. Also in their files was a will, handwritten by Randy Headrick, leaving his house, furnishings, land, monies and insurance to the ex-girlfriend's oldest child with her husband.

While she was in the area, Rhonda stopped by the Henagar Police Department and spoke to two of their officers who were distant relatives of Headrick's. One of the men had been working as a dispatcher since 1994 and up until the time of the murders in 1995, and said that Headrick had been a frequent visitor to the police department.

"He would talk about being in Vietnam," the officer said. "He told me one time about running down a pig trail and a gook jumped out in front of him. Randy said he stabbed him with his bayonet and picked him up off the ground with it while he was still running, and slung him to the side. Randy said something about looking into his eyes as he stabbed him.

"He talked about getting cow skulls and letting the meat rot off of them and then painting them. He talked about when he was in prison and said they had to move him from prison to prison because he would whip everybody there. He said he was a lethal weapon, that he could kill anybody with his bare hands."

The officer said that he had been promoted from dispatcher to a part-time patrol officer in July of 1994, then went full-time in January 1995.

"Someone came and got a warrant on Jill Shrader. I went up to Shane and Jill's trailer on Highway seventy-five to arrest her, and when I got out of my car, a gun went off in the backyard. It was dark and I couldn't see. In a minute, Shane came out of the front door and I asked him what the gunfire in the backyard was about. He told me he shot a TV in the backyard, and was trying his gun out. He said he had a small-caliber handgun, but I didn't see it."

The other Headrick relative who worked in the Henagar Police Department told much the same story as the first man.

"Before his wife and mother-in-law were killed, Randy used to come into the police department quite a bit and hang out. He would talk a lot about being in Vietnam and how he did a lot of hand-to-hand combat and how he killed a bunch of people while he was in Vietnam. He talked about when he got arrested in Texas for the weapons violations, and said that the police came and took his gun collection, which he claimed was over one hundred guns.

"I haven't been around Randy very much. He moved to Texas when I was small and didn't move back here until he got out of prison."

Yet another former Henagar police officer, who had gone to work as a sheriff's deputy in January 1995, was interviewed at the sheriff's department. He reported some of the things he had heard Headrick say while visiting the police department.

"Randy Headrick usually came into the Henagar Police Department about twice a week when I worked there in '94," the deputy said. "He talked about his military background and being in Vietnam and all the training he had and how he could kill people with his bare hands. He

talked about the Indian artifacts he was making out of
skulls, and he brought a few of those to the police department and showed them to us.

"He talked about being arrested in Texas for having an
unregistered firearm. I asked him how he got 'unregistered firearm' out of a pipe bomb; I had heard it was a
pipe bomb. He got mad about it. We would rag him
about it because we would catch him in a lie. He told us
when he got arrested that the police took his guns, which
I assumed was several from the way he indicated it."

Jimmy Phillips learned that one of the life insurance
policies Headrick had taken out on his wife, with Union
Labor Life Insurance Company, had been paid to him on
February 11, 1997, in the amount of $101,315.04. The
company representative that he spoke with agreed to
send copies of the records on the policy to him at the sheriff's department.

The evidence against Randy and Shane Headrick was
piling up with increasing speed. Interestingly, most of the
case against Shane was being made from statements that
had been uttered by his own brother, Randy, who thoroughly implicated Shane at every opportunity—without
any hesitation whatsoever. Betrayal of his own brother was
of no concern to him.

CHAPTER 45

The investigators' offices were not the only place where hectic activity regarding the case against Randy Headrick was taking place. District Attorney Mike O'Dell and his staff were rapidly preparing to make a major move in the case, and Rhonda Jackson and her fellow officers hurried to get the final pieces of the puzzle in place so that O'Dell would have everything he needed to proceed as he and his team planned.

On September 15, Rhonda Jackson and Jimmy Phillips went to the Jackson County Sheriff's Department and met with the deputy state fire marshal to look through his file and make copies of any pertinent information on the suspicious fire that burned Headrick's former girlfriend's home.

Rhonda also interviewed a man who had sold the ex-girlfriend a class ring, which she later sent back for repairs. The man also worked at Earthgrains bakery and knew Headrick and the woman were seeing each other.

"Randy came in and said she wanted him to pick up the ring for her, so I let him have it," he said. "He didn't sign anything."

The woman called later and asked about the ring, but Headrick had it and hadn't signed a receipt when he supposedly picked it up for her.

The names of two women, both former Earthgrains employees, had been given to Rhonda Jackson, with the information that they were well-acquainted with Randy Headrick and had talked to him often when they worked together. Rhonda met with the first woman at the Rainsville Police Department, where she questioned her about her knowledge of Headrick and what his behavior had been when she worked with him.

"I used to work at Earthgrains during the same time Randy Headrick worked there," she said. "Randy collected stamps and he brought a few to work, which I saw. He said he and his wife were having problems. He said she didn't like to have sex. He specifically stated that she didn't like oral sex. He said he was going to sell his stamp collection and get a lot of money, and then divorce Carolyn.

"He used to talk about being in Vietnam. He would talk about seeing bodies and seeing people die in bamboo traps.

"Randy implied that he thought me and another woman at Earthgrains had a lot of class. He said if either one of us would, he would take us out. I knew that Randy and his ex-girlfriend had an affair. I knew she had an affair with another man before Randy. I know Randy gave another woman at Earthgrains an engraved ink pen. I don't think she ever went out with Randy. She thought he was strange. I know his ex-girlfriend's house burned and she thought Randy did it."

Rhonda interviewed the other woman by phone, since she had moved to Arkansas. She said she had worked at Earthgrains for about three years, starting in 1992.

"I knew Randy and that woman had an affair," she said. "I tried to warn her not to have anything to do with him, but she wouldn't listen. I thought Randy was weird, and I was half-afraid of him. He came over to my house several times, and he brought me a hamburger once when I was sick. My husband was there at the time.

"Randy flirted with me, but he never asked me out. I

never had anything with him but friendship. He gave me a small green tennis bracelet; it didn't have any diamonds, and I don't know if it was real or not. He also gave me an amber-colored decanter and an engraved pen set.

"He talked about being in Vietnam and having a steel plate in his head."

September 17, 1998, was a milestone in the case against Randy Headrick and brother Shane. District Attorney O'Dell and his staff had made all the necessary preparations to move forward, and on that day a special session of the DeKalb County grand jury was called by circuit judge Randall Cole. The grand jury assembled at the DeKalb County Courthouse at 8:30 A.M. to hear the evidence against the Headrick brothers. Fifteen grand jurors listened as the district attorney's team presented their reasons why they believed the two men should be held responsible for the deaths of Carolyn Headrick and Dora Ann Dalton. The grand jury's foreman, Robert W. McCord, was a well-known and highly respected man in the county, a retired teacher who was an outstanding leader and organizer. Within a fairly short time, the grand jury decided that capital murder indictments would be returned against Randy and Shane Headrick.

William Randall Headrick was indicted on three counts, the first being that he intentionally caused the death of Carolyn and Dora Ann by shooting them with a gun, "in violation of the Code of Alabama, contrary to law and against the peace and dignity of the State of Alabama."

The second count charged Headrick with murdering Carolyn Headrick by "shooting her with a gun for a pecuniary or other valuable consideration, to-wit: life insurance proceeds."

The third count charged that William Randall Headrick "did solicit, request, command, or importune Waylon Shane Headrick to engage in conduct constituting the crime of murder."

Randy Headrick had been indicted for murder of two or more persons, murder for consideration or for hire, and criminal solicitation. A writ of arrest was issued, and although he was currently being held without bail at the Etowah County Jail on his federal firearms violation, Judge Randall Cole ordered there to be no bail in connection with his DeKalb County case.

Waylon Shane Headrick was indicted by the grand jury on three counts. The first count stated that he intentionally caused the deaths of Carolyn and Dora Ann by shooting them with a gun, and the second count stated that he caused their deaths by shooting them with a gun for a pecuniary or other valuable consideration. His third indictment was for murder of two or more persons, and murder for consideration or for hire.

The day of the grand jury indictments of Randy and Shane Headrick was the biggest day, up to that point, of Rhonda Jackson's career in law enforcement. After more than four years of painstaking work to find enough evidence that would bring about the indictments of Carolyn and Dora Ann's killers, Jackson saw that Randy and Shane Headrick were finally going to be brought to justice. All the nights of lying awake, praying for that critical break in the case, had finally ended, and Rhonda felt she had proved herself to the sheriff, the district attorney and her coworkers. They all could have told her, however, that there had never been a doubt in any of their minds that she could, and would, do the job, and do it well. She had always had their respect as well as their admiration.

There was still a lot of work ahead for Jackson and her team, but from this point on, that work would take on a new focus. The frustration of not being able to prove Randy Headrick's guilt had now been replaced with the satisfaction of knowing he would finally be held accountable for the brutal, murderous betrayal of his wife and mother-in-law.

There still existed some degree of doubt as to the extent of Shane's involvement, largely due to the fact that the bulk of the evidence against him had come from his brother, Randy. Randy's seemingly intentional implication of Shane could quite possibly fall into the same category as his claims of Vietnam heroism and his ability to commit murder and "get away with it."

On September 18, Rhonda Jackson and Jimmy Phillips flew to Arlington, Texas, where they met homicide detectives from the Arlington Police Department. They arrested Shane Headrick at his home at 4:05 P.M., only fifteen minutes after investigators Mike James and Clay Simpson had the satisfaction of serving the indictment on Randy Headrick at the Etowah County Jail back in Alabama.

CHAPTER 46

With Shane Headrick in custody and booked into the Arlington jail, Rhonda Jackson and Jimmy Phillips advised him of his rights before any questioning took place. Shane chose to waive his rights and agreed to make a statement and answer questions without the presence of a lawyer.

Shane insisted that he had told the investigators the truth, and said that he'd cooperated with them all along.

Jackson began the interview. "I asked him if it was still true what he said before, that if he did it he doesn't remember it. I asked him what that meant. He said, 'I don't know.'"

Shane said that he didn't remember what he'd said at the TBI office about seeing the murders like a dream. Rhonda asked him how he could explain failing the polygraph he took at that time if he didn't have anything to do with the murders. He told her that he guessed it was because he was nervous.

Phillips asked Shane why he took Jill to work and kept the truck on the day of the murders, and he said it was because he wanted to work on it.

"How are we going to prove where you were that day?" Phillips asked.

"I don't know," Shane said. "I went to the laundry

room that day at the motel, and I was at the pool, laying out in the corner. A white girl with a black baby was there, but I didn't talk to her."

Jackson reminded him that he had previously told the investigators that he had talked to the girl at the pool, but Shane said that she might not even have seen him that day. Then Jackson asked him if he had been using drugs that day. He admitted that he might have smoked a joint in the motel room.

Jackson then began firing a series of rapid questions at Shane:

"Did you shoot them? Did you kill Carolyn? Did you kill Dora Ann? Were you there? Did you drive?"

Shane answered no to all those questions.

"Where were you that day?"

"Atlanta."

"Did you go to Alabama that day?"

"No."

"Did you rent a truck?"

"No."

Jackson asked Shane why he got so upset and became violent with Jill when she would bring up the murders and question him about them. He said that he didn't get mad at first, but she kept bringing it up and he got mad then. When asked what he had told his new girlfriend, whom he was living with at that time, about the murders, he said that he didn't tell her much; she didn't want to know.

Shane was in tears, crying several times during the interview, but he still claimed that he didn't have anything to do with the murders. Jackson wrote out a short statement, including a sentence stating that he would sign a waiver of extradition. Then Shane asked if he could call his girlfriend before he signed it. After a ten-minute conversation, he told the investigators that he wanted to stay in Texas until his baby was born, in around thirty days.

Jackson wrote out another statement, which said he was not willing to sign a waiver of extradition. The second statement read, "I've told the truth. I don't have anything else to add. If I killed those two women, I don't remember it."

Shane had a problem with the wording of that statement, specifically the sentence "If I killed those two women, I don't remember it." A third statement was written that said, "I've told the truth. I did not kill Carolyn or Dora Ann. I didn't have anything to do with their deaths. At this time, I'm not willing to sign a waiver of extradition." He found that statement satisfactory and signed it.

When the investigators went to Shane's home to interview his pregnant girlfriend, she was understandably very upset about the situation and was rather hostile toward the officers. She said that Shane had told her that he didn't have anything to do with the murders, and she also said he had told her it wouldn't surprise him if Randy did it.

"I know Shane didn't have anything to do with this," she said.

Rhonda asked her how she could be certain about that—unless she had been with Shane on the day of the murders. Of course, she had to say that she had not been.

"This is all Jill's fault," the woman said. She claimed that she had a letter from Jill in which she had threatened them, and that Jill had come to another Headrick relative's house and threatened the people there with a gun.

"I know Jill is trying to get the reward money," she insisted.

The investigators wanted to locate and interview Randy Headrick's first wife, but she had moved from Arlington to an address in Dallas. The Arlington detectives said her new address had checked out to be that of an office building instead of a residence, so Jackson was unable to make contact with her.

When she called home that evening to check in with her family, Rhonda's husband told her that Jill Shrader had called and left a message on the answering machine saying that someone had threatened her. Rhonda tried to contact Jill at her home several times before she and

Jimmy Phillips left Texas, but could never get an answer. When Rhonda got back home to Alabama, Jill called her again and they talked about the alleged threats. Rhonda tried to soothe Jill's ruffled feathers and keep the situation in Texas as peaceable as she could. There was more than enough trouble in DeKalb County to keep the investigators occupied.

The following morning, Rhonda Jackson returned to her tiny, cramped office upstairs at the sheriff's department. She sat down at her desk, opened a drawer and pulled out two Alabama Uniform Incident/Offense reports. On each, she wrote the case number, time and date, and the victim's name: Dora Ann Dalton, on one sheet, and Carolyn Jean Headrick, on the other. On both forms, she listed the criminal offense as "murder" and wrote the defendants' names, William Randall Headrick and Waylon Shane Headrick. The original offense date was noted, as was the date of their arrests. Then Jackson had the tremendous satisfaction of finally writing, in bold script across the center of the form, **"Case Closed by Arrest."**

CHAPTER 47

The investigators had all worked long and hard to assemble enough statements and interview transcripts to convince the grand jury to indict Randy and Shane Headrick. Now their attention turned to finding even more information to help the district attorney and his staff build a solid case to take to the courtroom.

On September 23, 1998, a man came forward with a note he had found on his porch the night before, around nine o'clock. The note was from a Headrick family member, and was intended to be for the man's wife. It gave two different phone numbers where the family member could be reached, and said, "Please call. We're all being framed."

The man's wife was at work, so he returned the call. The relative said the sheriff's department had framed Randy Headrick, and wanted to know what time the man's wife and son had gone to Builders Supply and talked to Headrick on the day of the murders.

"I told her I thought Randy had an alibi at work," the man said, "but [the person I called] said that the sheriff's department had intimidated that witness."

The man turned the note over to Rhonda Jackson.

In order to get details on Headrick's truck lease, the investigators called the owner of Harbin Ford in Scottsboro.

He told them that William Randall Headrick had signed a two-year lease on February 25, 1995, on a red Ford F-150 pickup. The payments on the lease were $248.57 a month.

Shane's alleged involvement in the murders was still not pinned down quite as tightly as the district attorney and the investigators would like for it to be. Jimmy Phillips knew Jill's mother, and he talked to her in an attempt to find out what contact she'd had with Shane on the day of the murders.

"My husband called Mr. Headrick, Randy's father, four or five days before the murders to let him know that he was going to pick Jill's car up for her. My husband didn't call Mr. Headrick the day of the murders and tell him he was coming to get the car. A friend called my husband and told him about the murders, and told him not to come and get the car because the lady had been murdered.

"I tried to call Jill in Atlanta all day on the day of the murders. I didn't get hold of her that day, and I tried again on Saturday and was unable to contact them in Atlanta. I tried again on Sunday morning and Shane answered the phone. I asked him if he knew what was going on on Sand Mountain, and he said he hadn't heard from anyone on Sand Mountain. I then told him his sister-in-law and her mother had been murdered. Shane's response to this was 'Well,' and I told him to have Jill to call me back.

"In about five minutes, Jill called back and she was real upset and crying. Jill told me, to the best of my memory, that Shane was expecting it. I then told Jill not to go back over there with Shane, and she said that the people where she was would take her over there.

"I told her to get her clothes and come home, but she didn't."

There were so many different accounts, from so many different sources, on how Shane had first learned of the murders of Carolyn and Dora Ann, that it was going to take some time and effort to try and sort them out. The investigators knew that the timeline of events in Atlanta on the day of the murders was vital to proving Shane's involvement . . . or proving his innocence.

As for Randy Headrick, still cooling his heels in the Etowah County Jail, he'd had enough of his current accommodations and was ready to make a move. On October 13, he signed a Consent to Transfer of Case for Plea and Sentencing.

The consent read, "I, William Randall Headrick, defendant, have been informed that an indictment is pending against me in the above designated case." (Referring to the federal firearms charges brought against him by the ATF in the United States District Court for the Eastern District of Tennessee.) "I wish to plead guilty to the offenses charged and to consent to the disposition of the case in the Northern District of Alabama, in which I am under arrest, and to waive trial in the above captioned District."

Headrick would now wait to be transferred to the DeKalb County Jail, where he most likely hoped visitation would be more convenient for his family. Life in the jail, however, would be no bed of roses.

CHAPTER 48

The following day, Rhonda Jackson got a tip from a man in the Dalton family that someone else might be involved in the murders. He gave Jackson the name of the woman who gave him the information, and the following day Rhonda and Jackson County investigator Doyle York were on the woman's doorstep in Scottsboro.

The woman was willing to tell the officers what she knew, but there was apparently a great deal of alcohol involved in connection with her story, and her memory was rather blurred.

"I met Bubba in 1995, at Hunter's Lounge in Scottsboro, and we became friends. He came by my house a lot. He came by one night and was drinking. I don't remember how the conversation got started, but he told me that Randy Headrick asked him to participate in his wife's murder. They were riding around drinking when this conversation took place. They were on Sand Mountain. He told him no, that he drinks, but he's not like that. He thought Headrick was kidding.

"I don't know if it was at the same time or not, but he said he was driving by the lady's house and heard a gunshot and thought, 'Oh no, they've done it.'"

The investigators went straight to the Jackson County Jail, where Bubba was currently being housed. He was

flabbergasted to hear of his friend's account of their ine-
briated conversation.

"I dated her in 1996," he told the officers. "I used to
go to her house quite often and we would get drunk. I
don't remember saying anything to her about the Headrick murders. I don't know Randy or Shane Headrick. I've
never rode around with them. They never asked me to
participate in the murders. If I said these things to her,
I must have been so stoned that I don't remember.

"I didn't have anything to do with these murders. I told
her about someone shooting at me at Henagar in September or October of 1997. Maybe she got that mixed up. I
don't remember saying anything about the murders."

This was apparently yet another case of too much alcohol leading to tall tales and half-imagined stories,
which had plagued the investigation since its beginning.

During the first week of November, Shane Headrick was
transported to the DeKalb County Jail from the Dallas-Fort
Worth, Texas, detention facility, where he had spent the
time since his September arrest. Randy Headrick, after
pleading guilty to his federal firearms charges in Tennessee and waiving a trial, was still in the Etowah County
Jail waiting for the judgment in that case so that he could
then be transferred to DeKalb County.

Another busy holiday season full of thefts, DUIs,
wifebeatings and child abuse came and went for the investigators, and the new year brought continuing progress
in the Headrick case.

Judgment was set in Randy Headrick's federal firearms
case. He was ordered to pay an assessment of $450 to the
court and sentenced to twenty-one months for each of the
counts against him, to run concurrently. The way was now
clear for his transfer, but it would not come as soon as he
had hoped.

On January 8, 1999, DeKalb County Circuit Court judge
David A. Rains issued an order to transport Headrick for
an arraignment in the murder cases against him. Headrick's arraignment was set for January 14 at 1:30 P.M. in the

third-floor courtroom of the DeKalb County Courthouse. Judge Rains ordered the DeKalb County sheriff to arrange the transportation of Headrick from the custody of the Etowah County sheriff to the DeKalb County Jail. However, Judge Rains ordered that at the conclusion of the arraignment, Headrick would be returned to Etowah County.

Shortly after the arraignment, a Fort Payne city police detective, Andy Hairston, called to tell Rhonda Jackson that Tonya Headrick, Randy's wife, had landed herself in the Fort Payne City Jail for three days on a DUI charge and had made some statements to another inmate about the murders. The woman told Hairston that Tonya had said that her husband had killed his ex-wife and mother-in-law. He had shot them and stabbed them. Hairston brought Tonya out of her cell and was going to talk to her, but she told him she didn't want to make a statement without her lawyer present. Back into the cell she went.

Four days later, on January 12, Jackson, Phillips and Simpson went to the Fort Payne City Jail and interviewed all six women currently in the jail about anything they might have heard Tonya Headrick say about the murders.

One of the women was clearly not impressed with Mrs. Headrick's histrionics.

"I was in the jail cell next to her while she was in here," she said. "She was high when they put her in jail. She was screaming and hollering about her civil rights being violated, and that they had removed her medicine bag from around her neck. I never heard her make any comment about the double homicide at Henagar. She didn't make any statements that I heard about her husband, except that she had just got back from Birmingham, where her husband had gotten off of some gun charges."

Investigator Clay Simpson reinterviewed the woman who had told Hairston that Tonya Headrick had told her that her husband had committed the murders. She told Simpson that she had been arrested on January 8 and was put in a cell with Tonya Headrick. Tonya told her, she said, that she was married to Randy Headrick and that she and her husband's lawyer had "been out partying," celebrating because Headrick had only received a twenty-one-month sentence on his federal weapons charges.

"She told me that Randy Headrick had murdered the two women at Henagar, and had gotten by with the murders. I asked her if he had committed the murders, and she said yes, he did, but the police would not be able to prove that he did them."

CHAPTER 49

Shane Headrick had taken a polygraph back in April 1996, and during a meeting with the DeKalb County investigators, the TBI polygraph examiner discovered that some admissions made by Shane during his pre-polygraph interview had not been documented. Those statements were put into the record and added to the DeKalb County case files.

The examiner stated that Shane said his brother, Randy Headrick, had asked him to kill Dora Ann and Carolyn. Shane said Randy told him he wanted them shot, their tongues cut out and they be left with a spear in them. Shane said he told his brother he would not do it.

At one point during the interview, Shane began sobbing and said he didn't remember being involved in the murders. However, if he had been, he didn't remember it. He said it seemed as though he could see the murders taking place, but it appeared as though it was in a dream. He said that he could see a lot of blood at the house.

Investigator Mike James had been present during the pre-polygraph interview, and he heard Shane say, "I am not saying that I did not do this, but I am saying that if I did, I do not remember it."

Later on during the interview, James remembered hearing Shane state, "I can see it like it was a dream, but

I can't see myself in the dream, but there was a lot of blood. I just don't think that I could have done it."

Despite the grand jury indictment, Rhonda Jackson was not entirely satisfied with the amount of proof that had been gathered on Shane Headrick's involvement. The lion's share of information had come from his brother, Randy Headrick, who seemed to have set out to implicate Shane in the murders of Carolyn and Dora Ann. Jackson was determined to find everything she could to either confirm Shane's guilt or clear him of the charges against him.

On January 19, Jackson called the Chamblee, Georgia, Police Department to contact one of their officers and enlist help in once again obtaining detailed motel records from the Lodge on Buford, where Shane Headrick and Jill Shrader had stayed at the time of the murders. The officer, Captain Dave Perkins, contacted the motel and made arrangements for one of their staff to research all of their back records that were still in existence.

When the records were assembled, Jackson and Phillips went to Chamblee and met with Captain Perkins to obtain the registration cards from the motel for the time period requested. They then went to the motel to speak with the manager, who looked up further registration information for them. The officers took possession of registration records for all those motel customers who checked out between July 7 and July 15, 1995. According to the manager, all outgoing calls from the motel were recorded by computer, but there was no record made of incoming calls.

The investigators asked about a lady who did the laundry for the motel, for Shane had told them that he talked to her on the day of the murders. The manager told them there was no one currently working at the motel who had been employed in their laundry in 1995, and unless they had a name to work with, there would be no way of locating her.

The night manager, who was working at the motel in 1995, said that he didn't remember having any contact with Shane Headrick. Captain Perkins checked local police records and found there had been no contact with Shane or Jill by the police during their stay at the motel in Chamblee, and Jackson photographed the motel before she and Jimmy Phillips returned to Alabama.

One of the things District Attorney O'Dell requested from Rhonda was that she ask a member of the Dalton family to put down in writing a detailed account of how things were between Carolyn, Dora Ann and Randy Headrick in the time leading up to the murders and immediately afterward. This, he believed, would give him a clearer picture of what the last days of Carolyn and Dora Ann's lives were like, and what led up to the murders. He felt it would help him mount a solid prosecution. On February 9, 1999, Rhonda received a long letter that painted a sad picture of dashed hopes, betrayal and disappointment.

The relative said that Carolyn was a kind, gentle woman who never bothered anyone. She could not drive, did not work except as a caregiver, and had never been married. Carolyn was the oldest of Dora Ann's children, and the rest of the family agreed that it seemed as if life had pretty much passed her by. She was very timid and never went anywhere except shopping or to church. Carolyn had devoted her life to taking care of her mother, and they depended greatly on each other. Then one day the neighbor's son Randy Headrick moved in across the street with his parents, and he and Carolyn got acquainted. After seeing one another for a few months, Carolyn fell in love with him and they got married.

At first, the relative said, Headrick was as good as anyone could be to Carolyn and Dora Ann. The Dalton family all knew that he was on probation, but Carolyn believed him when he said he was innocent of the crime he'd been convicted of. The family accepted him because Carolyn loved him and they wanted her to be happy. When the parole officer came by, Carolyn and Dora Ann had only good things to say about him. Then his parole ended, and he began to change.

Headrick began to go for weeks without speaking to Dora Ann, bragging to the family about it, as though it were a game. He told the family that he had to treat Dora Ann that way, but never gave any reason for it. Dora Ann insisted that it didn't bother her as long as he was good to Carolyn.

The first thing that aroused the family's suspicion about Headrick's intentions was when he brought home a life insurance application from Earthgrains. The policy was on him, he told Carolyn, but he needed her signature. Carolyn was innocent about such matters, and didn't even question him about why her signature would be required on a policy that was for him. When the policy came in the mail, it was in Carolyn's name. She called a family member and said the life insurance company had made a mistake and issued the policy in her name instead of Headrick's. The relative suggested that she call the insurance company and have them check the application, and when she did, she was told that no mistake had been made. The application had been filled out and submitted in Carolyn's name. When Randy was questioned about it, he told her the insurance company had made a mistake, and she never mentioned it to him again.

Dora Ann had a savings account in her name and the relative's name, and she received a statement in the mail every month. One day, Randy picked up the statement and said, "See, Carolyn, your mother doesn't trust you enough to even have your name on her bank account. She has this other person's name on it, and you are the one who takes care of her." This wasn't news to Randy; he'd seen the bank statement many times since he and Carolyn were married. On this occasion, though, he made such an issue out of it that Carolyn told her mother about it. Soon Dora Ann went to the bank and closed out her account. She gave the money to Carolyn, who, in turn, opened another savings account in her name, but made the relative the beneficiary of her account. From then on, when the statements came, they came in Carolyn's name.

When Carolyn and Randy married, the relative said there was an understanding that they would live with Dora Ann. Carolyn told Randy that her father had wanted her to have the place if anything ever happened to Dora Ann, because she was the only one of the siblings that didn't already have a home of her own. Carolyn let Randy know that Dora Ann had made a deed, but had not recorded it. She had it made in Carolyn's name only, and her other children felt that it needed to have another name on it, regardless of whose it was. Everyone agreed this was in Carolyn's best interest. When Randy learned of the arrangement, he stopped doing anything toward the upkeep of the house. He even stopped mowing the yard. When it got mowed, he would pay Shane to mow it. This went on for weeks, and the only explanation he gave Carolyn was that his dad had told him he was breaking his back to fix up a place that one day would be Billy Jack Dalton's. Carolyn tried to make him understand that it would be hers, but he said that Billy Jack would take it away from her.

It wasn't long until Randy took Dora Ann and Carolyn to the courthouse, and Dora Ann recorded the deed.

"When she told me what she had done, I asked her if Randy was doing more around the house since she had it recorded," the relative said. "She said that he was working a lot more."

A few weeks after the deed was recorded, the relative received a phone call at work from Dora Ann. She was very upset because Randy had taken out an enormous life insurance policy on Carolyn with State Farm, and he was trying to get her to borrow against this policy. Carolyn got on the phone and said that Randy took out the policy because he wanted Dora Ann to be taken care of if anything ever happened to Carolyn. He promised that Dora Ann would never go into a nursing home and said that he would pay a private nurse to take care of her. Carolyn said that Randy had ordered blueprints and had promised to build her a house right behind Dora Ann's home. She said he'd told her the policy with State Farm was the type you could borrow money from. He had had the idea that he would get Carolyn to borrow the money for their new house instead of him, because even though he had a job, he had no collateral. Because Carolyn had collateral, which was Dora Ann's house, it was up to her to get the money. Dora Ann was terrified that Carolyn would lose their home because she knew that Randy had a way of manipulating Carolyn and getting her to do whatever he wanted.

"When Carolyn told me what he had done, it was like a bell went off," the relative said. "I talked to Dora Ann and told her that it sounded to me as if Randy was planning to kill Carolyn to collect all of the life insurance money. Dora Ann had thought the same thing, but it was something that she did not want to believe. You see, Dora Ann was the one that was sick, but Randy had it all planned out like Carolyn would die before her mother, which made no sense to me at all because Carolyn was the picture of health."

Not long after this, Carolyn began to change.

"She would call me and tell me that she didn't want Randy to hear her conversation, so she would go into another room. She told me that she wanted to sign the house and the savings account back over to her mother," said the relative. "She said that she didn't want anything to be in her name, but she never told me why."

Two weeks before the murders, the relative saw Carolyn alive for the last time. She said that she had forgotten to deduct the amount of the life insurance premium in the check register. Randy looked at the checkbook and became furious with her because he thought she had not paid the premium.

"She said to me, 'I don't know why Randy thinks he needs this insurance on me. We can't afford it. If it was not for Mother, we wouldn't have food to eat. Sometimes he only gives me seven dollars for groceries, but we have to pay the insurance premium. The policy is coming up for renewal in August, and I am not going to renew it.' I asked her if she had told Randy, and she said that she hadn't at that time, but she was going to. She said that Randy didn't even have the money to help Dora Ann to pay part of the monthly bills anymore, and that she couldn't see paying for something they couldn't afford."

Randy had made a big issue of telling the media that he loved Dora Ann, but the relative said that was a lie.

"He hated her. He wouldn't talk to her at all. He wouldn't eat the food she cooked. He even forbade her to ride in his car. He told Dora Ann, two months before the murders, that he was going to take Carolyn away from her and she would have to go into a nursing home. I thought this was strange, since this was the reason he led Carolyn to believe he was taking out the big insurance policy in the first place. If you love your mother-in-law enough to pay premiums on a policy with money you do not have, just so their future will be taken care of, then you are going to treat them as if you love them. You are going to eat their food, let them ride in your car and, most of all, you are going to talk to them."

Randy also repeatedly told the media that he loved his wife.

"This could not have been further from the truth," said the relative. "He hauled his girlfriend back and forth to work against Carolyn's wishes. He had an affair with this woman. He took items that he had given to Carolyn and gave them to her. He told people that he and Carolyn were separated and even went so far as to quit parking his car in Dora Ann's yard. On the few occasions that he took Carolyn out anywhere, if he ran into people he knew, he would ask Carolyn to duck down in the car so they could not see her. The list goes on and on, and none of his actions were those of a man that loved his wife. A man who loves his wife is going to take out enough insurance on himself to see that she is taken care of in the event of his death, especially if she does not have the means to take care of herself, as was the case with Carolyn."

Headrick never once tried to console the Dalton family. In fact, he did not even speak to them. He never once questioned how Carolyn and Dora Ann had died—it was as if he knew all about it. When the family was allowed to enter the house after the women's deaths, Headrick went straight into Carolyn's room. He sat on the edge of the bed and picked up her purse.

"I stood and watched him as he took out the check-book," the relative said, "and then he went into Dora Ann's room and got his and Carolyn's marriage license. He showed no sign of remorse whatsoever. He had completed his plan, and took only what he needed to start him on the path to collecting his money."

On one occasion, on Carolyn and Randy's anniversary, he had gone to the cemetery where his wife and mother-in-law were buried and put a dozen red roses on Carolyn's grave; the grave that bore a tombstone that her family had ordered to be engraved with the name, "Carolyn Jean *Dalton*."

The letter, which exposed Headrick's blueprint for murder in heartbreaking detail, made a powerful statement about life in the house on Shady Lane from the time before Randy Headrick moved in up until the time that Carolyn and Dora Ann were killed. DA O'Dell could not have wished for a more accurate and chilling account of the events leading up to the murders, and the behavior of the man who methodically put his plans into place to murder his wife and mother-in-law for the money he stood to gain by their deaths.

CHAPTER 50

Still unsatisfied with the ever-changing stories about how and when Shane had been told of the murders of Carolyn and Dora Ann, Rhonda Jackson got subpoenas issued on February 10, 1999, for the July 7, 1995, toll records for Jill's place of employment and for the toll records for two pay phones at the motel in Chamblee, from July 4 through July 11, 1995. Both subpoenas were faxed to the BellSouth Subpoena Compliance Center.

The following day, a woman who knew Randy Headrick was interviewed by phone. The woman, who had met Headrick through Red Crow at the Native American Connection in Chattanooga, said that Red Crow had wanted to bring Headrick into the store as a partner. Obviously, that idea hadn't gone over very well with the other partners in the business, who apparently weren't nearly as impressed with Randy Headrick as his mentor was.

The woman said she had seen Randy and Tonya Headrick at the Twenty-third Street Flea Market in Chattanooga once, before they got married. She said they were set up at the market, selling household items that they were displaying on the hood of their car. Among the items, she told Rhonda Jackson, were twenty to thirty books, mostly hardcover, on the subject of human sacrifice and the action of killing. She didn't question where

Headrick had gotten those books, she said, but they appeared to her to be evil.

Statements like this one kept coming in on a regular basis to the investigators as time for Headrick's trial grew nearer. For the most part, the majority of the statements were considered hearsay and were not conclusive proof of Headrick's guilt. But taken all together, they painted a frightening portrait of a man entirely capable of slaughtering his wife and mother-in-law in order to line his pockets with insurance money and live the high life with plenty of guns and girlfriends.

On July 22, 1999, Judge David A. Rains received a startling memo from attorney Bob French. It seemed that Tonya Headrick's grandmother had hired an attorney, Randy Brooks, of Anniston, Alabama, to defend Headrick's capital murder case. French told the judge that he and his cocounsel, Robert Ray, did not know Brooks was being hired. This would likely cause French and Ray, as court-appointed attorneys, to be relieved as Headrick's lawyers, and they both wanted to stay on the case. Headrick, who had at that time been temporarily transferred to the federal prison at Fort Leavenworth, Kansas, was a pauper, they said, and had no means himself to pay an attorney.

To the disappointment of the two lawyers, who had worked long and hard on Headrick's case for years, a court order was issued in early August that ended their involvement with Headrick.

"This Court previously appointed Mr. Robert T. Ray and Mr. Robert B. French to represent the Defendant in this case," the court order said. "It has come to the attention of the court that the Defendant's family has retained Mr. Randy Brooks to represent the Defendant, and that the Defendant desires to be represented by said retained counsel.

"It is hereby ordered that the order appointing counsel for the Defendant is hereby vacated and the Court hereby relieves attorneys Ray and French of any further obligations to the Defendant in this case."

Tonya Headrick's grandmother had successfully removed two of the most skilled and experienced defense attorneys in the Southeast from the Headrick case. Over the following months, attorney Brooks would proceed to bombard the court steadily with a continuous series of motions, none of which seemed to make a great deal of difference in the case against Randy Headrick.

CHAPTER 51

For the investigators and the prosecutors in the district attorney's office, the year 2000 brought stepped-up activity in the planning of Randy Headrick's prosecution. Rhonda Jackson and Jimmy Phillips were still not satisfied with the evidence against Shane Headrick, and many trips were made from Henagar, Alabama, to Chamblee, Georgia. All likely routes were taken and carefully timed, with the results compared with Shane's verified contacts and phone calls on July 7, 1995. It was beginning to look like Shane could not have had enough time to go from Chamblee to Henagar, help to commit two murders, then return to Chamblee within the time period he was unaccounted for.

Attorney Randy B. Brooks filed a Withdrawal of Motion for Mental Evaluation with the DeKalb County Circuit Court on January 4, on the grounds that Headrick was not raising any defenses of mental disease or defect. Brooks said he'd had several meetings with Headrick and had not had any difficulty in communicating with his client, and that Headrick was fully capable of cooperating in his defense.

The following day, DA Mike O'Dell filed a motion of his own, a Motion to Continue. The motion gave several sound reasons to continue Headrick's case.

Headrick had arrived in the custody of Sheriff Cecil

Reed's office on October 1, 1999, and had not been able to consult with his newly retained counsel, Randy Brooks, at that time. O'Dell pointed out that there had not been a criminal court docket in the county since Headrick's arrival, and February 14, 2000, was the first available trial week.

The primary reason for the Motion to Continue, however, was the scheduling of another capital-murder trial that had been set for the same date. A young Fort Payne man, John Betton, was arrested for murder on November 23, 1997, and had been in jail awaiting trial since that time. O'Dell maintained that the Betton case should be given priority due to the lengthy delay induced by Betton's appeal of his juvenile court transfer.

O'Dell also stated that Headrick's federal sentence was continuing to run and would be completed on February 11, and after that time, his presence would not be required in the federal prison system and he would merely be an Alabama inmate. John Betton's long-awaited trial for capital murder, Headrick's recent arrival in the county and a complete lack of prejudice to Headrick would be ample grounds to grant the continuance, O'Dell said.

"Wherefore the premises considered, the State requests that this Court, for good cause shown in open court, grant the State's requested necessary and reasonable continuance to a date beyond February 14, 2000."

The continuance must have certainly suited the purposes of Brooks, who began to prepare a long and winding stream of motions with which he would assail the Circuit Court of DeKalb County.

In early January, Rhonda Jackson had requested information on Randy Headrick's military service, particularly any training in specialized areas. She was certain that his many claims of Ranger training and instructing, and heroic, bloody Vietnam action, were false, and she wanted proof for the district attorney and his staff before Headrick's trial date, which had been scheduled for February

14, 2000. The irony of Headrick being tried on Valentine's Day for murdering his wife, who had loved him and his mother-in-law, who had supported him, was not lost on the prosecutors. It made them even more determined to bring justice for the family of the two women, and the continuance that was later granted in the case would allow more time to pursue several routes of interest.

When Headrick's military service records arrived, Rhonda Jackson's suspicions were confirmed. She already knew that he reportedly enlisted in the Alabama National Guard on November 16, 1973, at the age of sixteen, by lying about his age. He underwent basic training at Fort Leonard Wood, Missouri, and Fort Knox, Kentucky, and was transferred to the Texas National Guard, reportedly being listed as on active duty for one year with the 111th Armored Division at Fort Worth, Texas.

The records showed that during his time in the National Guard, Headrick qualified as a marksman with the M-16 rifle in February 1974. His military occupation specialty, or MOS, was as a motor transport operator. His specialized training was as a tracked-vehicle mechanic, with training in wheeled-vehicle maintenance and tracked-vehicle maintenance, and he'd had a course in race relations.

Military personnel records indicated that Headrick entered the U.S. Army on November 3, 1975, and received a discharge under other than honorable conditions on May 30, 1980, due to conduct that could be tried by court-martial. According to the records, he was in foreign service for one year, six months and twenty-eight days, and his highest rank was SP4. Headrick claimed he received his discharge because of going AWOL when his wife left him while he was in the army. They later reunited and remained married until September 1986.

None of the military records indicated that Randy Headrick had been involved in any way with the Rangers, Special Forces, or any other such specialized groups, or had received any training of the sort. In fact, his military career was unremarkable to the extreme. All Headrick's many stories about his military exploits and special training in combat, explosives, and killing methods were like so many of his other claims . . . total falsehoods.

CHAPTER 52

On February 11, Randy Brooks continued his onslaught of paperwork, filing a motion to reveal the deal or any incentives offered to potential witnesses.

Brooks and his client asked for a court order requiring the State to furnish a great deal of information. Among the items listed on the motion was any information that concerned any agreement or negotiations between the State of Alabama, or any law enforcement agency involved in the case, and any potential witness. The request included any information that involved an agreement for the disposition of any criminal case or the failure to bring a possible criminal case.

The motion also requested any information concerning any incentives paid to, or offered to, or discussed with any potential witnesses for the State. The incentives referred to, the motion said, would include any payment for expenses for the witnesses, any payment of motel, hotel, food or other expenses of that type, and any payment or expenses paid for any family members of any witnesses.

A court order was requested that would require the State to furnish the Defendant the name of any witnesses or any other persons that have made any claims for any rewards offered by the State of Alabama concerning the case, and the names of any family members or of any other

agencies that offered a reward in any way connected
with the case.

Brooks and his client also requested the information
concerning agreements, whether in the form of written
agreements, verbal agreements, or unwritten understand-
ings, specifically including agreements between an attorney for any witness, and any state agency.

"This information to be furnished in a timely manner,"
the motion concluded.

A handful of other motions followed on March 31, with
the first being a motion to suppress statements of the defendant. Headrick and his attorney hoped to have the
court agree to suppress as evidence the several statements that were taken from Headrick by law enforcement
on the evening of July 7, the morning of July 8 and the
afternoon of July 8, 1995. As grounds, they claimed that
the statements were illegally and wrongfully obtained in
violation of the Defendant's constitutional rights as protected under the Constitution of the United States, Constitution of the State of Alabama, and existing federal and
state case law.

Brooks claimed that Headrick's statements were not voluntary, and that he did not give a knowing intelligent voluntary waiver of his legal right to remain silent under the
circumstances.

Headrick and Brooks requested that an evidentiary
hearing be scheduled to determine the validity and con-
stitutionality of his statements, and upon the conclusion
of the hearing, that the statements be suppressed as evidence in the trial of his case.

The second motion filed that day asked the court for
an order requiring the prosecutor to make known the
criminal history of each witness they intended to call at
trial.

Motion number three, filed on March 31, requested a
court order requiring the production of the record of all
juvenile court proceedings involving any prosecution witness, due to the fact that the Defendant was charged in

an indictment with the offense of capital murder, and the prosecution had stated they would seek the death penalty in his case. They cited as grounds a Supreme Court decision that a defendant's right to probe into the influence of a possible bias of a prosecution witness outweighed the State's interest in protection of the confidentiality of a witness in the juvenile court record. The defense, they said, did not have access to the juvenile court records unless they were produced by the State of Alabama.

The fourth motion filed by Brooks on March 31 asked the court to make a pretrial determination as to whether Shane Headrick intended to invoke his Fifth Amendment privilege. Stated grounds for the motion were that the Defendant had information that Shane intended to invoke that privilege and not testify in Randy Headrick's case.

In the event that Shane did not testify, the motion said, it would be prejudicial to Randy Headrick to have references to Shane's possible testimony in voir dire or opening statements, or to have Shane called as a witness and invoke his Fifth Amendment privilege in the presence of the jury.

Attorney Brooks wanted to know beforehand whether or not Shane intended to testify in Randy's trial and, if he did not intend to testify, Brooks wanted to prohibit the State from making any reference to that in front of the jury.

Apparently, most of the flurry of motions filed on March 31 had something to do, in one way or another, with the possible testimony of Shane and Jill. Headrick must have thought their appearance on the witness stand could be potentially disastrous to him, and he sought to discredit them and prevent their testimony in any manner that he could.

On April 13, 2000, District Attorney Mike O'Dell filed a motion of his own, a motion of discovery asking the court to order the Defendant to permit the State to analyze, inspect and copy or photograph a long list of materials. These included books, papers, photographs, tangible objects, and reports or results of physical or mental examination and/or scientific tests or experiments made in connection which were in the possession, custody, or control of the Defendant. O'Dell wanted a look at everything Brooks intended to introduce as evidence at the trial or which had been prepared by a witness who was intended to be called at the trial, if the results related to the witness' testimony.

The district attorney's prosecutorial team was gearing up to receive a guilty verdict and intended to ask for the death penalty for Randy Headrick, and no stone was being left unturned in the search for every detail, statement or even the tiniest scrap of evidence that would help them achieve their goal. When Randy Headrick filed a motion to suppress his earliest statements on July 7 and 8, Mike O'Dell knew that proving at what time Headrick allegedly learned how the murders were committed was of extreme importance to the case.

CHAPTER 53

On April 25, 2000, each and every person who was present at the crime scene on the day of the murders was contacted by the sheriff's department to come in and give a statement as to whether or not they had discussed the method of the murders with Headrick that day prior to his first interview, or at any other time.

Deputy Jim Mays, the first county officer at the scene of the double homicide at Shady Lane, told his interviewers that on his arrival, he had secured the scene as best he could. He stated that he did not talk with any member of the Headrick family concerning the method in which the two women were killed.

Officer Darrell Collins said that he spoke with no member of Headrick's family concerning how Carolyn and Dora Ann were killed. He stated that he assisted Investigator Danny Smith during Headrick's questioning.

Reed Smith said that he and Winston Busby went to the residence of Carolyn and Dora Ann on the day that they were murdered. Smith said that there was no one at the residence when he and Winston Busby arrived, and that he did not discuss the method in which the ladies were murdered with anyone. Smith said he did not talk with any member of Headrick's family.

Deputy Mary Waters stated that she performed crime

scene security at the residence on the day of the murders, and that she did not discuss the manner of the women's deaths with anyone.

Deputy Johnny Brown secured the murder scene and, to the best of his knowledge, did not speak to any of the Headrick family. Brown stated that he did not discuss the manner of death with anyone except other law enforcement personnel at the scene.

Deputy Van McAlpin spoke with neighbors to see if they saw anything out of the ordinary on the day of the murders. He did not speak to any members of the Headrick family, and did not talk about how the two ladies had been killed with anyone.

Chief Deputy Eddie Wright did not say anything to any members of the Headrick family at the crime scene, and Deputy Lamar Hackworth said he helped keep the scene secure on the day of the murders. Hackworth said he did not talk about the way the victims had been killed with anyone except law enforcement personnel and did not speak to any member of the Headrick family. Hackworth said he questioned people in the neighborhood to see if they saw anything unusual.

Investigator Danny Smith stated that on the day of the murders he did not discuss the way the murders had been carried out with any member of the Headrick family. Smith said that he asked Randy Headrick if he had been told how his wife and mother-in-law were killed.

Deputy Tony Bartley said that he did not discuss the manner of death with anyone at the scene or any member of the Headrick family, and Joey Hester said he did not enter the crime scene at all because his task that day was crime scene security.

Richard Igou, who had been district attorney at the time of the murders, stated that he did not have a discussion with any member of the Headrick family on the day of the murders, and Winston Busby said that no member of the Headrick family was present at the time he was at the murder scene. David Smalley and Donald

Smith both said that they did not speak with any member of the Headrick family.

Reverend Joey Turman told Investigator Jimmy Phillips that he was at the Cabbage Bowl Restaurant in Ider, having lunch with his wife, when Kathy Porter rushed in to get help. Turman said that he went to the scene of the crime and went inside and saw Carolyn and Dora Ann's bodies. At that point, he called 911 from the house, having called them earlier from the Cabbage Bowl. Turman said that he never talked to Randy Headrick at the crime scene, later at the funeral or at any other time.

Kathy Porter told Phillips that she did not talk to Headrick at all on the day of the murders. She did not tell anyone how the victims were killed, because at that time she did not know herself. The only time she talked to Headrick was on the day of the funeral to see what clothing he wanted to bury his wife in, and they picked out her clothes that day.

Sheriff Cecil Reed told Phillips that he did not recall talking to any of Randy Headrick's family on the day of the murders. He did talk to the press concerning the case, he said, but not on the day of the murders.

"The main thing I remember that day," he said, "is when Randy drove past the road and turned around and came back and turned onto the dirt road and was met by law enforcement on the road. He was told what was going on, but I didn't say anything to him about how the victims were killed."

The most telling statement came from Terry Knowles, the man who sat with Randy Headrick on the back of his truck after Headrick arrived at the murder scene.

"I didn't discuss how the victims were killed with anyone," Knowles said. "I heard Danny Smith ask Randy if his prints would be on the murder weapons, and Randy said, 'Yes, I made them.' When Randy said this, he realized what he'd said and he became very quiet then. I also heard Danny Smith ask Randy how he knew what they were killed with, and Randy said that someone in his family had told him how they were killed."

With everyone present at the murder scene verifying that they had not told Randy Headrick or any member of his family how the two victims had been killed, it seemed highly unlikely that he could have learned so quickly what the murder weapons were, and would remark, "Yes, I made them." In fact, it would seem that the only person, other than law enforcement at the scene, who could have known at that time what weapons were used to kill Carolyn and Dora Ann was the person who committed the murders.

Matters were looking increasingly bleak for mounting any kind of successful defense for Randy Headrick when the case came to court. It was common knowledge that the district attorney planned to ask for the death penalty if Headrick was found guilty. Therefore, Headrick and his attorney began to give a great deal of thought as to what the wisest course of action would be, and how they should proceed in order to keep Headrick from taking a seat in "Yellow Mama," Alabama's notorious electric chair.

While Headrick languished in the DeKalb County Jail, trying to find a way to avoid a death sentence, one of the ironic coincidences occurred that often make true crime stranger than fiction. One of the first persons looked at as a possible suspect early on in the murders landed in the DeKalb County Jail, where he would keep company with Headrick for a time. John Mark Johnson, the Valley Head man who had long, dark hair, drove a red Chevy S10, had a criminal history that included time spent in a Florida prison for federal firearms violations, and was heavily involved in the local Native American community, had been brought to the attention of authorities early in the investigation. Johnson was quickly ruled out as a person of interest in the murders of Carolyn Headrick and Dora Ann Dalton, but he was arrested on a grand jury indictment in late February 2000 and booked on fourteen sex charges involving a juvenile female. The charges included first- and second-degree sodomy, first-degree rape and child abuse, all involving the same victim. Johnson would enter a guilty plea and be sent to prison, but he and Headrick shared some jail time while Headrick and his attorney planned their next move in their attempt to save Headrick from a death sentence.

Johnson's wife, Laura, who had also been questioned early in the investigation, died under mysterious circumstances on October 12, 1997, in a headline-making incident when she plunged approximately three hundred feet to her death from an overlook at DeKalb County's Little River Canyon National Preserve. She, Johnson and their daughter were at the canyon allegedly preparing to participate in a Native American purification ritual; authorities were told she slipped and fell from the overlook during the ritual. The DeKalb County investigators, the FBI and park service authorities found her death highly suspicious and continued to investigate it for several years, but no charges have yet been filed in connection with her death.

Headrick and Johnson must have had some very interesting conversations during their time together in the DeKalb County Jail. Both were highly intelligent; both shared a common interest in Native Americana and firearms; both had become grieving widowers. These amazing coincidences proved, to many of the sheriff's department personnel, that reality is, indeed, sometimes stranger than fiction.

CHAPTER 54

On May 11, 2000, DA Mike O'Dell issued an astounding four-page, single-spaced press release with the headline in large, bold letters: **HEADRICK SENTENCED TO 60 YEARS IN MURDERS OF WIFE AND MOTHER-IN-LAW.**

It was, without a doubt, the most gratifying press release O'Dell had ever prepared, and it marked the end of one of the most sensational cases northeast Alabama had ever seen. The press release also underscored Rhonda Jackson's tireless pursuit of justice for Carolyn Headrick and Dora Ann Dalton and their family, and her determination to bring down the ruthless killer who was convinced that he had gotten away with their murders. Randy Headrick's last-minute guilty plea came as a happy surprise to O'Dell and his team.

Despite the length of the press release, almost every media outlet that received it ran it almost in its entirety. It was the news that people had been hoping for so long to hear, and the day finally had come when Randy Headrick's own bragging had caused the doors of justice to slam shut, trapping him with his own lies and betrayals.

Mike O'Dell's press releases ordinarily ran around two to three paragraphs, but in the announcement of Headrick's guilty plea, he wrote a very complete summary of the entire case. Besides its detailed description of the crime and Headrick's apprehension, it also credited all those in his office and in the sheriff's department who had worked so long and hard to send Headrick to prison. The press release read as follows:

District Attorney Mike O'Dell announced today that William Randall Headrick has been adjudicated guilty in the gruesome 1995 murders of his wife, Carolyn Headrick, and his mother-in-law, Dora Ann Dalton. Headrick was sentenced to 30 years in the State Penitentiary in each case by Circuit Judge David A. Rains. The case was prosecuted by O'Dell and Deputy District Attorney Ben Baxley.

"These convictions have been a long time in coming," O'Dell said. "We believed from the very beginning that Randy Headrick was the killer of these two innocent women, and the focus never left him as our prime suspect. It was very frustrating during those first three years after the murders when we just didn't have enough evidence to charge and convict him. We remained patient, and we never stopped working on this case. We got a big break in August of 1998, when Headrick discussed the killings with a co-worker in Chattanooga. He believed he had committed the 'perfect crime' and couldn't keep from talking about it. Discussions he had with the individual at work led to additional information concerning the murders. All the clues led straight back to Headrick."

Investigative records indicated that the two women were shot in the head, stabbed with Indian spears, and had their throats cut. Autopsy and ballistic reports indicated that a .22 caliber revolver was used by Headrick. Mrs. Dalton was shot once in the head, while Carolyn Headrick was shot a total of three times. Both women were killed in the Henagar residence of Mrs. Dalton on July 7, 1995. Their bodies were discovered by another daughter of Mrs. Dalton.

"We were able to pinpoint the time of death to 12:15 to 12:30 P.M.," Deputy District Attorney Ben Baxley pointed out. "We located witnesses who saw a red Ford pickup truck back out of the driveway of Mrs. Dalton's residence at that time and speed away heading south. The witnesses later learned of the murders and came forward and told police what they observed. Randy Headrick drove a truck matching the description of the one observed speeding away from the residence at the time of the murders. We also learned early on that Headrick had attempted to kill his first wife with a pipe bomb in Texas several years earlier. Then came the most important piece of evidence, when we learned that Headrick had amassed a total of $325,000 in life insurance on his wife, Carolyn. In addition to the enormous amount of insurance, we found it compelling that Carolyn was a housewife with no outside income. The couple also had no children. It made absolutely no sense that he would have so much insurance on his wife—who didn't work—while he had only a minimal $25,000 on himself," Baxley pointed out.

(O'Dell added that, according to employment records, Headrick earned only $6 an hour as a woodworker in a local building-supply store.)

"His monthly truck payments were almost $250, and his insurance premiums averaged around $100 per month. Those amounts represented almost 50 percent of his total monthly income. We learned from various witnesses that the cost of the insurance was causing financial difficulties for the Headricks. We were told by family members that Carolyn was planning to cancel the insurance two weeks prior to her death, and financial records indicated that Headrick's truck payments were two months in

304   *Sheila Johnson*

arrears. In fact, the leased truck was subsequently repossessed about a month after he killed the women."

Police reports indicated that Headrick had been sexually involved with two other women over the eighteen months prior to the murders. Both women came forward and told police that during their affairs with Headrick, he had inquired of them whether or not their husbands were insured. In both instances he offered to "get rid" of their husbands. He also told one of the women that he and his wife were having marital difficulties as well as financial problems.

"Once again, Headrick couldn't keep his mouth shut," O'Dell said. "He told one of the women that if he could get rid of his wife and mother-in-law, he would have it made. He further stated to her that he had taken out an insurance policy on Carolyn because he was going to get rid of her, his mother-in-law, and the woman's husband."

On separate occasions over the eighteen months prior to the murders, Headrick told a postal employee that he knew how to commit the "perfect murder." He stated that he would do the killing himself, but he would have a perfect alibi. According to the witness's statement, Headrick said that "for enough money, an alibi could be bought." He further told this witness that he knew where to shoot someone and kill them instantly, and where to stab someone and cut their throat, also killing them instantly. Finally, he stated to this witness that he had insurance on his wife in the hundreds of thousands of dollars. The witness came forward to police immediately after learning of the murders.

"Headrick's brother Shane told police that on two occasions, within weeks of the murders, Randy Headrick had asked him to help kill his wife and mother-in-law," O'Dell pointed out. "Randy was very specific on how he wanted the murders carried out;

he wanted them shot, their heads cut off, and a spear stuck into each of their bodies. He offered his brother half of the insurance money for his assistance. His brother was also indicted for the murders, but we are reviewing the case against him. Recent investigative findings indicate that Shane Headrick may not have been involved at all. A decision on his case will be made soon."

(According to O'Dell and Baxley, the final pieces of the puzzle came when Headrick admitted to the killings to two separate individuals. One was the coworker in Chattanooga, while the other was a fellow federal inmate in the federal penitentiary in Fort Leavenworth, Kansas, while Headrick was serving a twenty-one-month sentence for a federal firearms violation. On both occasions, Headrick gave detailed information about the killings he had committed.)

"We moved forward with an indictment in early Fall of 1998," Baxley said. "We met with Sheriff Cecil Reed and the investigators he had assigned to this case, and reviewed all the evidence. It was then that we decided the time was right to charge Randall Headrick and seek to bring him to justice. His guilty plea and the convictions we have obtained against him for the deaths of Dora Ann Dalton and Carolyn Headrick are sweet indeed. I am certain that Headrick felt that he had 'beaten the system,' or pulled off the perfect crime he had become obsessed with committing, but he was wrong. Justice has prevailed. He has had several years of freedom he should not have enjoyed, but those days are over. He will be in the penitentiary, paying for these horrible crimes, for a very long time."

(O'Dell gave credit for the successful prosecution of Headrick to DeKalb County Sheriff's investigator Rhonda Jackson, who was lead investigator for the Headrick case.)

"Rhonda did an absolutely sensational job bringing this case to a point where Ben and I could proceed with the prosecution. She has worked tirelessly for many months, and over the past six to eight weeks, she has worked twelve to sixteen hour days, contacting witnesses and reviewing evidence with us. I could not begin to express how very proud of her we are. Sheriff Reed has been extremely cooperative with us in allowing Rhonda to work exclusively on this case, and it has paid very big dividends by getting this vicious killer off the streets for many years to come. Rhonda has learned a great deal from this case, and it will most certainly make her a better investigator. Her dedication and professionalism is unmatched in any murder investigation and prosecution I have been involved with. I salute her for a job very well done."

(Special praise was reserved for Deputy District Attorney Ben Baxley and Assistant District Attorney Bob Johnston.)

"Ben is an extraordinarily gifted prosecutor who has been a tremendous asset to this office," O'Dell said. "This is the third murder prosecution we have prepared for trial together over the last four months, and I must tell you we are both mentally drained. Someone pointed out that these convictions were the fourteenth and fifteenth consecutive successful homicide prosecutions by this office over the past three years. Ben has been a significant part of that success. It has been an honor to try cases with Ben.

"Bob Johnston has also played a very important role in these murder prosecutions. He is our 'rules expert,' and his work on the legal issues has been invaluable. Bob is such an ardent student of the law, so wise and knowledgeable. His goal is to be a judge one of these days, and as much as I will miss him, I believe he has the ability and temperament to be an outstanding jurist. He will bring great distinction to the bench."

(O'Dell's next words of praise were for Assistant District Attorney Scott Lloyd.)

"Scott has been the workhorse around the office as we have struggled to deal with all the murder cases we've been faced with. Scott has been the glue that has held my office together over these many months handling all the property offenses, walk-ins, child support cases, and District Court prosecutions. His willingness to handle virtually any, and all, matters unrelated to the murder prosecutions has freed us up to invest the time necessary for us all to be successful. Frankly, I am quite blessed to have a magnificent staff in both DeKalb and Cherokee Counties. Deputy District Attorney Ben Latham, who has been with the Cherokee County office for almost 35 years, has also had to take on a much greater role. He has been very gracious in his willingness to 'fill the gaps' left by our enormous homicide case load. The 'Team Concept' has, once again, served the citizens of these two counties exceedingly well."

O'Dell's lengthy, four-page treatise astounded all the members of the media who were not very familiar with the case, since Headrick's guilty plea had taken five years to come to pass and was looked at by some as "old news." However, for those reporters who had covered the murders from the very beginning, O'Dell's press release brought almost as much satisfaction as it brought to the investigators, the prosecutors and the family of Carolyn Headrick and Dora Ann Dalton. LaRue Cornelison, the *Times-Journal* writer who had reported so extensively on the case during its early months, was no longer in the newspaper business by the time Headrick was sentenced, but the outcome of the case was still a tremendous personal satisfaction to her. She had felt from the very first, when she interviewed Headrick and heard him saying that he wanted the killer found and punished, that he was actually the murderer. His demeanor during the interview was chilling, and she never for a minute doubted his guilt.

Randy Headrick's bloody betrayal of his wife and mother-in-law would be punished, as would his attempts to incriminate his younger brother, Shane Headrick. Shane, in fact, could also be looked at as a victim of his brother's betrayal. The confused, troubled young man had been a perfect mark for Randy Headrick's skilled manipulation all his life, and had it not been for the prosecution's determination to find the truth, Shane Headrick surely would have joined his brother in prison.

CHAPTER 55

On May 25, DA Mike O'Dell filed a motion in the DeKalb County Circuit Court to distribute the rewards that had been offered for information leading to the arrest and conviction of the person responsible for the murders of Carolyn Headrick and Dora Ann Dalton.

O'Dell told the court that during the early days of the investigation, the Alabama governor had authorized rewards totaling $10,000 to any person providing the information needed to make an arrest and conviction. In August 1998, O'Dell said, Terry Durham came forward with crucial information that led to the September 1998 indictment of Randy Headrick for the murders, and on May 11, 2000, Headrick was convicted following his guilty pleas.

Terry Durham made himself available to the state and the defendant's attorneys and investigators throughout the preparation of the case for trial, O'Dell said, and Durham's testimony directly led to the arrest and convictions of Randy Headrick.

O'Dell then requested the court to enter an order directing that the rewards authorized by the governor be paid to Terry Durham.

Five days later, O'Dell got his order. The court ruled that the reward money authorized by the governor—$5,000 for

information in each of the murders for a total reward of
$10,000—would indeed be paid to Terry Durham.

On June 21, Mike O'Dell sent out another press release
announcing that he had received the $10,000 reward
check from the governor's office. It was presented that
day to Terry Durham in O'Dell's office:

> "The selection of Durham came after a commit-
> tee of law enforcement officials associated with the
> case met and decided who the recipient of the re-
> wards should be," O'Dell said. "Ben Baxley was co-
> counsel with me and spent a great deal of time
> preparing the case for trial. His input was vital due
> to his knowledge of all our potential witnesses and
> their impact on the success of the prosecution. In ad-
> dition, Sheriff Cecil Reed and his lead investigator
> in this case, Rhonda Jackson, served on the commit-
> tee. Once the selection was made, we presented our
> decision to Circuit Judge Randall Cole, who then
> issued an order directing the money to be paid to
> Durham."

(In addition to this being the first time a reward had
been paid to a witness since he had been associated with
the district attorney's office, O'Dell commented on the
unique cooperation between the local community and
state government in all aspects of the case.)

> "Never before have I seen such a cooperative
> spirit involving state and local entities. The way the
> Henagar and Ider communities came together
> was incredible. They are great communities with
> very caring and compassionate people. It was very
> obvious that they were going to do all they could
> to bring to justice the murderer of Dora Ann
> Dalton and Carolyn Headrick. The manner in
> which the citizens raised an additional reward of
> nearly $13,000 is nothing short of miraculous. It

shows the tremendous love and affection these folks have for one another. I am very proud of each and every one of them."

(O'Dell credited Governor Don Siegelman's office for being very cooperative throughout the process of the Headrick case.)

"Our Governor has always proven himself to be a friend of law enforcement and our efforts to fight crime in this community. Once we informed him that the case had been successfully resolved, he processed the reward check very quickly. We are extremely grateful to Governor Siegelman for his part in this matter."

O'Dell also commented on all the witnesses who were scheduled to testify at the Headrick murder trial, had it taken place as planned.

"Although Terry Durham has been designated the recipient of these reward checks, he is not the only reason we were able to obtain a conviction for murder against Randy Headrick. We had over 30 witnesses scheduled to testify. Many of these individuals were private citizens just like Terry who could have chosen not to get involved; instead, at some risk to their own safety, they came forward—and remained steadfast—in their desire to see that justice was done. Each one was like a separate piece of the 'puzzle.' We are indebted to each one of them. It just so happened that Terry's role became the most significant of all. Without him, the pieces would not all come together—they didn't give us the final picture."

The $12,700 reward raised by the citizens of the Henagar/Ider area was also presented to Terry Durham at a special meeting at the Ider Church of God, the church that held Carolyn and Dora Ann so dear to its heart. The church members and so many others within the community, who had raised $9,805 of the reward within only thirty minutes on the day that collections began, were pleased to be able to award the money finally, for it meant Carolyn and Dora Ann's murderer was convicted at last. And they were glad the money went to a young man like Terry Durham, who, despite his fears for his own safety and that of his wife and children, came forward and did the right thing. To see the reward go to a young family man with ethics and the courage of his convictions made its presentation all the more satisfying to the many people who had contributed to the fund.

CHAPTER 56

Despite his guilty plea and his current address within the Alabama Department of Corrections at one of their finer facilities, Randy Headrick was not through with the court system yet. At the time he had entered his guilty plea, he also reserved his right to appeal the trial court's order denying his motion to dismiss the indictment. That motion was based on Headrick's claim that the state had violated the "anti-shuttling" and "speedy trial" provisions of the Interstate Agreement on Detainers (IAD).

The IAD's primary purpose is to address concerns that untried charges pending in other jurisdictions and difficulties in obtaining a speedy trial create uncertainties that interfere with and disrupt prisoner rehabilitation and treatment programs.

At the time of Headrick's indictment for the murders of Carolyn and Dora Ann, he was being held in the Etowah County Jail awaiting trial on his federal firearms charges. The DeKalb County Sheriff's Department sent a fax and a follow-up letter to the U.S. Marshal Service asking that Headrick be held for future state proceedings. Headrick pleaded guilty to the federal charges and was sentenced, then was given into the custody of the United

States Marshal to be transferred into the custody of the United States Bureau of Prisons.

While he waited for transfer, Headrick was temporarily returned to the Etowah County Jail and during that time was transported to the DeKalb County Circuit Court for arraignment on the state murder charges. He was sent back to the Etowah County Jail that same day.

In January 1999, Headrick filed a motion in DeKalb County Circuit Court seeking a court-ordered mental competency examination, and his request was granted. A request for temporary custody was filed with Fort Leavenworth officials, and Headrick was transferred from the federal penitentiary to DeKalb County on October 1, 1999. On January 4, 2000, Headrick withdrew his motion for a mental competency examination. The next day, the state filed a motion to continue his case beyond the 120-day period set out in the IAD. A trial date of May 15, 2000, was set, and Headrick's federal sentence expired on February 11, 2000. On that same day, Headrick filed a motion to dismiss the indictment, claiming the "speedy trial" provision of the IAD had been violated. Then, on April 27, he filed a motion to dismiss the indictment, alleging a violation of the "anti-shuttling" provision of the IAD.

Headrick's motions were denied, with the trial court ruling on May 4 that Headrick's transfer to Etowah County following his arraignment did not require the dismissal of his indictment because the September 11, 1998, hold that the DeKalb County sheriff had placed on Headrick did not constitute a detainer under the IAD.

Headrick's second motion was denied on May 5, with the trial court saying that even though a trial was not scheduled to begin within 120 days of Headrick's arrival in Alabama from Fort Leavenworth, dismissal of the indictment was not necessary.

"The State has shown good cause in open court with the defendant and his attorney present, why the commencement of the trial of this case should be scheduled beyond the 120 day deadline argued by the defendant," the trial court ruled.

Headrick entered his guilty plea to the two counts of murder on May 11, but reserved the right to appeal, and he presented his case to the Alabama Court of Criminal Appeals during its October Term of 2000 to 2001.

In its decision, the criminal appeals court held that a detainer was never lodged against Headrick while he was temporarily housed in the Etowah County Jail; therefore, the state did not violate the IAD when it returned him to Etowah County following his arraignment in DeKalb County Circuit Court.

In reviewing the trial court's May 5 order, which claimed the state had shown good cause for continuing the trial beyond the 120-day period specified in the IAD, the criminal appeals court noted that Headrick did not object to the trial court's order granting the state's motion for a continuance.

"The failure of a defendant to object to a motion for a continuance before the 120-day period expires, precludes appellate review of the issue," the court said.

The court's ruling went on to cover in detail each of the issues involved in Headrick's appeal, and the reasons for their final decision.

"We find no error in the trial court's order," said the criminal appeals court. "For the foregoing reasons, the judgment of the trial court is affirmed."

Randy Headrick had reserved his right to appeal, but that appeal had been denied. He would remain in the Alabama prison system, being transferred from one facility to another, for very many years to come. There would be plenty of time for him to reflect on the bloody betrayal of his innocent, trusting wife and her mother—the "perfect crime" that eventually went wrong because of Headrick's own inability to keep from bragging about what he had done.

CHAPTER 57

Although Randy Headrick's case had finally come to an end, there was still one loose end remaining to be tied up by DA Mike O'Dell. On July 6, 2001, he entered a Motion for Nolle Prosequi in the Circuit Court of DeKalb County, in the case of the *State of Alabama* v. *Waylon Shane Headrick*.

O'Dell asked the court to drop all charges against Shane, and the motion was granted on July 9. Shane Headrick was a free man, with no charges pending against him in the murder cases. The most lasting effect of his indictment for murder would be the memory of his brother's betrayal, Randy's many attempts to implicate Shane and the knowledge that he had been used as a pawn in an attempt to lessen Randy Headrick's sole responsibility for the murders. Experiencing the continuing pain of those memories would be Shane Headrick's life sentence.

EPILOGUE

In the years following the Headrick case, life has moved forward for those who were involved for so long in the apprehension and prosecution of Randy Headrick. Jimmy Phillips and Clay Simpson, the investigators who worked such long, hard hours on the case, are still with the DeKalb County Sheriff's Department, and Mike James has gone from being a top-notch investigator to serving as Sheriff Cecil Reed's chief deputy.

"It's a new challenge for me," he said of his job change, "but I miss the investigative work." With his talent for detective work, it is likely that James still keeps a close eye on all the cases under investigation, and his door is always open when his former colleagues ask him for advice.

Sheriff Cecil Reed, an icon in Alabama law enforcement, is still on the job, awaiting the completion of construction of a large and much-needed new law enforcement complex and county jail before he retires. It will feature state-of-the-art security equipment and plenty of new cells for the inmates, who have crowded the old county jail for so many years. It will also provide roomy new offices for Reed and his staff.

"I want to spend some time in that new office," Reed said.

Mike O'Dell, who was an assistant district attorney at

the time that Carolyn Headrick and Dora Ann Dalton were murdered, was elected district attorney during the years when the case was being investigated, following Richard Igou's retirement. O'Dell has successfully prosecuted some of the most sensational murder cases in recent northeast Alabama history, including the Judith Ann Neelley and Hayward Bissell cases, both of which drew national attention.

Reporters LaRue Cornelison and Stephen V. Smith, who both became deeply involved in documenting the Headrick case in their newspapers, have moved onto other career paths, but still have vivid memories of Randy Headrick. The multitalented Cornelison, so well-liked and respected throughout the law enforcement community, could have pursued almost any line of work she wished, and she is now working in the prison system as a correctional officer.

"I went from writing about them to babysitting them," she said.

In the same year he won an Alabama Press Association first-place award for his photo of Randy Headrick, Stephen V. Smith also won three other prestigious APA photo awards, including second place in the same category with the Headrick photo.

"That was a good year for me," he said.

Stephen moved on from his newspaper reporting, writing and photography to become the founder and president of WordSouth Public Relations, Inc., the first public relations firm in northeast Alabama, and one of the most successful.

Rhonda Jackson, the attractive, determined young officer who so carefully led the investigation of Carolyn Headrick and Dora Ann Dalton's murders—and kept such meticulous records of every single phone call, conversation and piece of evidence—is still serving as one of the investigators at the DeKalb County Sheriff's Department. Throughout the years, Rhonda has been blessed with a wonderful family and one of the most supportive husbands she could have ever hoped for. Dewitt Jackson, a commercial poultry farmer, has backed up his wife 100 percent during every step of her career, and she praises him for his support at every opportunity. During all the sleepless nights while Rhonda tried to find the missing piece of the puzzle that would send Randy Headrick to prison for the double homicide, Dewitt was right there, encouraging Rhonda and letting her know he had faith in her ability to get the job done. Dewitt was recently elected to serve on the DeKalb County Commission, and Rhonda supports his work just as wholeheartedly as he has always supported hers.

Shane Headrick does not live in Alabama, and it is hoped he has been able to make a peaceful, pleasant life for himself without too many memories of the past casting a shadow over it. He was used by a skillful manipulator who had bullied and dominated him as a child. Hopefully, he has been able to cast off the hold his brother had over him for so long.

The years have been tough at times for the Dalton family, but their faith in God and their closeness as a family has pulled them through. Things were probably hardest on Kathy Porter and her daughter, Kendra, who walked through Dora Ann's front door into a hellish scene, which haunted their nightmares for a long time. Kendra was especially traumatized by the experience, but her mother says she's been able to go on with her life and is now happily married with a family of her own and a career she loves.

At the end of the case, Kathy Porter wrote a letter to Rhonda Jackson that expressed her feelings toward the woman who had worked so hard to bring her mother and sister's killer to justice. She told Rhonda that she was very special to her, and that she felt the sheriff's department was lucky to have her on their staff. Kathy said that Rhonda had become more like a friend to her, always there when she needed to talk, and said how much she appreciated that. But most of all,

Kathy said, she appreciated Rhonda's dedication to God, which had meant so very much to her.

"The times that you shared a Scripture and mentioned us in your prayers have meant more than you will ever know.

"Thank you for not giving up."

As special as Rhonda Jackson is, there are countless other law enforcement officers around the country who are just as determined to bring criminals to justice. They work without ceasing, day after day, to help families like the Daltons to find closure and to see that the victims of violent crimes receive the justice they deserve.

To all of them, as well as to all of those who were involved in any way with the Headrick case, "Thank you for not giving up."